STRETCHED THIN

STRETCHED THIN

Poor Families, Welfare Work, and Welfare Reform

Sandra Morgen
Joan Acker
Jill Weigt

CORNELL UNIVERSITY PRESS   ITHACA AND LONDON

First published 2010 by Cornell University Press
First printing, Cornell Paperbacks, 2010
Printed in the United States of America

Library of Congress Cataloging-in-Publication Data

Morgen, Sandra.
    Stretched thin : poor families, welfare work, and welfare reform / Sandra Morgen, Joan Acker, Jill Weigt.
        p. cm.
    Includes bibliographical references and index.
    ISBN 978-0-8014-4774-7 (cloth : alk. paper) —
    ISBN 978-0-8014-7510-8 (pbk. : alk. paper)
    1. Oregon. Adult and Family Services Division.   2. Public welfare—Oregon.
3. Public welfare administration—Oregon.   4. Welfare recipients—Oregon.
5. Poor families—Oregon.   6. Social workers—Oregon.   7. United
States. Personal Responsibility and Work Opportunity Reconciliation Act of
1996.   8. Temporary Assistance for Needy Families (Program)   I. Acker,
Joan.   II. Weigt, Jill Michele, 1967–   III. Title.

    HV98.O7M67   2010
    362.5'56809795—dc22   2009028824

Cornell University Press strives to use environmentally responsible suppliers and materials to the fullest extent possible in the publishing of its books. Such materials include vegetable-based, low-VOC inks and acid-free papers that are recycled, totally chlorine-free, or partly composed of nonwood fibers. For further informa-tion, visit our website at www.cornellpress.cornell.edu.

Cloth printing   10 9 8 7 6 5 4 3 2 1
Paperback printing   10 9 8 7 6 5 4 3 2 1

Chapters 3 and 4 contain revised portions of Sandra Morgen, "The Agency of Welfare Agency Workers: Negotiating Devolution and the Work of Welfare Reform," *American Anthropologist* 103, no. 3 (2001): 747–762, reprinted with permission of the American Anthropological Association. Chapter 5 contains revised portions of Sandra Morgen and Lisa Gonzales, "The Neoliberal American Dream as Daydream: Counter-Hegemonic Perspectives on Welfare Restructuring," *Critique of Anthropology* 28, no. 2 (2008): 219–236, published by SAGE Publications, all rights reserved, http://online.sagepub.com; or of Weigt 2006. Chapter 6 contains revised portions of Weigt 2002 or of Morgen, Acker, Weigt, and Gonzales 2006.

Contents

Acknowledgments

The research and writing that went into this book over more than a decade racked up many debts—intellectual, institutional, and personal. Countless people deserve our thanks, but here we limit ourselves to those to whom our debts are greatest.

First, we thank all of those who shared their stories and perspectives on welfare with us. Many of them must remain unnamed because of promises of confidentiality. These include women and men who turned to Adult and Family Services (AFS), Oregon's welfare agency, for help and who allowed us to observe their encounters with agency staff or who gave precious time to be interviewed. Our deep appreciation goes to the AFS staff who let us witness their work and also granted us interviews. We hope their trust in us will be repaid, at least in small measure, by policymakers and a public who gain a broader, more critical view of welfare "reform" from reading this book.

The welfare administrators with whom we worked from 1998 to 2000 deserve our gratitude for the access they granted us, the information they shared, the work we did in partnership, and the funds they allocated to support the research. In particular we thank Sandie Hoback, Elizabeth Lopez, Donald Main, Jim Neely, Ellen Pimental, Sue Smit, and Ron Taylor.

Although the three of us wrote this book, our research team included many others who lent their time, energy, and valuable insights to the project, and we sincerely appreciate their contributions. We are most indebted to Lisa Gonzales whose talents as an interviewer, analytic skills, and passion for social justice are echoed on many pages of this book. Research team members Kate Barry, Suzanne

Williams, and Sonja Vegdahl dedicated hundreds of hours each to understanding the daily practices of welfare restructuring, observing, recording, and sharing their insights as fieldworkers.

Terri Heath served as project manager of the funded research we conducted in partnership with AFS, overseeing the countless steps involved in the survey portion of the study and working closely with AFS staff. Holly Langan, a single mother of three, was an excellent work-study student with our project while completing both an undergraduate degree and a master's degree in public policy. She also shared with us her perspectives as a former and current recipient of public assistance. Thanks also to Dr. Patricia Gwartney and her staff at the former Oregon Survey Research Laboratory for their professional work helping to design, conduct, and analyze the data gathered in the telephone survey of Oregon families who left or were diverted from welfare or Food Stamps in early 1998.

This research was done under the auspices of the University of Oregon Center for the Study of Women in Society (CSWS), and the center's excellent staff provided more kinds of support than can be accounted for here. Thanks especially to Cheri Brooks, Debra Gwartney, Shirley Marc, Peggy McConnell, Beth Piatote, and Lin Reilly. Our gratitude goes to CSWS for providing grant and project funds without which this project would not have seen the light of day. Other colleagues at the University of Oregon helped in large ways and small to sustain this very long-term effort. They include Leslie Harris, Ken Hudson, Anne Johnstone, and statistical consultant Robin High.

We are also deeply grateful to and inspired by a group of activists and advocates who have worked tirelessly in support of Oregon's low-income families. They shared information with us and set a high bar for both research and advocacy. Among those who lent the strongest and most steadfast support (as well as critique) are Michael Leachman and Chuck Sheketoff of the Oregon Center for Public Policy; Cassandra Garrison and Kim Thomas, both formerly of the Oregon Food Bank; and Lorey Freeman of the Oregon Law Center.

Our intellectual communities provided ideas, inspiration, and support. This type of work is never done in a vacuum and many more colleagues than are listed here listened, commented, and critiqued our work or helped by the excellent standards they set in their own scholarship. We particularly thank Judith Goode, Margaret Hallock, Catherine Kingfisher, Jeff Maskovsky, Leith Mullings, Ken Neubeck, Ellen Scott, Dorothy Smith, Barbara Sutton, and researchers associated with the Welfare Researchers Roundtable in Oregon.

Our largest debt at Cornell University Press is to former editor Peter Wissoker. He spent many years in conversation with us about the book, was encouraging (even when critical), and gave us exceptionally careful readings and strong editorial assistance. We were lucky to work with another talented editor, Fran Benson, in the final stages of getting this book into production, and thank her as well as manuscript editor Susan Specter, copy editor Cathi Reinfelder, and the entire production team at Cornell. In these difficult times for university presses we take none of this fine work for granted. We want to underscore how valuable such institutions are as an integral part of the process of producing and disseminating knowledge.

We each owe much to friends and family for their patience and fortitude over the decade we devoted to this project. In addition to those mentioned above we thank the following friends for support and wise counsel: Jocelyn Ahlers, Lynn Bolles, Ann Bookman, Karen Brodkin, Linda Fuller, Anthony and Eileen Giardina, Ellen Herman, Greg McLaughlan, Cathy Richards Solomon, Carol Stack, Lynn Stephen, and Nancy Tuana.

Special thanks go to our children, partners, and other family members for their support and for understanding that the time we gave this project came from an abiding belief in the importance of research as part of the much larger process of political and social transformation that matters so much to us. Sandi thanks Seth, Sarah, and Robert Long for their love, their patience, and the inspiration they offer in countless ways. Thanks also to Sandi's sisters Barbara Morgen and Betsy Glen and her father, Dr. Robert Morgen. Joan thanks her sister, Fran Kirch, and her three sons Mike, Dave, and Steve. Jill thanks Deklyn, Soren, and Reinhard Schlassa for their love, humor, encouragement, and collaboration over the many years of this project.

Prologue

In December 1998, a group of executive staff of Oregon's welfare agency, Adult and Family Services (AFS), traveled across the state to meet with groups of welfare workers in order to present important changes in agency priorities and explain their planned strategy for the upcoming legislative session. On December 10, at one of these meetings, over one hundred welfare workers spent several hours of a work afternoon in an auditorium listening to a highly orchestrated presentation by the agency's top leadership. With the full agency leadership team present, there was no doubt that this was an important event. The meeting began with one of the administrators unveiling the latest draft of the agency's new mission statement. Another explained key elements of the budget they had recently submitted to the governor.

Sandie Hoback, the agency's lead administrator, made the climactic presentation entitled "Winter Focus Priorities and Empowerment." Hoback is a charismatic white woman, then in her early forties. She had overseen the agency during most of its half-decade-long transformation into a welfare-to-work agency. Her presentation was designed to frame and elicit the support of agency staff for changes in what she called organizational "philosophy" and the practices she defined as "empowering" for both the agency's workers and clients. Hoback began by presenting and explaining a diagram that differentiated what were now to be understood as two distinct areas of work in the agency: "core business" and "expansion areas." *Core business,* which was supposed to consume most (75%–80%) staff time, included welfare-to-work/self-sufficiency activity, employment retention, and improved accuracy in the Food Stamp program.

Expansion areas, which were to take up less than a quarter of staff time, included the work of promoting "family stability" and wage enhancement. With "expansion areas" pictured on the periphery of the hand-out that displayed the organization's mission, Hoback's message to the assembled workers was clear: Focus on the core areas. It is this work, she claimed, that "has made Oregon a leader and is helping our families."

With the gradual unfolding of new welfare policies over the 1990s, Oregon's welfare workers, especially the agency's "case managers," now had different jobs than in the period before "reform." Previously their jobs centered on accurately determining client eligibility for the benefits the agency administered. Now the mandate for case managers was to promote and support employment by applicants for and recipients of Temporary Assistance for Needy Families (TANF), the nation's post-1996 "welfare-to-work" program. However, AFS was smarting in the wake of costly penalties imposed by the federal government because of a recent, unacceptable increase in errors in the Food Stamp program. Workers knew that some, though not most, such errors resulted in either over- or under-payments to families. Most errors, however, were minor clerical mistakes. Nevertheless, the state could ill afford these penalties, and Hoback was determined to convince workers that a redoubled effort to ensure accuracy in the Food Stamp program was necessary and consistent with the agency's new case management approach to public assistance service provision. However, she knew she had to persuade case managers that they could manage the requirements of the welfare-to-work program, do a better job of ensuring benefit accuracy, *and* accomplish both even as the TANF caseload was changing to include a growing proportion of hard-to-serve clients. "Hard to serve" is code among welfare reformers for clients who exhibit more "barriers" to employment than other clients, making them more difficult to get off the rolls and into employment.

Hoback urged the workers to reduce their expectations of what they should do *for* clients. Instead they were told to set high expectations, especially about employment, for their clients and to hold clients accountable for meeting these expectations:

> I am supporting you in understanding your limits. Your role is to sit with an adult in partnership and help them design a road map for themselves. You cannot take that journey for them....Expectations and accountability are really key.

"Understanding your limits" referenced the now more limited assistance available to clients, but also the approach of fostering self-sufficiency rather than providing public assistance, especially TANF. Hoback assured agency staff that this would be "empowering [for clients]." It would translate, she was confident, to the client "feeling they can do things....Often our clients don't set good limits for them-selves—your setting limits is good for them." Requiring clients to be accountable to agency goals was a positive step, she said, "accountability is not a dirty word."

The most significant change in organizational "philosophy" signaled by the new mission statement and diagram was the shifting of the agency's long-time goal of promoting "family stability" from the center to the periphery of the agency mission. Here Hoback was speaking to the widely felt tension among frontline workers between the agency's "work-first" mandate and the difficulties they faced in fulfilling that mandate, especially with clients who had more "bar-riers" to employment. She explained that "family stability" was no less important to the agency now, but that the agency now understood family stability to be an *outcome* of, not a *prerequisite* for, employment. In other words, case managers were no longer to see their task as helping families achieve "stability" by provid-ing resources to meet their basic needs so they could *then* focus on getting a job. Now, Hoback declared, it was employment that was to be seen as the route to achieving family stability.

Hoback also explicitly disparaged the previous model of human services as being focused on providing public assistance to families, defining that approach as reflecting an "old school social work" mentality that

> poured resources into families....Fix the family and then maybe move to work. I call this happy, healthy, *poor* families....This is a huge discon-nect. We know and researchers know that poverty is the number one correlate for poor family outcomes. So [pointing to the diagram, she continues] I come back to employment at the core....So I put family stability on the rim. It's important, but employment is center stage.

The echo of the new neoliberal approach to welfare is unmistakable: Welfare fosters poverty by promoting dependency on public assistance benefits, which results in families living below the poverty line. The implicit message was that Oregon's continuing success in caseload reduction necessitated this new under-standing of the relationship between "family stability" and employment.

In framing the new approach as empowering for both clients and workers, Hoback was careful to delimit the contours of the discretion welfare "reform" had given to case managers. Agency leaders had great faith in their workers, she assured them. "You are our strongest resource." Nevertheless discretion is not a "free for all." Workers were to use their discretion and flexibility to innovate, but innovation was to be largely channeled toward promoting employment.

Along with emphasizing the now common neoliberal belief in the value of employment and "personal responsibility," Hoback also reiterated the conservative view of government bureaucracy as static, as a source of inertia. "For too long in

government," she said, "structures [were] in concrete, we change. In an empowerment environment, structures change." She then enlisted agency workers in the
process of "reinventing" the agency by taking inspiration from the private sector.
She encouraged workers to routinely ask themselves, "How would a private business
approach this? There is a bread and butter part, but we have to expand, think about
the future, for us it's the same in the public sector....AFS is very good at inventing
our future." In addition to thinking *like* a business Hoback also talked about the
importance of strong partnerships *with* business. The new AFS, she trumpeted, is
a collaborator with employers and business and its "work preparatory activities
[should focus on meeting] the needs of employers who have job openings."

After her presentation, the audience asked a few questions and offered minor
suggestions. But then a veteran case manager, a white man who had been employed
at the agency for years, implicitly challenged some of her assumptions. He expressed frustration with the "empowerment" message and worried aloud about
the relegation of "family stability" work to the periphery:

> It is hard to feel empowered when, the best way to describe it…is some-
> times [it's] hard to adapt. But a lot of us *do* a lot of the family stability
> work. But we have to get it done when our caseloads are at ninety. It is
> still too much. Now the system is asking for more intense eligibility, case
> management, Food Stamp reviews daily, so the extra time to do expan-
> sion work is almost impossible. Where is the time?

Much is packed into his statement. He said what undoubtedly many of his
coworkers were thinking: that with caseloads averaging ninety per case manager
it is "almost impossible" to get to all the work defined under "core activities," let
alone to attend to the now peripheralized "expansion" areas. His statement that "a
lot of us *do* a lot of the family stability work" was his way of saying that when one
sits across the desk from a family in dire need, it is hard to consign the work of family stability to a postemployment future. He also tacitly contested the assumption
that workers could feel "empowered" by these directives given the time squeeze
they experience daily. His plaintive "where is the time?" was a way of saying it does
not feel empowering to be asked to do the "impossible."

Hoback responded by first acknowledging that the work they were engaged in
was difficult. But she stuck to the empowerment message, suggesting that workers
were being empowered to manage their time efficiently and to stick to agency priorities. She encouraged workers to see this as a challenge they could meet, and to
see themselves as contributors to Oregon's status as a leader in welfare reform:

> It is hard to move into new areas because it is hard to keep up with
> caseloads and it is tough to maintain. Yes, but I go back to, there is never

enough human resources. Daily—choose your priorities. I can do this overview, but day-to-day you are empowered to think through how to maximize on those things given your constraints. I know your work is not simple....I don't know any other way other than to experiment. No one is doing better than us. We are literally writing the book. We have to keep grappling, experimenting, learning from each other. I don't have an exaggerated sense of what you can do. We'll learn our way to the future.

In representing the new policies and priorities as defining a "new" agency, she attempts to elicit the workers' support to continue to make Oregon a national leader in welfare "reform."

She also normalized the difficulties workers faced by saying, "I have never known an organization adequately staffed after twenty years in human resources." In other words, inadequate staff resources are nothing new. So she recommended that they "set priorities" as a strategy for managing their time. Recognizing that it was hard for many workers to deny assistance to needy families, she cautioned them not to be too "heart-connected [to] clients." Instead she advocated "tough love" and the expectation of clients' accountability, defining these as being tantamount to "giving the client a compliment" because it showed that the worker believed they were capable of achieving what was expected of them. As evidence she used herself as an example, explaining that when "the governor asks me to do a task, it is intimidating...but I always take it as a compliment....Same for our clients." Ignoring the class and, in the instance of clients of color, racial and ethnic differences between herself and the low-income women who turn to AFS for help, she read directly from her own experience to frame the experience of being accountable to a mandate from above as empowering.

This meeting was not unlike the process of policy implementation that was taking place daily in the offices and cubicles in welfare offices in Oregon and across the country. As the agency's mission was changed by policy makers so too was the daily work of managing agency staff and of welfare provision. Implementing welfare restructuring involved much more than simply modifying rules or rewriting a mission statement. It required alterations in the most fundamental practices of agency staff—a process framed, required, and monitored by welfare administrators. A vocabulary of empowerment, self-sufficiency, and "personal responsibility" was used to help reframe the contraction of public assistance as something ultimately good for low-income families, AFS, and the state. This reframing was designed to garner the consent of public welfare workers who then participated in transforming both their own workplaces and the nature of the welfare state.

The policy terms under which welfare administrators redesigned AFS were prescribed, in large measure, by federal and state public officials. Being successful at welfare restructuring meant producing the results policy makers sought on the terms set by those policy makers. Their success as administrators depended on the effective implementation of policies by workers up and down the organizational hierarchy and the acquiescence of workers and clients to neoliberal rules of engagement. Getting workers' cooperation was facilitated by framing the mission, goals, and procedures of the agency in the most positive terms possible. In meetings like this one, welfare administrators functioned as cheerleaders for the new policies to inspire and facilitate implementation by agency staff, framing the agency's new mission and practices as empowering, both for workers and clients. How this process unfolded and its effects on both those who administer Oregon's welfare programs and the nominal beneficiaries of the program is the subject of this book. At the end of the 1990s, when the meeting we chronicled above took place, the goals of employment and self-sufficiency seemed feasible to those at the top who formulated the policies. But many poor families subjected to the new policies were stretched thin, trying to make ends meet on low-wage jobs or struggling to comply with tough, often unrealistic mandates. Welfare workers were also stretched thin as they tried to implement these policies despite high caseloads and resource limitations that interfered with their ability to help their clients.

In 2009, with the country in a deep recession, our nation's social safety net is even more frayed. The welfare policies enacted in the 1990s failed to anticipate and prepare for an economic crisis of this depth. Yet these realities appear to be less visible, or, perhaps, to matter less to policy makers than the problems on Wall Street. In these difficult times many safety-net programs for ordinary people are out of reach or fail to help significant proportions of those who are income eligible. But TANF tops the list: in 2008 only 21 percent of families nationally with incomes low enough to qualify for TANF actually received benefits (DeParle and Erickson 2009)[1] In contrast, nationally, 67 percent of families eligible for Food Stamps received benefits and 73 percent of eligible, uninsured children received government medical benefits (ibid.).

Despite the shocking reality of silent and unmet need, we have heard no clamoring for the reform of welfare reform. In this book our goal is to look past the dominant rhetoric about welfare restructuring to assess the real consequences and mechanisms of the 1996 "reform." This close examination of the realities of welfare restructuring lead us to suggest changes in welfare policies designed to promote greater economic security and well-being for our nation's most vulnerable families and for the country as a whole.

QUESTIONING THE SUCCESS OF WELFARE REFORM

When the Personal Responsibility and Work Opportunity Reconciliation Act (PRWORA) became law on August 22, 1996,[1] its architects celebrated what they called the new "consensus" on welfare: that cash assistance should be temporary and contingent on recipients' seeking and finding employment. Framing the policy as consensual ignored the inconvenient truths that many policy makers and antipoverty advocates disapproved of welfare "reform" and that precious few of those most directly affected had much opportunity to weigh in on this radical change in the nation's social safety net. Then, as now, assessments about the assumptions and consequences of welfare "reform" were far more varied and disputed than the label "consensus" suggests. This book recognizes and focuses on *differences* in experiences, interpretations, and assessments of welfare reform. We believe an analysis of the varied realities and accountings of welfare restructuring helps to look back at a critical moment of policy change and also ahead, to how welfare policy can be changed to better address the needs of poor families and the nation.

Kim Smith,[2] a white mother of one toddler and another child in second grade, who lives in a suburb near one of Oregon's larger cities stopped receiving Temporary Assistance for Needy Families (TANF) early in 1998. She was excited: She had completed her general equivalency diploma (GED) and secured financial aid that would enable her to start classes for an associate's degree in health services at a nearby community college. TANF rules in Oregon meant she was ineligible for TANF because full-time schooling did not fulfill the program's work requirements. Smith had been on and off welfare when her children were younger. Most

1

of that time she combined part-time work with welfare, the low-wage jobs paying so little that her family still qualified for assistance. But now, through postsecondary education, she saw herself working toward a better-paying job.

It was hard to make ends meet that year, but Food Stamps, a housing subsidy, some financial help with child care from a student block grant, and her family's coverage by the Oregon Health Plan (OHP, or Medicaid) meant she could scrape by. But growing financial problems forced Smith to get a part-time job. She began working as a cocktail waitress for $7.00 an hour plus tips, but the job came with no benefits. Still, she could be with her children during the day when she was not at school, and her mother helped by watching the kids for free while she was at work at night. A few months later her mother fell ill. Smith was unable to manage on her own and was forced to drop out of school. She hoped it was only for a while, but in the meantime she had to pay back $1,800 in financial aid because she had not finished the semester. She felt she had no choice but to put her educational goals aside for the time being: "It's too much, school, and it's too long for them [her kids] to be, for us to be tight on money and me to be stressed out going to school."

She increased her hours to full-time and worked four late nights a week as a cocktail waitress. She took care of the kids during the day, but she got little sleep. On the nights that she worked, her children stayed with friends or relatives. When her income went up slightly, her share of the OHP premium went up and her Food Stamps were cut. "You end up having less," she sighed, during one of the three times we interviewed her face-to-face. She fell behind on her premium for OHP and lost coverage for a while; she was terrified one of the children would get sick. Two years after leaving TANF, Smith was struggling financially and could not see how she would get back to school. Welfare rules that excluded her from TANF eligibility if she attended college presented a huge catch-22, as she told us:

> They'll pay for your day care to work a minimum wage job for the rest of your life....Because at a minimum wage job you'll never be able to afford day care yourself anyway. But they won't pay for someone, for day care for a year or two for them to go to school and get a degree so they could become more successful.

For Kim Smith, who had plenty of work experience, Oregon's transition to a "work-first" welfare program meant that her plan of getting the education she needed to get a better job had become what seemed an impossible dream.

The stress and frustration Smith experienced was not unusual among mothers who were on public assistance at the time of this transition. Details differed, but hardships were similar. Linda Perkins, an African American single mother of two children, one five and the other ten, worked as head housekeeper at a motel. She, too, made $7.00 an hour and received no benefits from her employer. The job had irregular, unpredictable hours. She found a better job as a housekeeper in a home for elderly patients. The pay was $8.00 an hour, she was guaranteed forty hours a week, and the job provided health coverage. But her eldest son was having serious behavioral problems at school. Perkins worried about him a lot and sometimes had to leave work when the school called saying he was having problems and she needed to pick him up. When stress-related high blood pressure began to affect her health, a school-associated social worker recommended that she quit her job for a while in order to get her son's behavioral problems stabilized. An understanding welfare worker allowed her to get back on TANF without engaging in the requisite job search for a period of several months, and her son began to improve.

Soon her case manager began pressuring her to return to work. Perkins wanted to work, but she feared that the cycle of difficulties she had faced for years would return with her return to employment. Her ongoing difficulties making ends meet contributed to the stress she felt:

> What is hard is that you work long hours, for very little pay....And I'm always frustrated, and I know that the therapist told me that the reason why my son has behavior problems...is because he feels my stress. And I'm always stressed out. There is not a point or time that I am not stressed about worrying about how I'm going to pay for this, how I'm going to do that. You know? There is a constant ball of stress....I think that if I was able to make more money, spend more time with the kids, that I would not, that I wouldn't be so stressed out and neither would my child.

On the other side of the desk, welfare restructuring changed the work of welfare provision as well. Instead of determining eligibility for and administering public assistance, welfare workers' jobs were now focused on promoting the employment of their clients and moving them off TANF. This has remained true to the time of this writing. Many find this new definition of their work exciting and their jobs more fulfilling, including Elana Lopez, a Latina case manager with twenty-four years of work at the agency:

> It's been excellent, I believe, for my clients, and I think for us it has been satisfying....We haven't just pushed paper....But we really helped somebody in their lives to hope that they will have a good life....That you made some kind of intervention, a point of impact, a positive thing in people's lives, and in our whole culture as a result of it.

But case managers will tell you that welfare "reform" has not been excellent for everyone. Thomas Dennison, a white case manager we spoke with, expressed his concern that some needy families are not getting the help they need:

> We can't say that it is all positive, that everybody that needs help is get-ting help and that everybody that has been disqualified deserved to be disqualified. You know there are people out there that are legitimately hurting who can't get help now or feel they can't get help now.

Moreover, the fact that case managers now carry caseloads upward of ninety clients each makes it nearly impossible to meaningfully address each client's needs. And that is producing significant work pressure and stress, as Tammy Hill, a veteran white female worker confesses:

> I never have a day when I feel good about where I am with my caseload, and I feel uncomfortable...[with] the time pressures.

Yet state welfare administrators and local welfare agency managers have approached welfare restructuring in Oregon enthusiastically. Christy Kahoe, a white female branch manager assessed "the whole welfare reform...as [being] a real positive move for the state." Compared to other states, she continues, Oregon has "taken a real humanistic approach to this and just really looked at what we can do to really help our clients, so that is one of the reasons why we have been so successful." Two other branch managers, Cyrus Todd, a white man, and Anna Borelli, a white woman, described Oregon's new welfare program as "visionary" and "forward thinking" respectively. They endorse the oft-repeated claim by the agency's lead administrator that Oregon is a "national leader" in welfare reform, in large part because the program "empowers" both the workers who implement and the clients who are served by a program based on the philosophy that "work is always better than welfare."

These women and men are a few of the over one thousand people we encoun-tered between 1998 and 2000 in our research on welfare restructuring in Oregon. In this book we examine their different experiences and their interpretations of those experiences in considerable depth. The voices and experiences of those most directly living welfare "reform"—clients and workers—have generally been overshadowed by the triumphant voices of many policy makers eager to call welfare reform a grand policy success. One such policy maker is Mike Leavitt, former secretary of the U.S. Department of Health and Human Services (DHHS). In 2006, on the tenth anniversary of the congressional passage of the new welfare law, Leavitt applauded welfare reform for bringing "significant improvements in the lives of many Americans by helping them break the cycle of dependency and encouraging them to pursue self-sufficiency" (U.S. DHHS 2006). He dedicated his agency's efforts to finishing the "unfinished business of welfare reform by helping more Americans find jobs that will *lift* them from the welfare rolls" (U.S. DHHS 2006). Here, Leavitt makes explicit the goal of welfare reform. It is not to help *lift* families out of poverty but to reduce the reliance of the economically insecure on the welfare state.

Within the public policy community, however, there are others who issue more sobering assessments of both the goals and the level of success of the new welfare policy. Dr. Avis Jones-DeWeever, former director of Poverty, Education, and Social Justice Programs at the Institute for Women's Policy Research, warns that

> Lost amid all of the 10th anniversary celebratory discussions that equate caseload reduction to welfare reform success is the on-the-ground reality of families continuing to live at the margins, struggling to make it, but in recent years, falling further and further behind (2006).

Her focus on the continuing realities of poverty and economic insecurity that millions of low-income families now face as the social safety net has been dramatically contracted paints a very different picture than Leavitt's focus on the achievement of caseload reduction.

Groups with diverse structural relationships to the welfare system, especially in terms of their political interests and their power and influence over policy and institutional practices, vary in their appraisals of welfare restructuring. These assessments offer a challenge to the claim that there is a broad "consensus" that welfare reform has been an unbridled "success." Clearly race, class, and gender differences and inequalities are woven into the relationships people have to the welfare state and are, therefore, deeply implicated in these diverse perspectives.

Groups that define success as caseload reduction—often policy experts, politicians, and state welfare administrators—have ample evidence to support their claims. Nationally TANF caseloads were cut in half between 1996 and 2000; caseloads fell even after the recession of 2001 resulting in "a decrease from 4.6 million families receiving TANF in 1996 to 2.1 million in 2002" (Urban Institute 2006, 1). TANF caseloads continued to decline in the next, far deeper recession beginning in 2007, reaching 1.6 million in June 2008 (U.S. DHHS 2008). Employment rates for single mothers grew steadily, at least during the economic boom that coincided with adoption of the new welfare law, rising from 60 percent of single mothers in 1994 to 72 percent in 1999 (Moffitt 2002, 1). However these rates fell during the recession of 2001, down to 69.8 percent by 2003, and remaining at 70 percent through 2007 (U.S. Bureau of Labor Statistics 2008). Single mothers experienced a greater unemployment increase than other working parents or workers generally (Sherman, Fremstad, and Parrott 2004). National studies of the outcomes of policy changes in welfare in the mid- to late 1990s consistently showed that about two-thirds of adults leaving TANF found jobs. For example, in our study, of those people who left TANF, 71 percent were employed twelve to fifteen months after leaving the program in 1998.

But a deeper look shows a less positive reality: Of those who had jobs, only 58 percent had been working steadily during that time (Acker et al. 2001). Moreover, finding a job, even in the prosperous economy of the late 1990s, did not usually mean an escape from poverty. In Oregon, 55 percent of TANF leavers still had family incomes below the poverty line twelve to eighteen months after leaving the program (Acker et al. 2001). Leaving welfare for employment often meant increased income for these families (Cherry 2007), but most remained poor and economically insecure. The national poverty rate fell from 13.7 percent in 1996 to 11.3 percent in 2000—not even close to matching the dramatic decline in welfare caseloads—but then climbed steadily after 2000 (Kilty 2006).

Twelve years after passage of PRWORA, the reform "successes" of the late 1990s seem even more incomplete and fleeting. The great majority of families who left or were diverted from TANF have household incomes either below or near the official poverty line, reflecting the low wages and limited benefits of available jobs, anemic wage growth, and more often horizontal than vertical job mobility.[3] Improvements in the rates of poverty and of employment of poor single mothers in the mid- to late 1990s were largely reversed after 2000 in the wake of the recession and then the "jobless" recovery (Parrott and Sherman 2007), and the recession beginning in 2007. Thus, the "success" of welfare reform is more complex and contested than the audible public discourse suggests.[4] It is important to examine closely both the political claims and the realities and perspectives of those most intimately affected by welfare restructuring.

In this book we explore the lived reality behind the success claims by looking at how welfare "reform" was implemented, experienced, and interpreted on the ground in Oregon in the late 1990s. by the human service workers in Adult and Family Services (AFS),[5] the Oregon state welfare agency, and the low-income, primarily female-headed families who turn to the agency for assistance when they are facing hard times.[6] We argue, as have others, that these experiences with the actualities of welfare restructuring were, and are, profoundly shaped by conservative family values and a belief that an unregulated ("free") market will produce a viable path to self-support and individual/familial independence (from the state)—what is often termed *neoliberalism*.[7] Welfare restructuring was also based on a fundamental, class-inflected change in social expectations of mothers of young children: They are now expected to be breadwinners first and caregivers second, unless, of course, they have husbands who bring home an adequate wage to support them and their children. In 2005 Congress reauthorized TANF (implemented in 2006 once signed by President Bush). Provisions of TANF's reauthorization, enacted as part of the Deficit Reduction Act of 2005 (DRA), made the "work first" basis of federal welfare policy more stringent and coercive.[8] Although the reauthorization debates were often heated, the bottom-line assumption of policy success was rarely publicly challenged, at least by those whose power and privilege enabled their voices to be heard.

Welfare restructuring was never simply about terminating Aid to Families with Dependent Children (AFDC). The program only cost the nation about 1 percent of gross domestic product (GDP) from the 1980s through the 1990s (Steuerle and Mermin 1997). Rather, welfare "reform," was just one, albeit highly visible, step toward much broader changes in redistributive public policies, a paradigm shift from a Keynesian, redistributive national welfare system to a market-oriented, minimalist (welfare) state in which redistribution is downsized and privatized. Proponents of welfare "reform" actually had their eyes on much bigger prizes: privatization and cuts/cost containment of massive entitlement programs such as Social Security, Medicaid, and Medicare and the further subjugation of social policy to the imperatives of free market capitalism. Given that proponents of this larger paradigm shift often point to the "success" of welfare reform in their arguments for a further privatized, devolved, and limited social safety net, it is imperative that we examine closely how this paradigm shift, its purported "success," as well as its consequences were produced. This we do as we explore how welfare restructuring was and is actually implemented and enforced, how support for these changes has been articulated and produced, and how questioning and dissent have been expressed, muted, and answered.

As we write this book, the U.S. economy is faltering in the wake of the most severe economic crisis since the Great Depression: massive job loss and unemployment growth, the housing/mortgage crisis, declining rates of health insurance coverage, enormous stock market losses, and ever more gloomy economic forecasts week after week. Millions more families are facing economic hardship and insecurity, and there are many indications of ongoing need for a restored, stronger, and more accessible social/economic safety net. Studies such as this may point to areas of weakness in the power of the dominant beliefs, and thus to areas for potential change in the conservative, anti–welfare state opposition to ensuring adequate basic social and economic supports for everyone. By examining the experiences of those most closely affected and involved, we illuminate the myth of successful "reform" and consider alternative public policy directions that would better promote broad economic well-being and security and reduce the growing economic inequalities that we, and many others, see as undermining democratic citizenship.

Our Research Questions and Research Strategies

Three general questions about welfare restructuring illuminate different experiences and interpretations of the implementation of welfare "reform" at the local, day-to-day level and what this suggests about the broader changes in public policy.

1. How do groups differently positioned within welfare-state processes experience and interpret welfare restructuring, especially the radical shift from income maintenance to mandated paid labor, taking into account differences in race, gender, and class relations? Given the diverse opinions of those most closely involved—administrators, clients, and workers—how are the claims of success framed and maintained? How are contradictions between these "successful" policies and the seemingly less successful social and individual realities handled? How do individuals differently located within the welfare state and by gender, race, ethnicity, and class both accept and contest the ideologically charged assumptions underlying the new policy framework?

2. How are these new policies actually produced, implemented, and transformed into practical actions in daily life in welfare organizations? How is "success" produced as concrete procedures and measurable outcomes? Other research tells us that victories on the ideological or even the policy levels do not automatically translate into material, everyday procedures.[9] Actual practices must change if policies are to become more than empty statements of belief; that is, if they are to have the desired outcomes. Policies can become actualities or they can be sabotaged at the site of implementation. In the case of welfare restructuring we ask: How were changing expectations of women and ideas about the economy, poverty, and welfare translated into actions and concrete experiences in the lives of welfare recipients, welfare workers, and administrator?. We also seek to understand how race, class, and gender relations shape and produce differences in these actions and experiences.

3. Finally, given the complex consequences of restructuring for families that need public assistance and the state agencies whose programs constitute vital links in the social safety net, we ask: What is the reality behind the accepted definitions of success and the underlying assumptions and issues at the center of the now-dominant public policy framework? To answer this question we explore the concrete realities of the ongoing reproduction of a very low-wage labor force (Piven and Cloward [1971] 1993), adding to the already considerable research on the human, social, and political consequences of welfare restructuring.[10]

Our answers to the questions we pose are based in large part on extensive data from our multimethod, multisite study of welfare reform in one state, Oregon, during the 1990s. Oregon was widely viewed as a national leader in welfare reform, charting a path to "work-first" policies early in the 1990s even before PRWORA passed in Congress. We were among dozens of teams of researchers who studied the effects of welfare restructuring at the state-level, recognizing that welfare devolved to states meant that the actual welfare programs, as well as the economic and political realities of states (Winston 2002), differed enough to warrant fine-grained analysis of these different contexts.

Because welfare reform was so controversial (despite claims of consensus), a great deal of research was conducted, at least in the several years immediately after PRWORA's implementation. Much of this research, especially that conducted by policy evaluation researchers who constitute the core of the "poverty research industry" (O'Connor 2001), relies heavily on quantitative analysis of large data sets (administrative and survey data) to examine caseload decline, employment and income patterns, and family "outcomes" among former and current recipients of public assistance.[11] Other research, more often conducted by academic social scientists or scholar-advocates, has looked more broadly and, often, deeply, at the consequences of welfare state restructuring, low-wage jobs, and lack of access to affordable health- and child care and housing for low-income families.[12] These latter studies often use or supplement quantitative methods with qualitative research, providing more nuanced and complex accounts of the survival struggles of the single mothers who have borne the costs of late-twentieth-century economic restructuring and neoliberal social policy. These examples of what Jeff Maskovsky and Judith Goode call "the new poverty studies" (2002) challenge the rhetoric of policy makers and the paradigms of mainstream poverty researchers that both ignore how gender, race, and class relations in contemporary capitalism are implicated in the production of poverty and economic insecurity. A much smaller group of researchers have focused on the impact of welfare restructuring on welfare workers, examining processes of implementation and the impact of policy changes on the work of welfare provision.[13]

Our study is unusual in examining the multiple and varied experiences and perspectives of clients and former clients and welfare workers, and it also explores changing welfare policies and practices as they are guided by the welfare administrators who make the initial translations of national prescriptions into state policy or who manage the implementation of the local work of welfare. Thus, we develop a more complex analysis than most other accounts of welfare restructuring. This study illuminates the tremendous changes mandated by PRWORA as these are actually manifested in practical activities, crises, and, sometimes, solutions in the everyday lives of those on the front lines of public assistance.

We spent three years, from 1998 through 2000, examining the process of welfare change on the ground in Oregon and the production of policy "success" as it played in multiple sites. We began our research in 1998 with a year of ethnographic fieldwork in three local welfare offices (called "branches" in Oregon). We chose these branches[14]—referred to in this book by the pseudonyms Bridgetown, Woodside, and Coastal—so we could observe the practices of welfare reform in communities with different local economic conditions and client and staff demographics. Because Adult and Family Services (AFS) gave its local offices considerable responsibility for welfare-to-work program design, the work of welfare for staff and experiences of clients differed among locations. We observed a wide variety of meetings and interactions—including individual meetings between case workers and clients, group workshops that clients were required to attend, staff meetings and trainings, and interactions in waiting rooms and reception areas.[15]

During the fieldwork we conducted in-depth interviews with almost all (95 percent) of the staff across the organizational hierarchy in each of the three branches, including clerical workers, family resource managers, case managers, supervisors, and some of the non-AFS employees who provided subcontracted job readiness services in the branches through the Job Opportunities and Basic Skills program (JOBS).[16] During these 126 interviews we discussed the nature of individuals' jobs, their experiences as workers, questions about service provision and branch organization, workers' attitudes toward clients and welfare "reform," and questions about their racial, gender, class, educational, and occupational identities and backgrounds. The interviews, which averaged about ninety minutes, were tape-recorded and transcribed verbatim.[17]

In addition to the ethnographic work in the branches, a second phase of the research focused on the experiences of clients and ex-clients of the agency, including their interpretations of the consequences and "success" of welfare restructuring. Here we interviewed a large, statewide, random sample of agency clients chosen from a group that had each left or been diverted from[18] TANF or Food Stamps during the first three months of 1998. We followed their experiences over two years, drawing on three sources of data: telephone surveys, in-depth interviews, and administrative data First, we conducted telephone surveys of the statewide random sample of women and men at two points in time after their exit or diversion from TANF or Food Stamps.[19] At twelve to fifteen months after exit or diversion, we interviewed 970 people; six months later we reinterviewed 757 of this group of women and men.

Second, we conducted in-depth, in-person interviews with a subsample of this larger group. The first in-depth interviews, with 75 women and 3 men, took place in between the first and second telephone survey interviews. The second in-depth interviews (65 of them) were completed closer to the two-year post exit or diversion mark. Two-thirds of the participants in this phase of the study identified racially as white, and one-third identified racially as African American,

Latino/a, Native American, Asian American, or mixed race. Thirty women from this original sample were interviewed a third time in 2001–2002.[20] These interviews were for a separate study and took place closer to four years after these clients left TANF in 1998. (See chapter 5 for more detail about these samples.) Third, we had access to extensive administrative data provided by AFS and the Oregon Employment Department for the full statewide random sample.

Perspective Matters

Anaïs Nin is credited with saying "We don't see things as they are, we see things as we are." A central theoretical and organizing principle of this book is that perspective matters, that ideas and assessments of welfare restructuring are shaped in complex ways by social location and by particular theoretical and political assumptions and values. This view follows directly from a wealth of feminist scholarship, especially feminist discussions of epistemology and much scholarship by feminists of color.[21] As we argued above, our book is distinguished from many others on welfare "reform" because we designed our research to examine the varying experiences and perspectives of the various groups most directly affected by welfare, with attention to their relations with each other, their positions in the welfare state, and how those positions intersect with gender, race, and class to produce differences among and within these groups. Different perspectives often produce different interpretations of the same actions and events: Paying attention to multiple perspectives enriches our understanding of how the paradigm shift from income maintenance to work-first welfare is assessed.

Our focus in the substantive chapters of the book is on the welfare state employees and clients who are "in the [welfare] system." Although their perspectives are crucial in the implementation of policy, theirs are not the only perspectives that matter. Indeed, as far as the actual process of making and assessing public policy goes, their perspectives matter far less than those of policy makers— politicians in Congress, state legislators, and governors—or of the well-connected lobbyists and think tanks that help shape policy agendas. The views of policy makers, still overwhelmingly white, elite men (Center for American Women and Politics 2008), are driven by political ideologies and parties, partisan think tank policy reports, the media, their own values, and their interpretations of public opinion.

The policy makers and researchers, including ourselves, who study welfare have very different vantage points from those who experience, assess, and know welfare in ways that are much closer to the ground; that is, those who are "in the system." Our point is not that these vantage points should necessarily be privileged over those of researchers, policy makers, or even antipoverty advocates. It is rather, as reflected in the title of this section, that "perspective matters," including the various perspectives that emerge from what different groups know or believe due to their different positions in the welfare state. We will understand complex social issues best when we examine them from multiple perspectives and experiences.

There is no singular perspective that emerges automatically from the position of client, welfare worker, or even welfare administrator. Indeed, we see them more as categories within which we can observe both differences and patterns of similarity. We will look to gender, race, and class to help understand how those engaged with the welfare system are positioned within the structure of the welfare state. Where a person is positioned determines how much access one does or does not have to certain information and experiences. The stories we tell in the following pages are intended to illuminate the complexity of the impact of positionality on experience and perspective.

Positionality and perspective also matter for understanding the other sources of information about the welfare system. Welfare administrators, clients, and workers are members of the public, and as such their perspectives are influenced by their own experiences as participants "in the system," but also by what policy makers say and by what they "know" from how these issues are framed and reported by the mass media. An extensive body of research focused on media coverage of poverty and welfare demonstrates that poverty and welfare are given gender, race, and other characteristics in and by the media, in terms of representations of *who* is seen (literally) as poor and/or on welfare and in the promulgation of explicit or implicit assumptions about *why* they are poor.[22] This research demonstrates how media images and reportage have depicted the poor as the welfare-dependent, as (disproportionately, and pictorially almost exclusively) African American, as not "working," and as families plagued by every manner of behavioral and attitudinal dysfunction. This pattern has continued since welfare "reform," although added to the consistent pattern of reportage, a newer story line has emerged, framed almost exclusively to answer what has been deemed the core question: Has welfare reform been a success? In general the media "answer" has been a resounding echo of policy makers' "Yes" (Avery and Peffley 2003; Schram and Soss 2002). And as we detail in chapters 3 and 5, media representations of welfare recipients and of welfare restructuring are echoed in some of the attitudes and interpretations offered by agency workers and recipients themselves.

While the media frames stories about welfare and poverty in terms of the success of reform, poverty itself only rarely "makes news," the exceptional example of reporting in the immediate aftermath of Hurricane Katrina notwithstanding[23] (deMause and Rendell 2007). And those stories generally give the microphone to policy makers and researchers much more often than to those who live in poverty or provide direct services to the poor. When the poor are featured in news stories, what they say is "severely circumscribed…poor people…telling generic stories of suffering," while it is left to "experts" to interpret the causes and solutions; not surprisingly non-Hispanic whites and men are disproportionately chosen as the "expert" sources" (deMause and Rendell 2007). In a study of welfare reporting in the *New York Times* and the *Washington Post*, policy makers connected to government represented 58 percent of the sources, and other "experts" (mostly researchers) another 14 percent; recipients of welfare constituted 10 percent of sources and frontline human service providers were only 3 percent of the sources cited (Lens 2002). Clearly the story of welfare restructuring is impoverished when the perspectives of those most directly affected are effaced or so highly circumscribed by media sound-bites and the ubiquitous framing of the issues.

As researchers we too participate in filtering, selecting, and representing the different perspectives of those we study; we are not a transparent "pass through" for their voices. We have tried to be true to the stories, images, explanations, and experiences we witnessed and heard about, but our social locations as individuals and our theoretical perspectives as scholars surely shaped our vantage points, analytic strategies, and conclusions. In other words, *our* perspectives mattered too. In the appendix we discuss briefly our social locations as individuals and how our different political, generational, and class backgrounds affected the research.

Our understandings of the complex experiences and dynamics we studied are inflected not only by our positions in the matrix of gender, race, and class relations but also by the knowledge we have accumulated as social scientists and activists and by the theoretical assumptions and frameworks we brought to our work. As feminist scholars we did not ignore the fact that the vast majority of the people most directly affected by welfare reform are not generic welfare "recipients," as they are usually referred to in welfare agency documents and in much other research on welfare reform. In fact, the vast majority of potential, current, and past recipients of welfare are *women* who are poor. They are also women who have racial identities and who are racialized in the perceptions and interactions they have with welfare agency staff. Furthermore, welfare workers are also predominantly women, although they have more economic security than their clients. Their work in the agency positions them in a matrix of power relations in which gender, race, ethnicity, and class shape access to power, resources, and differential opportunity. Our work emerges from and is meant to be in dialogue with other feminist theorists who use an *intersectional framework* to understand power, difference, identity, and experience in women's lives.[24]

Intersectional theories "require that research findings be understood in relation to the distribution of power in the production of inequality [and] the simultaneous examination of multiple dimensions of inequality and difference" (Dill and Zambrana 2009, 193–194). This theoretical framework theorizes gender, race, and class as "simultaneous processes, socially constructed, historically and geographically specific and involving material, ideological and psychological elements which create and recreate unequal economic and power distributions" (Acker 2006, 39). Through this lens we understand that race, gender, and class inequalities are woven into the history and overall structuring of welfare states, into the structure of particular welfare programs, into the relative legitimacy of public provision of various kinds, and, of course, into efforts to change those programs.

Much of the literature on welfare in the United States either presumes or ignores the reality that poverty, economic inequality, and the gendered and racialized nature of class relations emerge from capitalist processes; that is, they are neither forces of nature nor inevitable ways of organizing economic life (Folbre 2001; Nelson 2006). Ironically, most research on poverty and welfare "does not define itself as an inquiry into the political economy and culture of late 20th century capitalism" (O'Connor 2001, 4). Our goal is to do just that. Moreover, we analyze capitalism not as an abstract, megaforce "out there," but as particular social relations, practices, policies, and assumptions that are peopled, embodied, and enacted in daily life in the context of significant and growing social and economic inequality.

Thus, our analytic strategy is to start "on the ground," to pay attention to and analyze the actions, practices, and values of those agency personnel and clients who, on a daily basis, transform policies written into texts or verbal messages into material benefits and experiences in the context of capitalist workplaces, communities, and political processes. In our view, the analysis of practices—of "on the ground" actions and procedures—is necessary to understand what social scientists often abstractly refer to as "structures" or "forces" (Smith 1987, 2005). Theories and ideologies, such as beliefs about the desirability of government supports for low-income families, become actual in the "doing," in the processes of translation into practices that affect the situations of those involved. This approach can also show how local practices in disparate places are interrelated, how relations among levels of power are organized, and how the potentials for interpretation and resistance vary.

Additionally, as researchers we shared a critique of *how* research on poverty and welfare policy has been, and was being, produced in the aftermath of welfare policy changes. Most federal funding for research on poverty over the past half century has been allocated for "purposes of measurement, program evaluation and policy analysis…based on methods derived from economics, and steeped in a market-oriented worldview" (O'Connor 2001, 213–214). The topical obsessions of this research have been the individual and behavioral characteristics of the poor and, particularly, their use of public assistance (Morgen 2002; O'Connor 2001).[25] So we designed our research to gather data on a much broader range of concerns than many similar studies, and we sought to provide extensive opportunity for both welfare clients and workers to define and discuss the issues that they believed were most salient. Moreover, having the opportunity to spend months in the agency watching workers interact with clients, each other, and managers gave us a strong foundation for understanding what we heard from both workers and clients in interviews. Our shifting angle of vision also helped us to appreciate the various, often conflicting, pressures on those who occupy different positions within the welfare state, the subject of this book.

Place, Politics, and Power

Our research was based on welfare "reform" as it was lived in the particular economic, political, social, and demographic realities of Oregon in the mid- to late 1990s. In the conclusion we consider changes post 2000, but our data for this period is far less rich. Based on reading an extensive literature about welfare restructuring in other states and communities, we believe that our findings resonate broadly with what researchers have documented elsewhere. However, it is important to note some of the ways Oregon differs from some other states.

Oregon is a comparatively small state (by population), a more rural state than many, and compared to the country as a whole, whiter and more racially homogeneous. During the period of our study, people of color represented 12 percent of the state's population, less than half their proportion in the U.S. population (Oregon Progress Board 2000, 2). In 1998, 88 percent of Oregonians were white, 6 percent were Latino, 3 percent were Asian American, 2 percent were African American, and 1 percent was Native American (ibid. 2000, 2). Oregon's racial and ethnic makeup is, however, rapidly changing. In particular, the state is experiencing a relatively high rate of increase in the Latino population, an increase of 144 percent between 1990 and 2000 (Padin 2005, 52).

As in the nation as a whole, poverty rates in Oregon are significantly higher for women than men, for single parents than married-couple households, and for African Americans, Native Americans, Latinos, and immigrants compared to non-Hispanic whites. In 1998, 10 percent of non-Hispanic white Oregonians were poor compared to 22 percent of Native Americans, 27 percent of Latinos, and 30 percent of African Americans (Oregon Progress Board 2000, 7). The racial composition of Oregon's TANF caseload mirrors (with variations discussed below) the distribution of poverty in the state.

Understanding the racial composition of TANF caseloads is important, in part, because researchers have found a strong correlation between the racial demography of TANF caseloads (especially a higher proportion of African Americans as TANF clients) and the likelihood that a state enacted "tougher" welfare policies, especially shorter time limits, family caps, and coercive sanction policies (Soss et al. 2001). Thus, Oregon's lower-than-the-national-average proportion of clients of color on TANF may help explain what some have defined as a "kinder and gentler" version of welfare reform in the state. In addition, most of Oregon's poor families, because they are white, do not face exactly the same challenges endured by women of color, in Oregon or nationally—challenges that follow from the ways racism profoundly marks the lives of low-income women and families of color.

Because welfare restructuring devolved to states significant flexibility to redesign their public assistance programs and because states differ markedly in the strengths of their economies, their political cultures, and the racial, ethnic, and class makeup of residents, we recognize the importance of keeping the particulars in mind as we move from our research on Oregon to our recommendations for the nation. Nevertheless, as we suggested above, despite program and local political-economic differences, key aspects of welfare restructuring were replicated in state after state: explicit and implicit criteria of "success," stringent work requirements, time limits (although the length of time varied), the contingency of benefit receipt based on compliance with agency rules, the availability of work supports and subsidies to (temporarily) help bridge the gap between low wages and family needs, and benefit exclusions for both documented and undocumented immigrants.

Oregon's welfare policies and programs were influential among its sister states in part because Oregon initiated welfare "reform" earlier than most states. Its caseload decline was among the nation's highest, something welfare administrators in the state were proud of (see prologue). Oregon was one of only four states to obtain waivers to its AFDC program in 1992, and the state secured an additional waiver just before PRWORA was passed in 1996. The 1996 waiver meant that in the first five years (1996–2001) after PRWORA was enacted (when we studied the program), Oregon was not subject to all provisions of the federal legislation. Unlike some states, Oregon did *not* adopt some of what antipoverty advocates consider among the most draconian policies: the family cap (denying or limiting increases in the TANF grant for children born after a family goes on TANF), allowing no exemption from work after the birth of a child, shorter lifetime limits on receipt of TANF than the federal law (of five years), or the severest sanction policies for noncompliance. Among states Oregon falls roughly in the middle in terms of the severity of its sanction policies: fourteen states (and the District of Columbia) had policies that ranked as low (severity), eighteen (including Oregon) as medium, and nineteen as high (Crouse 1999). Oregon's policies on provision of services to immigrants are like those of a significant number of states that are relatively more than less generous.

On the other hand, Oregon was among the most restrictive of states in other ways. Oregon adopted a policy subjecting new mothers to work requirements when their baby reached the age of three months, earlier than most states. Moreover, unlike at least some states, Oregon did not allow recipients to pursue a two-year postsecondary education as an "allowable activity" for work requirements. Oregon also has a number of policies that compare unfavorably with many other states in terms of getting more money into the hands of its clients, including both a comparatively limited earnings disregard policy[26] and the state's decision not to "pass through"[27] much of what it collects in child support for families on TANF. Oregon leaders also supplanted spending from its TANF block grant, more than most other states, diverting funds that would otherwise have been spent on low-income families to general funds programs such as child protective services and education (Leachman, Merten, and Sheketoff 2005).

In terms of the people whose lives we studied, this research mirrored, in key ways, research being conducted about the experiences of ex-TANF recipients in other states. Most of the research on welfare funded during this period focused on families that left cash assistance (called welfare "leaver" studies).[28] This was especially true of the millions of dollars in funding provided by Congress to assess welfare-to-work. These dollars were allocated only to state welfare agencies (and their chosen partners). We partnered with AFS in submitting one of these proposals. Although that study was not ultimately funded by DHHS, agency administrators, keen to do the research and apparently pleased with our collaboration in the drafting of the proposal, decided to use state funds to do a somewhat scaled-back version of the proposed study. After much discussion among ourselves and with the agency, we agreed to conduct this study as a "partnership" (the term that was used) with the agency. As we discuss more in chapter 1, the terms of the partnership involved joint decisions over important facets of the research design, with our role defined as "independent researchers" who retained ownership of the data and independence from the agency in the analysis of data.

Our study is perhaps most unusual in our decision to include welfare administrators among the groups we studied. This decision was made during the study as we realized how incomplete this study would be without attending to their perspectives. What we learned from and about agency administrators was not, with the exception of interviews with branch managers, through formal interviews. Rather, it came from informal discussions with and observations of them while we were proposing, and then planning and carrying out the other facets of the research. We also drew on extensive documentary evidence, including public documents or data produced by and about the agency during the 1990s, media stories about the agency or welfare reform in Oregon newspapers during the 1990s, and information about Oregon's welfare program collected by federal agencies and other researchers.

In addition to the three years of data collection (1998–2000), we were active participants in state-level policy discussions for several years following the completion of the study. We met with, presented data to, and discussed our findings with agency administrators, antipoverty advocates, state legislators and legislative committees, and other members of the public. These were not only occasions to *disseminate* study findings; they also served as further opportunities to learn about the varying perspectives of various groups positioned differently vis-à-vis the welfare state.

In this book we pay particular attention to the interweaving of gender, race, and class as these shape the experiences of welfare restructuring. Struggles over welfare policy since the 1980s have deep roots in a long, contested history of conflict over ameliorating poverty and in the ideologies and practices of globalizing free market capitalism, nationally in the United States and transnationally. Because of this it is important to explore welfare restructuring in the larger context of the history and current realities of poverty, inequality, and changes in capitalist economies. It is to this larger historical and political-economic context that we now turn.

HISTORY AND POLITICAL ECONOMY OF WELFARE IN THE UNITED STATES AND OREGON

To understand welfare restructuring in the late 1990s, it is important to understand the history of the contested but fundamental interconnections among an evolving capitalism, poverty, and assistance to the poor. This context is essential to make sense of the political energy and rhetorical excess that often propel public discussions of the poor by the more affluent. This brief detour into history is also important background for sorting out the complexity of positions that seek to define good public policy: how much, in what forms, and under what conditions should public assistance be given to the poor (Polanyi 1957). Social welfare programs in capitalist states are shaped by the demands of powerful economic elites and represent political compromises hammered out between these elites and organized labor, political leaders, and social movement advocates. Thus, the issues at stake in contemporary debates about welfare are not new. These debates reflect the contentious ideological, political, and material assumptions that have been and remain present in many economic and political developments and in the theories and ideologies that justify and explain those developments.

"Welfare" has been continually restructured over the two-hundred-year history of industrial capitalism in the United States. Some moments of restructuring have been so thorough that they effectively constitute public policy "paradigm changes" or, using Sanford Schram's term, new "policy regimes" (2006). The restructuring of welfare in the 1990s is one such moment. The people whose lives we followed are participating in this paradigm change even when they do so reluctantly. They were actors in historically grounded processes in which capitalist economies recurrently produce poverty and low incomes; those who suffer the resultant poverty struggle to cope somehow; and states, under political pressures, deal, in varying ways, with the resulting problems. To understand the experiences of those in our study, we need to see them within this history, although our account in this chapter is necessarily brief and schematic.[1]

As industrial capitalism emerged in the early nineteenth century, a paradigmatic transition took place in both the United States and England: Poor Law reform resulted in significant changes in the provision of poor relief. As Karl Polanyi (1957) argues, these reforms eliminated previous access to support or provisioning from local public sources, as inadequate as it often was, and made the "able bodied" poor completely dependent on the vagaries of uncertain labor markets. Politically, Poor Law reform was meant to control low-wage labor and to force the working-class poor to work for any wage offered.[2] The ideological rationale for these changes was that relief to the "able bodied" was believed, by elites, to undermine independence, discourage diligence in paid work, and encourage indolence and vice. These claims resonate eerily with the discourse of "welfare reform" a century and a half later.

During the nineteenth and early twentieth century in the United States, such poor relief policies shaped the programs offered by the local governments and private charities that provided minimal aid to the poor. The ideology and practices of relief typically distinguished between groups defined as either the "deserving" or the "undeserving" poor.[3] The deserving poor, then regarded as the disabled, the blind, the infirm elderly, and white widows or abandoned wives, were largely exempt from the assumption that immorality or sloth caused their financial woes. But the able-bodied poor, including mothers of color and white women who were neither widows nor abandoned wives, were judged responsible for their own poverty and undeserving of charitable aid. In the United States, in particular, these distinctions encoded a variety of racist and sexist assumptions about the morals, human worth, and proper place of men and women, whites, and people of color.[4] Other than some modest reforms won during the Progressive Era (1880s–1920s) (including Worker's Compensation and Mothers' Pension programs), there was no meaningful challenge to the Poor Law ideology and its underlying classical liberal views until the economic crisis of the 1930s (Piven and Cloward 1993).

From the New Deal to the War on Poverty

The first significant expansion of social provisioning accompanied by a fundamental paradigm shift took place in the midst of the Great Depression, when political and economic elites faced massive social unrest and the declining legitimacy of capitalism. In the wake of protracted, intense popular protests, the viability of the mostly unregulated market and inadequacy of available assistance gave way as demands for change became impossible for policy makers to ignore. The wage as the primary means of distribution crashed not long after the stock market crashed in 1929; unemployment and poverty skyrocketed. These developments created the political conditions for a broad challenge to the ideas that the poor were responsible for their own misery and should be coerced into proper labor market behavior.

In 1935 the landmark Social Security Act was passed, establishing the basic infrastructure of the U.S. welfare system in the form of social insurance, means-tested programs, and work relief programs. Even in the face of this crisis, many corporations did not relinquish their claims to nonresponsibility (Acker 2006), opposing most New Deal measures and effectively limiting their scope and scale (Piven and Cloward 1993; Sunstein 2006). Their main allies were southern congressmen intent on defending their states' highly racialized low-wage labor markets (Quadagno 1994). The Social Security Act established a central role for the federal government in providing poor relief and economic security programs, including partnerships between the federal government and states in funding and regulating social welfare (and the poor). These programs were designed to affect relations of distribution and redistribution in fundamental ways, drawing on Keynesian principles that justified activist federal government intervention in the market. Such intervention, Keynesians argued, would benefit the larger economy by spurring consumption, which would promote production (demand-side economics), contributing to the widely accepted goals of full employment, shared affluence, and, thus, social stability and economic growth.[5] These New Deal programs—compromises between disparate political interests dominated by powerful white men—confirmed and reinforced long-standing gender and racial divisions and inequalities (Quadagno 1994).

The liberal U.S. welfare state was built on two unequal tiers—social insurance programs and means-tested public assistance programs; gender and race inequalities consigned most women and people of color to the means-tested programs.[6] The social insurance programs were designed as contributory "wage replacement" programs. At the inception of these programs, most women and people of color were ineligible to participate because the occupations to which they were largely restricted—domestic and agricultural labor, much human service work, and government employment—were excluded from coverage in the legislation. The less generous and more stigmatized tier included means-tested programs such as Aid to Dependent Children (ADC),[7] renamed Aid to Families with Dependent Children (AFDC) in the early 1960s.[8] Eligibility for these programs was ostensibly based on need (means-testing), but, in practice eligibility was also shaped by race-, class-, and gender-inflected state and local social norms about who deserved support. ADC institutionalized the assumption that worthy mothers should be supported to raise their children in their own homes. While this reinforced the gender division of labor and the traditional family ethic (Abramovitz 1996), it nevertheless recognized as socially valued the care work provided by worthy (i.e., white) mothers (Pateman 2005). Many income-eligible women did not get ADC, stymied by state regulations that excluded applicants from "unsuitable" homes or whom officials or employers deemed "employable"; in practice this excluded many African American, Native American, and Latino women and many immigrant families.[9]

Despite extensive federal involvement and investment in the economy, high unemployment and economic insecurity persisted well into the 1940s. It was only after the United States entered World War II, sending millions of men overseas and priming the economy through war-related production, that the economic crisis ended. What followed was a sustained period of economic growth for U.S. capital, with Keynesian tax, labor, and welfare policies promoting economic growth and considerable income redistribution. Congressional passage of the G.I. Bill at the end of World War II constituted a major, though often unrecognized, expansion of the welfare state. The G.I. Bill provided tuition and a family support allowance for returning veterans to pursue education and a vast veterans' mortgage program that subsidized home purchases for many, mostly white, male veterans. Again, gender and race exclusions limited who benefited from this expansion of public assistance (Brodkin 1997; Williams 2003).[10] So, while the white middle class expanded as public subsidies supported suburbanization, home ownership, and occupational and income mobility for white men, families of color and white women not attached to men with access to the G.I. Bill, failed to reap the benefits of this form of public welfare.[11]

Gender, race, and class inequalities have been integral to the production of poverty and differential economic opportunity throughout U.S. history. In the mid-twentieth century, as the white middle class was expanding, the "Other America" (as an influential book of the period referred to the poor) included up to fifty million Americans, including most African Americans, Native Americans, and Latinos (Harrington 1968). In 1964, as popular unrest intensified in the United States, especially in poor African American communities, the Democratic administration of Lyndon B. Johnson expanded social welfare programs again, launching the "War on Poverty." The 1964 Economic Opportunity Act, the establishment of Medicaid and Medicare in 1965, and other social spending led to another period of significant expansion of the welfare state, including new means-tested programs, new jobs and economic opportunity programs, and innovative community-based social services. From 1965 to 1972, federal antipoverty and social welfare expenditures more than doubled (Katz 1996, 266). Access to AFDC, especially for families of color, grew as a powerful welfare rights movement secured changes in program policies and practices.[12] Ideologically, these programs recognized, sometimes quite explicitly, that poverty was produced by extant and historical race and gender discrimination, lack of economic and educational opportunity, the failure of low-wage employers to provide pensions and health insurance, and other structural failings. This period of public policy was different from the past in that the welfare state was expanded *and* because the program was specifically defined as an essential dimension of an explicit anti-poverty policy.

Federal investments in antipoverty programs paid off. Poverty rates were cut in half between 1959 and 1973 (Mishel, Bernstein, and Allegretto 2007, 284), and improvements were felt even among groups with historically very high rates of poverty. For example, poverty rates among black children dropped from almost 66 percent in 1965 to 39.6 percent in 1960 (Spriggs 2007). Among female-headed families with children, poverty rates fell from almost 60 percent in 1959 to below 40 percent in 1979 (Mishel, Bernstein, and Allegretto 2007: 287). Further improvements might have occurred, but political realities intervened as the policy framework that addressed poverty through public investments, regulation, social welfare, and antidiscrimination policy came to a screeching halt with the rise of the political power of the Republican right wing and the election of Ronald Reagan in 1980.

The Campaign for Welfare State Reform

The assault on the U.S. welfare state that climaxed in the paradigm shift that is the focus of this book began in earnest with the election of Ronald Reagan in 1980. A dramatic shift in public policy ensued, as the "Reagan Revolution"[13] sought to contract public spending, especially for social programs; slash taxes, especially on businesses and investment income; and challenge key policies enacted in the previous decade that involved the federal government in supporting antidiscrimination and equity policies. Conservatives legitimized social program budget cuts by claiming that the "war on poverty" had been lost. But the U-turn in public policy had less to do with an objective assessment of "war on poverty" programs than with the growing hegemony of conservative and neoliberal ideologies and policy agendas.[14]

Conservatives took aim at the liberal "equity" agenda, challenging the underlying social analysis that defined race and gender discrimination and economic inequality as major causes of both poverty and the continuing disadvantages experienced by white women and people of color. Instead, the new policy architects focused on rebuilding declining U.S. economic and political power, supporting traditional morality and "family values" and cutting "big government" (i.e., the welfare state). The highly audible leaders of the rising Republican right wing, a mix of fiscal and social conservatives, argued that a free market, shed of excessive regulation and a high tax burden, would unleash prosperity, allowing America to regain its global position as an economic and political leader.

Aid to the poor was vilified for ostensibly having failed the poor and the nation by promoting dependency and enabling promiscuity, teen pregnancy, single parenthood, matriarchal African American families, and the growth of an urban "underclass." Right-wing thinkers and policy makers identified two main villains in their antiwelfare ideology: (1) the poor, especially the inner-city African American poor, whose poverty was allegedly the fault of individual pathologies or familial deficiencies and (2) misguided and expensive government social programs that failed because they perpetuated dependency and poverty. Conservatives argued that the nation could not afford to support those who refused to support themselves, especially when those needing support were sexually promiscuous, lacked work discipline, lived in "broken" families, and failed to value marriage and self-sufficiency.

A racialized discourse about welfare queens, an inner-city "underclass," and cross-generational welfare dependency took root, fertilized by vehement right-wing Republican politicians and advocacy organizations and blossoming in the media (Hancock 2004; Gilens 1999), the poverty research industry (O'Connor 2001), and the culture at large.[15] The combination of racist imagery and assumptions about poverty and welfare with an antitax political rhetoric that blamed social programs for soaking up "hard earned" tax dollars, reinvigorated old arguments about the deserving and undeserving poor and social nonresponsibility.

Changing assumptions about gender and families were also entangled in the attack on welfare. Even as social conservatives bemoaned declining family values, the growth in women's labor force participation, especially among mothers, began to further erode the cultural assumption that the public has a responsibility to support poor mother's care work. In Reagan's first term, social welfare programs were cut drastically. In his second term the administration promoted a variety of changes in social welfare policy, including tightening program eligibility, increasing work requirements, and giving states more flexibility in how they met federal program mandates. In 1988 Congress passed the Family Support Act (FSA). This legislation began in earnest the process of transforming AFDC from "a program that helped single mothers to stay home with their children into a mandatory work program" (Abramovitz 1996, 357), focusing both on employment for single mothers and financial "responsibility" by absent fathers.

Although there had been experiments with work-promotion programs in earlier periods (Piven and Cloward 1993; Mittelstadt 2005), the Family Support Act created unprecedented opportunities for states to encourage or require welfare recipients to participate in employment, jobs training, or education. The FSA reinforced the view that poverty was an individual problem resulting not from capitalism, racial or gender discrimination, or failures of the market, but from the poor choices, values, and behaviors of individuals and families and the alleged dependency-producing impact of intergenerational poverty and welfare (Naples 1997; Fraser and Gordon 1994).

With Bill Clinton's election in 1992 the employment mandates of the FSA were accompanied by important changes in tax and minimum wage policies designed to "make work pay." Clinton had campaigned on the promise to "end welfare as we know it," but before he could advance his vision Republicans took control of Congress in 1994. Once again welfare "reform" became a priority for the right wing intent on dismantling or privatizing social programs. The issue united social and religious conservatives concerned about "family values" with fiscal conservatives intent on cutting taxes and limiting government (Weaver 2000; Haskins 2007). Congress passed welfare "reform" as the Personal Responsibility and Work Opportunity Reconciliation Act (PRWORA) in 1996, a restructuring of welfare designed by Republicans in Congress and signed by a Democratic President who agreed in principle (if not with each provision) with a bill that abolished poor mothers' entitlement to cash assistance and subjected them to a new time-limited, "work-first" policy paradigm. PRWORA represented a fundamental change in the political landscape, as the center of the Democratic Party shed much of its commitment to the legacy of the New Deal and a redistributive/activist welfare state.

PRWORA replaced AFDC with Temporary Assistance for Needy Families (TANF), a time-limited program that makes receipt of public assistance contingent on compliance with work requirements. The end of the right, or entitlement, to aid if certain conditions were met was the most radical element in this legislation. A number of provisions of PRWORA, including expanded child care and health care subsidies, were designed to "make work pay." PRWORA also devolved considerable authority to states to design their TANF programs, changed federal funding into a block grant, legislated a five-year lifetime limit for receipt of cash assistance, and held states accountable for targeted reductions in caseloads and proportions of clients meeting work requirements. The Act also excluded most legal immigrants (and all undocumented immigrants) from eligibility for various forms of public assistance and promoted marriage and stringent child support enforcement.

Welfare restructuring represented the triumph of market fundamentalism and a public policy paradigm that enshrines the assumption of nonresponsibility of the state and capitalist enterprises for the sustenance of those living and working in the United States.[16] While we are focusing here on the United States, welfare restructuring is a global phenomenon. The assumption that states should not interfere in the operation of markets either through regulation, excessive taxation, or the provision of forms of assistance that constitute an alternative to provisioning via employment became the driving force of economic and social policies in many countries of both the global North and South (Harvey 2005).

As we have discussed, over much of the twentieth century, welfare state programs played a key role both as social safety nets and as a mechanism of income redistribution, thus aiding low-income families and modulating, to a limited degree, the income inequality produced by capitalist market processes. The social policy paradigm that emerged with the New Deal, continued with the postwar GI Bill, and intensified during the "war on poverty" is, thus, distinguished from both earlier and later periods in U.S. history. During the several decades following World War II, the growing affluence of the nation was more equitably shared than it has been since. Real family income essentially doubled for families across the income spectrum, with the highest *rate* of income growth enjoyed by those in the lower and moderate income brackets. This pattern was sharply reversed after 1980. Not only has real income growth for most families in the lower- and middle-income brackets been comparatively sluggish, income and wealth growth for the wealthy has been nothing short of staggering (Phillips 2002; Mishel, Bernstein, and Allegretto 2007).

It is against this backdrop of history and political economy that the stories we tell and the analysis we offer of the "success" of welfare restructuring is positioned. Most of the women and men we encountered are unlikely to see themselves as part of this larger story of shifting political-economic realities and ideological presumptions. The daily experience of seeking, providing, or having to live with the consequences of changes in public assistance consumes their attention. Moreover, neither the larger culture nor the culture of the welfare agency—whether for workers or aid seekers—fosters critique or even questioning of the "way things are." But as readers and citizens, and, for us, as writers, questioning *is* very much in order, and doing so with the hindsight of history helps foster greater insight about both what has happened and what alternatives might be in the economic and political interest of this country.

Overhauling Welfare in Oregon

Welfare "reform" in Oregon was deeply enmeshed within national and state politics concerning welfare, economic development, poverty, taxes, race, and gender. Welfare administrators had to navigate a complex political terrain as they managed their agencies, secured funds for their programs, and responded to regulation and monitoring by a variety of political actors. While the particulars of this political history are specific to Oregon, the basic argument resonates with the broader tale of the politics of neoliberal welfare restructuring nationally.

Welfare restructuring is part of a larger political process of neoliberalization that began in the 1980s when Oregon experienced its worst recession since the Great Depression. By the end of the decade Oregon's per capita income was 8 percent *below* the national average and real annual wages plummeted as family wage jobs in the timber and fishing industries disappeared, replaced (partially) by jobs that were less plentiful and lower waged (Oregon Progress Board 1989, 2). In 1989 Neil Goldschmidt, the Democratic governor, convened a group of state leaders to craft a strategic plan to build "statewide capacity for long-term, well managed growth" to foster Oregon's successful competition in the global economy (Goldschmidt 1989, 1). The plan, *Oregon Shines*, charted a neoliberal course for economic development, focusing on attracting new businesses to the state. This was to be facilitated by developing a "superior workforce," enlisting social service and educational institutions "to serve competitive economic objectives," maintaining Oregon's natural environment, and distinguishing Oregonians as characterized by an "international orientation" and as "unusually adept in global commerce" (Oregon Progress Board 1989, I-2).

The plan targeted public resources to the goals of the economic development plan, emphasizing investments in those "public facilities and services that directly affect business opportunities and costs," *reducing* the costs of doing business in the state (Oregon Progress Board 1989, I-2). The public services targeted were "roads, ports and utilities, and services which enhance the quality of the human environment, including schools, police and fire protection, and parks" (Oregon Progress Board 1989, I-2). Nowhere does the document propose investment in human services despite a passing reference to Oregon's high rates of child poverty. This plan for public investment was not gender-, race-, or class neutral in its impact. The priorities chosen and used to shape state budget decisions involved relative divestments in programs for low-income Oregonians who, as nationally, are disproportionately women and children and communities of color.

An "innovative" public-private partnership emerged from this plan: the establishment of the Oregon Progress Board. This board was to develop and monitor what were called the *Oregon Benchmarks*, "a set of quantifiable indicators for the economy, communities and the environment [that] define Oregon's strategic goals as measurable outcomes, with targets for improvements" (Oregon Progress Board 2002). During the next two Democratic gubernatorial administrations, these benchmarks were adopted as state policy. State agencies, including the Oregon Department of Human Services (ODHS), were mandated to reshape their missions, goals, and objectives in relation to relevant benchmarks and to develop "performance measures" to measure their effectiveness and efficiency in meeting those benchmarks. The Oregon Benchmark system was lauded nationally, winning the prestigious Innovations in Government Award in 1994 from the Ford Foundation/Kennedy School of Government (Harvard University).

Alongside what many saw as a promising path of innovation in government and public policy, another set of developments were brewing that dramatically affected pubic policy in the state. In 1990 Republicans gained control of the Oregon House of Representatives for the first time in twenty years, and voters passed two ballot initiatives that were to have profound effects on social welfare. Measure 5, a property tax limitation modeled on California's Proposition 13, significantly reduced the ability of local governments to raise revenue through property taxes. State government was required to replace the lost local revenues, ultimately creating a great strain on the state's general fund and pitting advocates for human service funds against the highly organized and more popular advocates for K–12 education. Measure 7, or the "Full Employment Program," proposed a six-county pilot program to subsidize employers for hiring people who applied for AFDC or Unemployment Insurance. Employers would be permitted to use public funds to temporarily hire employees at subminimum wages (could pay as little as 90% of minimum wage) and employees in this program would become ineligible for supplementary public assistance (including Food Stamps) because these funds would be diverted to employers to pay the subsidized wages.

Measure 5 and Measure 7 were both sponsored by right-wing individuals/advocacy groups that increasingly, since the early 1990s, have used the state's initiative system to push a series of antitax, "limited government," antilabor, and "pro-family" (i.e., mainly antigay) agendas.[17] The primary sponsor of Measure 7, Richard Wendt, CEO of a southern Oregon woods products manufacturing company, was closely linked to the conservative think tank, the American Institute for Full Employment (AIFE).[18] AIFE's creed committed the organization to "the principles of individual liberty, limited government, the free market, and the values of productive work in creating healthy families and communities" (1996, 1) The AIFE website and educational materials explicitly defined "full employment" as part of a longer term goal to dismantle the full range of government safety net programs. Private companies, instead of low-income families, were to receive public funds through public/private partnerships to subsidize jobs and minimal training for "American workers, and especially those who, sadly, have been conditioned to accept public assistance as a substitute for the opportunities and rewards of paid work" (1996, 1).

Measure 7 could not be implemented without the state being granted waivers from the federal government to allow them to modify federal programs. The newly elected Democratic governor chose not to request waivers for this program, one she had vigorously opposed. Two years later, Measure 7 sponsors filed a lawsuit against her to force her to seek the waivers. A compromise program, called JOBS Plus, was ultimately adopted as a six-county pilot workfare program approved by the Republican-controlled state legislature, enacted in 1993.[19] Although some of the more regressive provisions of Measure 7 were modified, the basic intent of the measure—to promote rapid labor force attachment— was implemented. An editorial in the state's leading newspaper, *The Oregonian,* revealed that the program resulted from "close negotiations" between Adult and Family Services (AFS) and Measure 7's private-sector sponsors (1993). These "close negotiations" enabled a right-wing think tank to have a place at the policy table that helped to shape welfare-to-work programs in Oregon. Soon afterward the Republican-controlled state legislature expanded the pilot JOBS Plus program statewide. Although JOBS Plus did not replace the JOBS program, the program became an option that welfare workers could use at their discretion with clients.

In retrospect, Measure 5 had a greater impact than Measure 7 on Oregon's welfare programs. When efforts to raise state taxes to make up for Measure 5 requirements for state funding of K–12 education failed, state agencies were forced to cut their budgets. In 1993 Democratic Governor Barbara Roberts, facing a projected 15 percent reduction in funding for state programs except public schools, ordered all state agencies to submit budgets 20 percent *below* their current service level. But she promised that 10 percent of these proposed cuts would be forgiven if agencies could demonstrate progress on one or more of the seventeen Oregon Benchmarks. The benchmark chosen by AFS to pitch for budget reduction forgiveness was "to increase the percentage of adults who are self-sufficient," or in, pragmatic terms, to reduce the AFDC caseload.

The goal of caseload reduction also emerged from the report of a legislative work group to recommend changes to the state's public assistance system to meet the objectives of "empowering individuals to avoid or escape conditions of poverty, supporting and strengthening families to care for themselves[, and] creating economic opportunities by linking economic development with human services." Two years later they released the report *An Investment Opportunity: Redesigning Oregon's Public Assistance System to Reduce Poverty by Placing More Oregonians in Jobs* (Oregon Welfare Reform Work Group 1995). In the meantime, Republicans gained control over both houses of the state legislature. They passed Senate Bill 1117, which drew *selectively* on the recommendations of the committee's report, prioritizing the goal of family self-support, code for welfare caseload reduction.

The new policy required almost all welfare clients to participate in the state's JOBS program, placed strict restrictions on teen parent's housing arrangements, and expanded the controversial JOBS Plus program statewide. It became the basis for the state's waiver request to the federal government for a welfare-to-work program that significantly modified the regulations affecting AFDC, a waiver that was granted in March 1996, five months before Congress passed federal welfare legislation. The waiver allowed Oregon's welfare program to be bound by some of its own rules rather than all of the new federal TANF rules enacted in PRWORA the following summer of 1996.

The waiver differed from federal policy in key respects. Oregon *was* to be held to high rates of participation in the JOBS program, but the state was not required to adhere to the federal five-year time limit for receipt of TANF. As a result the five-year time clock did not "tick," as long as participants were deemed to be in compliance with the "employment development plans" developed with or by their case managers. On the other hand, Oregon was able to implement a strong "diversion" program that was designed to prevent applicants from getting on TANF. Upon application for cash assistance, most clients had to participate in a month-long job search called the "assessment process" (see chapter 3 for extended discussion). During assessment the family did not receive TANF, but case managers could, at their discretion, provide cash assistance to the family. Diversion, or assessment policies resulted in significant caseload reduction *before,* not after, receipt of TANF (Gonzales, Hudson, and Acker 2007). Oregon's rules required new mothers to seek and accept work once their babies reached the age of three months. TANF block grant monies underwrote not just the TANF grants but the "transitional" and work support assistance many clients received once they were employed, including Employment-Related Day Care (ERDC) and extended Medicaid coverage. The waiver also allowed the state to make certain decisions about teen parents and provided substance abuse and mental health services for clients whose caseworkers mandated such services.

At its core Oregon's welfare program was employment-focused, defined success in terms of employment outcomes, and allowed the state to "reinvest" the funds saved through caseload reduction for services that prevent TANF use and encourage rapid attachment to the labor force. In addition to the "carrots," the incentives for clients to seek and accept employment, the agency also had in its arsenal a powerful "stick," a system of penalties and sanctions on clients who did not cooperate with the employment development plans (EDPs) they had to sign in order to get any help. These progressive sanctions ranged from financial penalties that reduced their TANF grants to, in rare instances, removal of the entire family from the grant.

The processes that resulted in Oregon's welfare-to-work program were highly politicized. In Oregon, as nationally, far right think tanks and advocacy organizations and a rightward moving Republican Party took aim at welfare as an initial step in dismantling the larger welfare state. When the Democrats controlled state government, welfare restructuring was wedded, at least rhetorically, to the goals of poverty reduction and neoliberal economic growth. Once the Democrats lost control, welfare caseload reduction goals superseded the language of poverty reduction. The phrase "living wage jobs" disappeared from agency documents, replaced by language claiming that *any* job is better than welfare and that low-wage jobs are a "foot in the door" to better jobs. As the Republican majority solidified in Oregon, and in the wake of voter-passed initiatives that squeezed the state financially and mandated rapid labor force attachment strategies, Oregon's welfare programs moved more firmly away from investments in education and training and toward diversion and employment-focused programs. The federal waivers secured in 1996 gave the agency more coercive tools, including sanctions and penalties. The combination of firm work requirements, new policies to make employment "pay" (e.g., increased support for child care, the extension of Oregon Health Plan to employed families, etc.), and coercive diversion and sanction policies gave welfare administrators and workers a new set of tools to change both the mission and the day-to-day work of welfare in Oregon.

The most dramatic moments of change in welfare policy in the United States—in the mid 1930s, the 1960s, and the 1990s—were each inextricably linked to much broader changes in the nation's economy and political landscape. Welfare "reform" in the 1990s was valorized as a successful public policy that allegedly "made sense" at a particular moment of capitalist development, characterized by increasing income inequality, growth in the low-wage (but not the family-wage) sector of the labor market, and an ideological shift in the degree to which corporations or the State accepted any responsibility to promote or support the economic security or well-being of workers and families. In the next five chapters, we subject the narrative of welfare reform as successful to the varied lived realities of different groups for whom this policy change was very much an "up close and personal" story. But it is important to keep the longer history of policy shifts we discussed in this chapter in mind throughout and to recognize how much is at stake both for these groups and the nation as a whole in the kind of social welfare programs we choose as a society.

VELVET GLOVES, IRON FISTS, AND ROSE-COLORED GLASSES

Welfare Administrators and the Official
Story of Welfare Restructuring

The "official story" of welfare restructuring—that is, the narrative that has been widely circulated to the public—has been largely written by and from the perspective of the State[1] actors who promoted, legislated, and/or implemented welfare "reform" and have declared it to be a policy "success." Welfare administrators, especially those who lead their agencies or work at the state level, always play key roles in the public policy processes that impact their agencies, mainly as they shape the framing, implementing, organizing, and assessing of what it means to "do welfare" everyday. Welfare administrators work at the nexus of complex, often conflicting, demands and expectations as they create and manage welfare restructuring. Compared to welfare workers and clients, they wield a great deal of authority and control as bosses, managers, and agency heads. However, the parameters of their authority and control are also constrained by their own positions within political and institutional hierarchies and relations.

Those who occupy the highest positions within their agencies are accountable to mandates and expectations from federal and state elected officials and federal and state human service agency heads and executive staffs. Less directly, but still significantly, they are also enmeshed in political processes in which powerful elites, policy advocates, and the unions that represent their workers contend for influence about organizational goals and practices. Within welfare agencies, top-level administrators and high- and midlevel managers occupy different administrative positions with varying degrees and kinds of power and authority within the organization hierarchy (e.g., state, district, and local). The diversity of jobs filled by people called "administrators" and the fact that these people vary in terms of their own race, ethnic, gender, and class backgrounds means that there is nothing close to a singular perspective of administrators about welfare reform.

Nevertheless, given their leadership and managerial positions, welfare administrators experience, interpret, and assess welfare restructuring differently than the welfare workers they employ or the clients Adult and Family Services (AFS) serves. And, as a group, welfare administrators differ from both welfare workers and clients because their gendered and racialized class positions provide them with greater power, privilege, and resources. Administrators' salaries are higher than those of the workers they manage, and certainly put them in a more privileged position on the class spectrum from the poor families who use agency services. AFS administrators, like their counterparts in other states, tend to be more racially diverse and have a higher proportion of women than is true in many other state agencies.[2] Nevertheless, as in the majority of U.S. workplaces, the highest levels of the organizational hierarchy are disproportionately filled by whites and men than is true of its lower reaches. In 2000 almost 60 percent of "mid- or upper-level" managers in the agency were women and almost 20 percent were persons of color.[3] However this management category includes twenty different job classifications that differ greatly in the degree to which they give managers control over policy. Unfortunately the data do not specify the percentages of women or persons of color at the *highest* levels of management where the greatest power resides.

During the 1990s both of the lead administrators of AFS were white, as was the head of the Oregon Department of Human Services (AFS was one division within the department) and the vast majority of the policy makers to whom these agency heads were accountable. Stephen Minnich, a white man, oversaw the first half-decade of welfare restructuring as AFS chief administrator. When Minnich left, he was replaced by Sandie Hoback, a white woman, who served in that position from 1996 until 2001. Hoback, who joined AFS in 1988 as an assistant regional manager, served as the welfare reform coordinator under Minnich before rising to the top post. She was widely known and respected as the chief architect of Oregon's approach to welfare "reform."

The economic, social, and organizational distance between administrators and agency clients and between administrators and their frontline workers is significant. This relative distance inoculated top administrators from the most immediate, and often the most difficult, circumstances of the clients directly affected by the policies they created and administered. The nature of their responsibilities means that they often encounter the consequences of their policies after individuals, cases, and client-staff interactions are transformed into statistical information and aggregate policy outcomes. Local administrators, on the other hand, occupied positions *between* these organizational leaders and the frontline welfare workers they manage and clients they are responsible to serve.

What we learned about these differently positioned administrators is drawn from three main sources. We observed the work of local (branch) managers in the three offices in which we did fieldwork in 1998. We also interviewed the eight operations managers in these branches. Our relationships with agency leaders, and with the group of state-level managers with whom we worked when we were doing our research on clients who left or were diverted from the TANF and Food Stamps programs, gave us access to some critical information about their work and their perspectives on welfare reform. But we did not conduct formal interviews with them. We learned what they thought and did through our interactions with them, as well as observations of administrators in a variety of public and private meetings. Additionally, we draw on public texts prepared by or under the authority of these administrators to give us a third source of information about how administrators framed and defended their policies. Having access to these administrators gives us a broader view of welfare restructuring than is available to researchers who limit (or have their research limited to) studies of clients and/ or welfare workers.

In this chapter we examine how agency administrators framed welfare policy changes in Oregon in the 1990s. Analyzing this "official story" helps reveal how agency leaders managed the image of the agency as it was implementing a politically inflected public policy. It focuses on the strategies they deployed to represent welfare restructuring as a "success" to their own employees, the state legislature, and the public. As the title of this chapter suggests, we use the metaphors of the velvet glove, the iron fist, and rose-colored glasses to evoke particular organizational practices that were crucial to the overriding goal of constructing and sustaining both the agency's claims of success and the cooperation and consent of agency workers in implementing welfare "reform." We end the chapter much closer to the daily work of welfare reform, focusing on the branch managers who navigated the complex terrain between the official story and the daily realities of welfare "reform."

The leadership of Adult and Family Services envisioned and implemented welfare reforms in Oregon earlier, and perhaps more avidly than their counterparts in many other states, as we detailed in chapter 1. In the early 1990s, AFS secured a series of federal waivers to experiment with welfare-to-work programs that deviated from federal AFDC regulations. They explicitly saw themselves as national leaders in reforming welfare, proud to be ahead of the policy curve both in piloting welfare-to-work programs and posting early and dramatic caseload reductions by the mid-1990s, *before* Congress passed PRWORA. Indeed in 1996 Oregon already ranked third among states in welfare caseload reduction (Harris

1999, 10) and soon took second place, just behind Wisconsin. The state also compared favorably to other states in the percentage of clients leaving welfare for paid employment and in the proportion of the TANF caseload that met the mandated work requirements. Although caseload reduction was clearly the driving force of welfare policy, agency leaders framed the program as focused on promoting employment and "self-sufficiency."

AFS administrators routinely expressed great pride in Oregon's version of welfare "reform." They pointed to Oregon's comparatively high rate of TANF caseload decline and claimed that Oregon achieved this goal with a more humane approach to welfare reform than most other states. As one example of the kinds of public representation of their program that was common, agency head Sandie Hoback penned a guest editorial published in newspapers across the state in 1999, appearing under the headline "Oregon uses kinder approach to welfare" (Hoback 1999). Responding to a spate of national news stories that showed that TANF clients were being dumped off the welfare rolls across the country as states were struggling to meet federally mandated caseload reduction targets, Hoback reassured Oregonians that these kinds of practices were not happening in Oregon. Taking off from Oregon's tourism slogan—"things look different here"—Hoback reassured readers that welfare reform also looks different in Oregon.

Two of the more controversial provisions of PRWORA were the time limits and sanctions that both helped produce caseload reduction. Hoback compared the federal five-year time limit and many other states' "rigid two-year time limits" with Oregon's "high expectations" for clients, explaining that Oregon clients who cooperate with the employment plans developed by their welfare workers are not subject to arbitrary time limits (1999). Referring to the practice of sanctioning clients, a powerful tool for reducing caseloads, Hoback assured readers that while Oregon's sanction policy *can* mean a family loses their grant in as few as five months, this "full family sanction" is imposed in less than 1 percent of cases and then only if the agency could prove that the children would not be harmed by the loss of welfare.

Another theme in the editorial is the agency's core belief and rationale for welfare reform: that "work beats welfare," that clients are better off financially when employed compared to receipt of cash assistance. Hoback supports this argument using dollars and cents as evidence. She compares the well-below-the-poverty-line income of a family on welfare with the financial resources allegedly available to a "typical" household headed by an employed parent; in these calculations, the agency assumes that in addition to wages each family receives supplemental income from the federal Earned Income Tax Credit (EITC), child support, Food Stamps, and other public supports that, with wages, raise a family's total income above the federal poverty line. In contrast to the abandoned families in the national news stories, Hoback argued that Oregon's poor families are better served and doing better. These themes constitute some of the core arguments administrators used to define their program as successful and humane.

Welfare restructuring in Oregon involved changes in policy and its implementation over the 1990s. Some changes responded to state or federal legislation and mandates from the U.S. Department of Health and Human Services (responsible for TANF and a host of other programs) and the U.S. Department of Agriculture (responsible for the Food Stamps program). Others were AFS initiatives. Still others were policy accommodations to budget realities determined by policy makers outside the agency (e.g., the governor, state legislators, Congress). In chapter 1 we provided a brief history of those changes. There we argued that welfare reform nationally, and in Oregon, was a highly politicized process, a laboratory for conservative and neoliberal policy makers for whom welfare-to-work, privatization, and the contraction of public assistance for the poor served larger political and economic aims. However Oregon's top welfare administrators consistently portrayed welfare policy changes in the state as nonideologically driven "reform." They depicted themselves as developing an approach to welfare based on a research-informed understanding of "what works." How and why they maintained that position is our focus in the next section.

Rose-Colored Glasses: Defending Welfare Restructuring

The claim that Oregon's welfare policies are based on research about what works, rather than ideology, was articulated forcefully at our first meeting with AFS leaders. We were gathered to ask the agency's permission for us to conduct fieldwork inside the agency. Hoback was clear: "We are proud—we have honed the Oregon approach through good research to get where we are. We are driven by what works—not ideology. We want to resist mightily being part of ideological debates." However, as we discuss below, how research was used and the ways it made a difference are far more complex than Hoback's statement suggests. This theme—of a nonideological, research-based approach to welfare reform—was reiterated in a number of documents, including a widely distributed document prepared by AFS called "A Short History of Welfare Reform in Oregon" (1997). This document was included in packets for state legislators when agency budget or other policy issues were being debated, and it was often one of the handouts agency officials used when they made other public presentations during the period of our research. This short history, shown below, exemplifies how the agency represented both the direction and the rationale for key policy choices in Oregon's welfare reform process.

A Short History of Welfare Reform in Oregon

Early 1980s: The original, or "old JOBS program begins. *It is purely a work-search program, with the aim of caseload containment.*

1988: The Legislature authorizes the "new JOBS" pilot program. *It is a highly voluntary program stressing long-term education.*

1990: A study of the "old" and New JOBS programs is issued by Deloitte Touche. *It finds that New JOBS is three times as expensive, has greater client non-compliance, and participants do not have significantly greater success finding work or earning higher wages despite receiving extensive education.*

October 1990: The federal "Family Support Act" goes into effect, requiring all states to set up JOBS (Job Opportunities and Basic Skills) programs. *Oregon's approach is based on its experiences in "old" and New JOBS. It is unique in its local planning and its emphasis on partnerships with community colleges, JTPA, public schools, the Employment Department, etc.*

1990–1992: National research continues. *It repeatedly shows that long-duration, education-based approaches are not as effective as "work attachment" models that stress frequent job-search activities.*

July 1992: Oregon is granted innovative waivers to the Family Support Act. *These allow AFS to require more clients to participate in JOBS; require all teen parents to finish high school; and require JOBS participants to be in drug, alcohol, or mental health treatment if needed.*

July 1993: The Oregon Legislature approves the JOBS Plus pilot program as a six-county pilot. *AFS requests waivers from the federal government.*

November 1994: The JOBS Plus pilot program begins, after federal waivers are approved. *This public-private partnership becomes part of the existing JOBS program in six counties, paying clients a wage while they work in subsidized training positions with local businesses.*

June 1995: Oregon's welfare reform bill, Senate Bill 117, is passed by the Legislature. *Among its provisions: almost all welfare clients can be required to participate in JOBS, teen parents must live in a supervised, safe place, and JOBS Plus is expanded statewide.*

July 1995: The provisions of SB1117 are incorporated into the "Oregon Option Welfare Reform Waiver Request," submitted to the federal government. *The waivers also sought permission for the state to retain and reinvest some of the federal savings from its caseload reductions, which normally would return to the federal government.*

July 1996: The Oregon Option waivers are implemented after federal approval is received in March.

August 1996: President Clinton signs a far-reaching federal welfare reform law, HR 3734, which includes "block-grant" funding of state programs. *Oregon is able to continue operating under its Oregon Option waivers and will receive additional federal funding because of its caseload reductions.*

The document begins with a reference to two early versions of Oregon's welfare-to-work programs, both pioneered during the 1980s. They described the first program, the "original or old JOBS" program, as "a work-search program, with the aim of caseload containment." The second program, the "new JOBS pilot program," is described as "a highly voluntary program stressing long-term education" (AFS 1997). The document then explains the decision to move away from investments in voluntary job training and education by citing "program evaluation research conducted by Deloitte Touche (1990), a national for-profit professional services firm."

The Deloitte Touche findings are summarized as showing that the "new JOBS" approach was costlier, had greater client noncompliance, and did not result in "significantly greater success [for clients in] finding work or earning higher wages despite receiving extensive education" (AFS 1997). The document then refers again to research, citing unspecified "national research" that "repeatedly shows that long duration, education-based approaches are not as effective as 'work attachment' models that stress frequent job search activities" (AFS 1997). This research is marshaled to explain why Oregon sought "innovative waivers" to the Family Support Act that, beginning in 1992, enabled the agency to *require* more clients to participate in the JOBS program, more teen parents to complete high school, and more clients identified with substance abuse or mental health problems to comply with mandated treatment. The rest of the short history focuses on state legislation and Oregon's decision to apply for federal waivers for a "work first" welfare-to-work program the state implemented in the mid- to late 1990s. These legislative inputs into welfare policy are described matter-of-factly, eliding the highly political processes discussed in the preceding chapter that significantly influenced the direction of welfare reform in Oregon.

This document is interesting both for what it says and what it does not say. It suggests that Oregon's decision to abandon the *human capital* approach to welfare reform (which emphasizes longer-term skill-building activities) and to opt instead for the *labor force attachment* approach (which emphasizes short-term job assistance designed to help people find jobs quickly) was based on research that showed the superiority of the latter approach. What the document does not mention is that agency leaders received the study at almost the same moment that Oregon voters passed two ballot initiatives, Measures 5 and 7. Both measures, albeit in different ways, dramatically affected the direction of social welfare policy (see chapter 1). Measures 5 and 7 were both advocated and bankrolled by right-wing groups that sought to promote "free market" public policies and limit government spending on public services. In the context of lengthy political negotiations over implementation of Measure 7, the state's looming fiscal crisis in the wake of Measure 5, and the capture of the Oregon House of Representatives by conservative Republicans, the "work first" (labor force attachment) model of welfare reform was far more politically feasible, research or no research to suggest its superiority.

But is it even accurate to read the Deloitte Touche study as supporting the labor force attachment strategy? The study compared clients at seven "new JOBS" program sites, each of which were piloting human capital investment strategies for welfare clients, with seven well-matched "old JOBS" sites that did not. Researchers found that clients at "new JOBS" branches were on cash assistance for slightly longer (less than one month longer) and that a somewhat higher proportion of "old JOBS" clients (43.1%) than "new JOBS" clients (38.5%) were employed at the end of the evaluation period (1990:10). Because of "enriched services" and the slightly longer period during which clients received cash assistance the "new JOBS" branches spent almost twice as much on full-time job placements as did the "old JOBS" branches. However, a higher proportion of the employed "new JOBS" clients enjoyed higher wages (1990:12). While overall employment rates were slightly higher at old JOBS sites, the authors conclude that the new JOBS employment *trend* appeared to be more favorable, with what the authors called a "higher rate of increase in the probability of employment over time" (1990:12).

Rather than determining that the "new JOBS" pilot programs were not as successful, the Deloitte Touche study authors concluded that because the pilot programs were still so new (less than eighteen months in operation), no definitive conclusions about the long-term impact of the program were yet warranted. And they recommend *continuing*, though not expanding, the program and reevaluating after more time, and some modest suggested program improvements were made. Nevertheless, AFS administrators chose to emphasize the tiny differences in employment outcomes and the more significant differences in program costs rather than the findings that clients who got education and training appeared to be getting higher-paying jobs and that the trend in job placements appeared to be shifting in favor of the "new JOBS" sites.

They also ignored robust findings from a survey of clients in both types of programs that showed much higher support for the "new" than the "old" JOBS program: 80 percent of "new JOBS" participants believed that the program would help them to get off welfare compared to only 43 percent of those in "old JOBS" sites (1990:13). Thus, when they used this study in the "short history" document to justify their decision to promote "work first" welfare reform, they were reporting the research results selectively to support politically produced policy decisions.

Long-time welfare policy researcher Kent Weaver argues that policy makers use research more as "ammunition" to justify policy choices than as "an independent source of information that affects their preferences and priorities" (Weaver 1999:5). He suggests that policy makers "pick and choose research that bolsters their pre-existing (by constituency pressures or personal values) policy preferences while rejecting and even casting doubt on research that goes against those preferences" (Weaver 1999:5). This is exactly what we witnessed in Oregon. AFS administrators' use of the Deloitte Touche report was not the sole example of this. We saw Hoback and other members of the AFS leadership team rather consistently look at research on their "work-first welfare" policies through the lenses of rose-colored glasses.

A second example of the deployment of research by agency administrators concerns a large national comparative study of welfare-to-work programs conducted by the Manpower Demonstration Research Corporation (MDRC).[4] The Portland JOBS program was one of eleven program sites studied that explicitly compared labor force attachment program strategies with human capital strategies that focus on longer term skill-building activities, including basic education and other education-focused activities. The MDRC study in Portland[5] followed over 5,000 single-parent AFDC recipients. Between February 1993 and December 1994 applicants for AFDC were randomly assigned to either a "program group," with required participation in job search and training activities, or a "control group." The latter were neither subject to participation requirements nor did they receive the same level of services or supports as the program group.

MDRC released two reports based on this research, one after two years of research and another after five years. In both reports Portland's JOBS program garnered strong praise. Indeed MDRC designated the Portland program as the top performance program of the eleven sites "in terms of employment and earnings gain as well as providing a return on every dollar the government invested in the program" (Freedman et al. 2000, ES-3).[6] Comparing programs and program results across states and sites, MDRC concluded that a "mixed approach," drawing on a combination of human capital investment (education and training) and labor force attachment strategies, yielded the best results. They defined the Portland program as an exemplar of this mixed approach.

AFS administrators proudly disseminated the MDRC study results widely—to the legislature, the press, their workers, the public, and, later, to us as researchers—using the study as evidence that their program was working. Nevertheless, they interpreted and used these results selectively. In materials presented to a legislative committee with oversight of their budget in 1999, agency administrators trumpeted their program: "Oregon's JOBS program 'produced effects on employment, earnings and welfare receipt that were among the largest ever found for large-scale mandatory programs,' according to a report issued in June 1998, by the Manpower Demonstration Research Corporation" (AFS 1999:1–7). But they emphasized *particular* results of the MDRC study: (1) that program group members got better jobs than control group members (based on the criteria of full-time employment, higher average hourly pay, and a greater likelihood of receiving employer-paid health insurance); (2) that these superior results were found even among clients with more "barriers" to employment; (3) that the program saved money (because program group members received cash assistance for less time); (4) that the increase in GED receipt in Portland rivaled rates in other sites with education-focused programs; and (5) that the program design and implementation reflected strong partnerships with local service providers and excellent services (AFS 1999: 117, 1–8).

Agency administrators applauded the researcher's conclusions about program success, attributing success to "a model based on high performance, ongoing evaluation and continuous improvement to achieve its mission" (AFS 1999: 1–39) and to the philosophy of welfare reform and the specific agency practices they had developed. They did *not* cite MDRC's important caveat that Portland's "unusual success" was

> likely to be due to a *combination* of factors.…Portland's caseload was not as disadvantaged as some of the populations in the other…sites, and the labor market in the Portland area during the follow up period was strong, allowing people to find and obtain "good" jobs. Furthermore, Oregon has a history of progressive social legislation, including generously funded welfare programs and a state minimum wage that is higher than the federal standard. (Scrivener et al. 1998, ES-21)

In failing to mention these factors, none of which are integral to welfare practices per se, agency leaders omitted key contextual conditions that were essential parts of the ingredients of success. They also neglected to mention that the particular mix of services, resources, and strong local labor market available to clients in Portland was not true for clients in most of the rest of the state.

Moreover, by the late 1990s, important features of the program that had earned praise from the MDRC researchers no longer characterized even the Portland program. Specifically, training programs had been watered down, workers were less encouraged and less likely to transmit the message that clients "hold out" for higher-paying jobs, and branches began to rely more heavily on diversion to attain the desired job placement or caseload reduction goals. In other words, administrators used the MDRC results to claim success for a program that was never fully implemented statewide and that, when they were using it as evidence of a successful approach, had been substantially changed even at the original sites.

If in fact Oregon's welfare policy was influenced by what research such as the MDRC study had found, the agency should have stepped up efforts to replicate the Portland sites' successes, rather than moving away from the lauded program model. However, as in the early 1990s, AFS leaders were navigating a highly constrained, ideologically charged *political* terrain. Measure 5 impacts on the state budget continued to drain resources that might otherwise have been available for state services, including human services. Republican control of the state legislature meant that when the legislature passed welfare reform legislation in the mid-1990s, that legislation included strong diversion and sanctions provisions and unabashedly promoted "work first" not job training, basic education, or the option of postsecondary education for TANF clients, or even the much praised "mixed approach." The economy was booming in Oregon and low-wage jobs went wanting for applicants. Welfare-to-work policies helped channel low-income women and men toward the low-wage jobs that were the fastest growing part of the labor market, and "work first" welfare reform produced the TANF caseload decline and jobs placements that helped to put Oregon on the map as a leader in welfare reform.

The third example of the tendency to look at research through rose-colored glasses hit close to home. During the course of our partnership with the agency, we encountered a series of difficulties resulting from differences both in how the agency and our research team interpreted findings from our study and in how to use those data to evaluate program success. The first significant problem emerged midway through the research. The agency asked us to submit an interim report on data from the first telephone survey we had done with clients who had left or been diverted from either the TANF or Food Stamps program in the first quarter of 1998. They asked only for the raw data. We complied with their request, although with some hesitation because we believed part of our job was to analyze the mountain of data and because the ongoing study was only in its midway point. A few days later they sent us a draft of a press statement they had decided to release, using a few pieces of data to trumpet program success. We were surprised and dismayed. In addition to fearing that release of the data would compromise a study in process, we were most concerned with *what* the press release said. Put simply, they proclaimed welfare-to-work in Oregon a success story.

We responded immediately, pointing out that such a press release was premature and inaccurate. In a memo to agency administrators, we said:

> We are concerned that the press release does not accurately reflect the basic findings of the TANF leavers portion of the study. More specifically, it selectively emphasizes the "good news" and does not suggest where the problems lie for the families who have left cash assistance. Our hope is that we can come up with a press release that both AFS and CSWS [Center for the Study of Women in Society] believe is true to the data. (CSWS Welfare Research team memo, January 18, 2000)

One specific inaccuracy was the press release's lead sentence reporting that 97 percent of respondents said that their families were better off working than on welfare.[7] The 97 percent figure did not represent the entire sample; the question had been asked only of those who were employed. We suggested that if they wanted to report overview data on family well-being, they could use the answers to the question: "Looking back to one year ago [when they would have been on cash assistance or Food Stamps or had just been diverted from TANF] would you say that, overall, you and your family are doing better, worse, or about the same?" Those results were pretty good, showing that 60 percent said they were doing better, 11 percent said things were worse, and 29 percent said things "were about the same." Or, we offered, they could use responses to a question that polled respondents about their family's well-being at the time of the survey. Forty-four percent of respondents responded either "good" or "excellent," and 56 percent said they were either "fair" or "poor." Either of these questions, we argued, would give a better sense of the overall fortunes of these families than the data they had chosen to use.

We also advocated that the press release focus on what *our* initial analysis suggested were the two "most striking" findings of the study: that 64 percent of TANF leavers are currently employed and that 72 percent had household income before taxes that were below the poverty line. We also pointed to extensive data in the survey that showed that many families were struggling to pay bills, continued to be eligible for and needed public programs (Food Stamps and Oregon Health Plan), needed but did not have health insurance, and had been forced to turn to food pantries or soup kitchens.

After more back and forth, our agency partners corrected some of these inaccuracies, but they continued to use the 97 percent figure in their public pronouncements about the study, and they refused to change the tone to reflect the more mixed results warranted by the data as a whole. Just days later Sandie Hoback used the disputed 97 percent figure in her weekly e-mail update sent to all AFS staff. In addition to using the statistic out of context, she interpreted as a "97% *approval rating,*"

> A Great Way to Start an Update: There aren't many things that get a 97% approval rating, but our work in moving people into employment is doing just that. A newly released study found that 97% of former clients who are working believe they are better off than when they were on welfare. (Hoback 2000, 1)

After we read Hoback's "Update," we sent another memo to agency leadership reiterating our concerns and asking for a telephone conference to discuss how the data were being used. We noted that even after we had pointed out their inaccurate use of the 97 percent figure, agency leaders continued to use it out of context and, sometimes, inaccurately. Our memo repeated our conviction that it was important to give agency staff a fuller picture of both the "good" and the "more sobering news," and we specifically challenged the legitimacy of using the 97 percent figure as "an approval rating."

Nevertheless, the day after we sent this memo, the director of the Oregon Department of Human Services (ODHS) issued the following triumphant report to the entire DHS staff under the headline "Work: Better than Welfare":

> We now have the benefit of good research on the outcomes we've achieved with welfare reform. *What it shows is what we have believed:* the majority of individuals and families who leave welfare are in a better position…(Weeks 2000, emphasis added)

His words echo Weaver's observation that predilection fosters interpretation. Like Hoback, Weeks picked only select positive findings to report: that 64 percent of participants were employed, that 70 percent earned more now than when they were hired, that 80 percent work thirty or more hours per week, that 68 percent had been in the same job for six months, that 83 percent reported job satisfaction, and that 48 percent of those employed had some form of employer-provided health insurance. He concludes, "The good news in this report is that most of our former clients agree work is better than welfare" (Weeks 2000). As researchers we found this practice troubling.

A year later we presented the agency with the completed study, a two-volume (almost 350 pages) final report.[8] We developed an Executive Summary with key findings that spanned what, by now, we were used to thinking of as both the "good" and "bad" news about the consequences of welfare restructuring on the families we surveyed. But agency leaders did not widely disseminate the Executive Summary we prepared. Rather, they developed their own, calling it the "highlights" of the study. Again they selected data to strongly emphasize the "good news." For example, the agency summary omitted statistical data that completed a picture of the range of responses to particular questions. For example, in pointing to data about wage enhancement between 1998 and 2000, they chose to note that nearly 50 percent of the sample experienced an increase in earnings. What they omitted was that 24 percent saw their wages decrease and 27 percent had so little employment that an earnings trajectory could not accurately be plotted. Most important, they failed to include our final recommendation:

> The state of Oregon, and these families, would be well served by intensified efforts to reduce poverty, sustain and improve safety net programs and foster more living wage jobs across the state. (Acker et al. 2001, iii)

Our general conclusion based on an extensive review of the data was neither a ringing endorsement nor a denunciation of welfare-to-work policy. Rather, like many other studies of welfare restructuring done in the aftermath of PRWORA, it recognizes that poverty reduction takes more than moving families off welfare rolls and into low-wage work and that public assistance programs continue to be vital for a large proportion of the one-quarter of the U.S. labor force whose earnings place them within or below 200 percent of the federal poverty line.[9]

However, neither poverty reduction nor economic security were goals of neoliberal welfare restructuring. TANF caseload reduction, employment of former recipients of public assistance, and the goal of self-sufficiency constitute the framework within which programs were designed and assessed. That welfare administrators in Oregon and nationally were so willing to accept the ideological premises of neoliberalism goes a long way toward explaining the framework they adopted to plan, implement, and assess welfare policies and practices.

"Accountability Is Not a Dirty Word": But Accountability to Whom and for What?

Social welfare agencies have always had to gather, process, and report reams of data about their programs in order to comply with a host of reporting requirements and as part of a political process in which they struggle to garner the resources they need to provide services and sustain their organizations. Because TANF (and AFDC before it) is jointly run and funded by federal and state governments, welfare administrators have long spent a considerable part of their time and agency resources producing the administrative data necessary for filing the many required reports. With devolution of more responsibility for TANF to states, the collection of administrative data took on new importance. These data now had the potential to spell trouble for states. If they showed that states were not meeting the caseload reduction and work participation targets set by federal and state policy makers, for example, states stood to lose resources. If data leaked about negative consequences for vulnerable families, the media and antipoverty advocates would be armed with powerful ammunition administrators would have to answer to. If results were not positive enough, it might be hard to sustain the enthusiasm of their own staff for policies that some proportion of workers worried about.

In this context we examine how Oregon welfare administrators made decisions about their own data gathering and presentation; that is, how they decided what to collect and what they reported forthrightly to those to whom they are accountable. As Hoback said so plainly in the meeting with workers that we depicted in the prologue: "accountability is not a dirty word." But the question is: To whom were these administrators most accountable and for what? In Oregon administrative data mattered because the state had adopted an innovative "results driven" public policy process called the Oregon Benchmarks, discussed above. State agencies, including the Department of Human Services, were mandated to reshape their missions, goals, and objectives in relation to relevant benchmarks and to develop "performance measures" to measure their effectiveness and efficiency in meeting those benchmarks.

AFS administrators had some latitude in their choice of performance measures, but some of them were hardly discretionary given federal and state mandates for welfare reform that emphasized targets or quotas for caseload reduction and for job placements. Moreover, Oregon's receipt of the Oregon Option waiver from the federal government had subjected the entire state TANF caseload to the JOBS program, provided additional supports for clients who secured employment, and required the agency to specifically measure program success *by the degree to which employment outcomes were met.*

Under the waiver, the state promised to address certain benchmarks, most notably, "[reducing] the percentage of children and adults living in poverty and [increasing] the percentage of adults who are self-sufficient." Among the "measurable goals" the agency was required to meet during the 1996–1998 biennium was reduction of the AFDC caseload from 40,000 to 33,000 through "self-sufficiency efforts" and reduction of the percentage of children living in poverty from 11 percent to 9 percent. The goals for 1998–2000 included further reductions in the caseload (to 20,000) and in the percentage of children living in poverty (to 6%).[10]

It is instructive to look carefully at the specific "measurable goals" (including the official "performance measures") AFS lead administrators chose to represent and assess agency programs. Listed below are these goals and "measurable" outcomes.[11] Chief among those are job placements, TANF caseload reduction, enhanced child support collection, and others including high school completion by teen parents and several measures of agency efficiency and diversity. But note that AFS administrators chose *not* to adopt poverty reduction as a performance measure for their agency despite the fact that this was one of the Oregon Benchmarks that had a clear relevance to agency programs.

Adult and Family Services Goals and Performance Measures, 1996–2001 (performance measures in italics)

1. Helping people find and keep jobs
   - Total job placements
   - *Percentage of families who are off welfare 18 months after TANF case closure due to employment*
   - *Wage at placement for full-time jobs*
   - *JOBS Plus*

2. Family stability and access to services
   - *Percentage of teen parents in school*
   - Teen pregnancy prevention

3. Preventing the need for public assistance in future generations
   - *TANF families per 1,000 Oregonians*
   - Programs for working families (Oregon Health Plan, Employment Related Day Care)

4. Providing accurate, timely benefits

5. Assisting families in obtaining child support payments
   - *Total child support collections*
   - Establishing paternity

6. Working in partnership with the community
   - *Program benefits, program delivery, and administrative*
   - *Percentage of eligibility decisions processed on time*

7. Providing staff with training to do their jobs accurately and effectively
   - *Diversity in the AFS workforce*
   - Staff training

The choice of these goals and specific performance measures helped structure the collection and presentation of administrative data by the agency during the critical years of welfare restructuring. Four times a year the agency published a quarterly performance report that presented administrative data and included agency interpretation of how that data demonstrates agency performance. And, as we discuss in chapter 3, these performance measures were used to prioritize what was important for managers and workers as they implemented state policy.

Given the importance of reducing poverty both as a state goal and as an ostensible correlate to welfare reform, we questioned the agency's failure to hold itself accountable to the goal of poverty reduction. We asked agency leaders why they had decided not to measure results by looking at poverty reduction directly, something that made sense to us as social scientists. They told us that reducing poverty was a goal that required action far beyond AFS and that they did not believe the agency should be held responsible for reducing poverty but only for promoting self-sufficiency and getting people into the labor force. Therefore, despite the importance of poverty reduction as a state goal and implicit rationale for welfare reform, they chose not to hold themselves accountable to poverty reduction as a measure of agency or program success.

Although poverty reduction did not make the list of key agency goals, this aim was mentioned in the first two years (1996–1997) of quarterly performance reports, although it was relegated to the reports' appendices. The language they used linked poverty reduction to welfare caseload reduction, claiming that "the success of AFS and our partners in reducing the welfare caseload translates into fewer people in poverty" (AFS 1996, 1). After 1997, language about poverty reduction is even harder to find, mentioned only in passing as the agency reiterates the assumption that employed families have incomes above the poverty line when wages are combined with multiple other forms of public assistance and subsidies.

In the AFS presentation to the state's Joint Committee on Ways and Means Human Services Subcommittee in February 2001, the agency linked four of the performance measures to the Oregon Benchmark goal of increasing the "percentage of Oregonians with income above 100% of the federal poverty level." These measures were (1) total job placements as a percentage of the TANF caseload, (2) the percent of families who do not return to welfare within eighteen months of case closure due to employment, (3) the average wage for full-time job placements, and (4) the number of TANF families per 1,000 Oregonians. Administrators argued that these measures *indirectly* address the goal of poverty reduction. More direct measures, however, were possible but not chosen.

Depicting their program and its results as successful was crucial for AFS administrators. Undoubtedly, agency leaders chose performance measures they believed they were most likely to be able to meet, measures that would bolster their image as a successful agency. From the perspective of welfare administrators, TANF caseload reduction became a viable substitute for the goal of poverty reduction. Oregon was, after all, very successful in reducing its AFDC and TANF caseloads during the mid-to-late 1990s. Unfortunately, as we detail in the introduction, they were not as successful at helping to translate "self-sufficiency" to a corresponding reduction in poverty rates, especially among children, even though the economy was booming and state lawmakers had raised the minimum wage twice. A study from the Oregon Center for Public Policy reported that the percentage of working families with children that were poor soared from 9.7 percent in the late 1980s to over 15 percent in 1996–1998 (Thompson and Leachman 2000, 44, 47). U.S. Census data indicated that 15.8 percent of Oregon's youth were poor in 2000–2001, a statistically insignificant difference from 1999–2000, when it was 16.8 percent (Thompson and Leachman 2002). Given the benchmark targets for the percentage of children living in poverty of 9 percent in 1998 and 6 percent in 2000, these data measuring poverty reduction in the "results-driven" framework would not have made the agency look particularly successful.

Looking closely at how AFS presented data about jobs, wages, and poverty reveals much about the assumptions agency leaders made and the interpretations they conveyed to those to whom they were accountable. For example, given the agency's fundamental assumption that "work is better than welfare," they needed to prove at least this assumption with actual data. The measure they chose to report for this in the quarterly performance report was the "average wage for full-time job placement." They then used this average wage as part of a calculation of "estimated spendable income for a single-parent family with two children." This calculation included the average wage for that reporting period, supplemented by the estimated value of other resources they presumed the family would have: Food Stamps, child support, and monthly earnings from the Earned Income Tax Credit (EITC). Using this calculation, report authors claimed that families with employed breadwinners would have an estimated disposable monthly income above the federal poverty line. They compared this favorably with the below-the–poverty-line incomes of families living on public assistance.

The calculation that compares employment to welfare so favorably was partially a result of the administrative decision by policy makers to freeze the amount of the cash grant (AFDC/TANF) at its 1991 level throughout the entire decade and into the twenty-first century. Thus, the buying power of the grant was guaranteed to decline annually despite demonstrable growth in the costs of food, utilities, child care, housing, and other necessities. Freezing the grant was another way they compelled families to leave the TANF rolls as the grant became ever more stingy and inadequate.

Agency researchers also made other questionable assumptions in their calculations, assumptions that antipoverty advocates in the state repeatedly contested both privately and publicly. For example, in 1996 agency researchers estimated that each employed family would receive an average of $208 monthly in child support. In reality only a small proportion of the TANF caseload received court-ordered child support, despite intensified child support enforcement as part of welfare reform. Their figures also counted an average of $273 per month for families from the Earned Income Tax Credit (based on one-twelfth of the full EITC) even though families receive only 60 percent of the estimated annual amount on a monthly basis (the other 40 percent coming as a tax refund). Furthermore, despite their optimistic calculations, at least one of every four job placements monthly were not in full-time jobs. Thus the resources available to these families fell well below the agency averages used in their calculations. Many clients lived in areas without an adequate supply of full-time, decently paid jobs. In addition, given the need to balance employment and care responsibilities, many single mothers "chose" part-time employment as a way of managing their multiple responsibilities. Even among full-time job placements, between one-quarter and one-third (depending on the year) were in minimum wage jobs, hardly jobs that could come close to sustaining families.

Antipoverty advocates consistently pointed out many of these faulty assumptions in public forums and to the media. They presented alternative calculations showing that many families who left welfare for employment earned very low wages and faced serious economic hardship. They also pointed out that because of income eligibility criteria, families whose incomes rise, even a little, can experience significant reductions in benefit levels (the "cliff effect") and become ineligible for supports, including child care subsidies, Food Stamps, and the Oregon Health Plan (see fuller discussion in chapter 5). For these families, despite rising incomes, overall household resources often declined, undermining family economic security (Tapogna and Witt 2002).

Finally, as we and Oregon's antipoverty advocates pointed out, even the modest wage gains the agency was able to document, were *not*, in large measure, attributable to their programs. For example, the average wage at placement for a full-time job grew by $1.49 between 1995 and 2000, rising from $6.11 to $7.60. But most—$1.00—of that increase resulted from two voter-approved increases in the minimum wage, from $5.50 to $6.00 an hour in January 1998 and from $6.00 to $6.50 an hour in January 1999. This leaves a mere forty-nine cent increase resulting from raises or securing better jobs over the five years of the strongest economy in Oregon in decades. This 8 percent wage increase compares unfavorably with the 11 percent increase for U.S. workers in the lowest-wage percentile between 1995 and 2000 (Mishel, Bernstein, and Boushey 2003, 128). In other words, former TANF recipients in Oregon did not fare as well as other very-low-income workers during the boom years at the end of the 1990s.

In summary, we argue that administrators' choices of what to measure and how to interpret data slanted their interpretation of welfare reform in ways that allowed them to claim statistical success when, as we argue throughout this book, the picture is far more mixed and complex. In arguing that they intentionally put a positive spin on these performance measures, we are not suggesting that they were deceitful. These managers were working in a highly constrained neoliberal environment in which besieged government agencies were forced by political reality to emphasize efficiency, to use cost-benefit analyses to justify program decisions, and to pay greater attention to the "bottom line." In addition, the highly politicized discourse about welfare in the mid- to late 1990s, the right-ward shift in Congress and in the state legislature, and fiscal realities meant that particular outcomes were valued, especially caseload reduction and job place-ment. Not being "successful" in this environment would likely have meant even leaner agency budgets, a result that would have had negative consequences both for agency workers and the clients they served. We conclude that agency leaders had chosen to wear rose-colored glasses as they read that research.

The choices administrators made about what to count, what to present, and how to interpret data about welfare reform made the realities of gender sub-ordination, racism, and class inequalities almost *invisible* in the discourse. The public texts AFS produced rarely mention that the vast majority of their clients are women. Nationally 90 percent of adults receiving TANF between October 1999 and September 2000 were women (U.S. DHHS 2000). The random sample of TANF recipients in our study included 93 percent women. Over and over the single mothers who are the majority of their caseload are referred to in agency documents as "applicants," "clients," "parents," "people," "Oregonians," or heads of "families." Clearly agency administrators are not unaware that their clients are not just any "people." Usually in their documents, there is a brief description of "Oregon's Welfare Population" that notes that "most families on welfare are single-parent households" and that among these "92% are headed by women," and "79% are white, 8% are African American, 8% Hispanic, 3% Asian and 2% Native American" (AFS 1997:4). But once this description is offered, race and gender disappear from both the language and the analysis of data.

When white women, women of color, and poor mothers are transformed by organizational discourse and practices into "people" or "clients" or "household heads" the particularities and realities of social inequality endemic in a society characterized by continuing racism, sexism, and class inequality are effaced. The neoliberal transformation of mothers into generic "heads of household" and "able bodied workers" fosters agency practices that ignore that the "people" they work with everyday do not have the same opportunities, advantages, experiences, and resources that many of those who are not poor take for granted. Furthermore, these "clients" who are organizationally defined as "heads of household" and "able bodied workers" struggle mightily to be good mothers as they face the responsibility (and usually the desire) to provide the unpaid care work their children need under very difficult circumstances and without anything close to adequate resources.

In fact, gender and race *do* matter and affect the women whose lives we studied. These women had mean monthly earnings that were 70 percent of the earning of the few men in the study (Acker, Morgen, and Gonzales 2002, 48–49). This amounts to the difference between earning $966 per month and $1,348 per month, which translates into a gender difference in degrees of hardship. Moreover, occupational segregation by gender and race affected the jobs the women could find. As we discuss more fully in chapter 5, the jobs held by most women we studied were in the low-wage clerical, service, or retail sectors of the labor force. And very few of these jobs were "good jobs in terms of earnings and benefits" (Morgen et al. 2006, 86).

But paying attention to race and gender as these textured the experiences of "clients," "people," and "heads of household" was not part of either the data gathering or reporting that agency administrators did themselves, asked for from us, or focused on when we presented data, at least as far as we could tell from how they used the data. Nor were the ways gender, race, and class affected families' fortunes explicitly addressed as part of policy development, training, or program implementation. AFS adopted a gender- and race-neutral analysis of the lives and circumstances of their "caseload." In this way welfare administrators actually promote the paradigm that roots poverty and economic insecurity in the failings of individuals rather than in the ways economic and political elites structure the economy, the labor force, public policy, and the ideological frameworks through which most of us understand our lives.

AFS administrators also ignored some of the key recommendations of our research. Our report concluded that the primary goals of welfare policy ought to be "the reduction of poverty and the enhancement of economic security of this nation's most vulnerable families" (Acker, Morgen, and Gonzales 2002). We recommended policies to promote living-wage jobs, strengthen the social safety net (especially in terms of child care, housing, and health care and for legal immigrants), encourage higher education and quality job training, and address the particularly high rate of poverty among single mothers. AFS leaders drew selectively also on the research-informed conclusions that we offered as promising paths for welfare policy. Clearly they had trouble incorporating perspectives that did not fit well with their framework or that veered from their sense of to whom and for what they were accountable.

The Production of Cooperation and Consent: Velvet Gloves and Iron Fists

Promoting neoliberal welfare policy entailed an active process of eliciting the cooperation, consent, and enthusiasm of frontline workers for the new policies. As the mission of AFS changed in the early 1990s, spurred by the budget reduction consequences of Measure 5, agency leaders took steps to transform the "culture" (their term) of the agency. They halved the number of management staff to channel more resources into frontline work with clients. They developed a new position, case manager, responsible for services designed to promote client employment and self-sufficiency. As we discuss more fully in chapter 3, case managers differed from other agency workers in that they were to provide case management services, not just determine eligibility for and manage the provision of benefits. Believing that an agency culture overly governed by a five-hundred-plus-page policy manual weighed down with Byzantine eligibility rules was not conducive to the new policy environment, agency leaders devolved more authority to local offices and advanced the idea of "principle-based decision making," an alternative to the eligibility-based decision making that had reigned for decades. We discuss this in greater detail in chapter 3, but here it is important to note that this change gave case managers much more discretion about who would receive TANF and under what conditions.

Local-level managers and work teams were "empowered" to develop JOBS programs that fulfilled agency goals and drew on the available resources and partnerships of their own communities. This devolution of key aspects of program design, as long as they led to outcomes consistent with the agency's mission, was a hallmark of Oregon's welfare reform process and was hailed by some external observers as bold and effective (Michaux 2008). Training was an important vehicle for promoting organizational change, including "nuts and bolts" workshops and other workshops designed to address the values, beliefs, and expectations of welfare-to-work programs.[12] Managers began to look for different qualities in new hires, seeking staff with "people skills." They also tended to hire workers who appeared enthusiastic about the new welfare policy. This transformation of agency culture and staff was at the heart of the actual practice of implementing the new welfare regime in Oregon, a fact Hoback understood well:

> Our greatest innovation is the significant culture shift inside the agency. Our workers were transformed from eligibility workers to case-workers. (Sandie Hoback, quoted in Stuart 1997)

Given the shift to "results-oriented" practices, agency leaders also sought to drive home the importance of the performance measures that they had adopted as indicators of agency success. Each month, workers were greeted with new charts enumerating the job placements, caseload reductions, and benefit accuracy rates (especially for Food Stamps) for individual branches and the agency as a whole. (Note that data were posted only on a few of the performance measures, signaling those that the agency deemed to be priorities.) These charts were posted on bulletin boards, but sometimes, when a branch or the agency's accomplishments were below administrators' expectations, managers devoted time in staff meetings to discussing the results.

Agency leaders also sent intraagency memos and e-mail "updates" to staff communicating, explicitly and implicitly, what they believed was important. "Updates" often began with "good news" about agency performance, the successes of an individual office in caseload reduction or program development, or expressions of appreciation for the good work of staff. The general tone was of a cheerleader, praising, but leaving no doubt about what was expected. An example was Sandie Hoback's "update" mentioned earlier in this chapter, in which she cheered on workers with her interpretation of our research as indicating the alleged "97% approval rating." Agency administrators and managers believed that while many, perhaps most, workers generally supported the new program direction and goals, they also surmised that worker enthusiasm and the degree to which they were implementing these changes was uneven. Moreover, at critical moments of policy change or development, agency leaders sometimes met face-to-face with groups of frontline workers to transmit directly the changing values, expectations, and practices as part of their evolving effort to manage agency culture.

One such pivotal moment in agency culture change revealed an iron fist inside the glove of "empowerment." In late 1998, during the year we were doing fieldwork in three branch offices of AFS, the agency faced a major issue: a "crisis" (their term) in the Food Stamp program (see chapter 3). The food stamp crisis resulted when the U.S. Department of Agriculture (USDA), which funds and has oversight of the federal Food Stamp program, found that Oregon's error rate in Food Stamp eligibility determination was too high. They threatened to assess a penalty of millions of dollars on the state. Agency leaders went into crisis mode, requiring new and time-consuming procedures. Workers felt betrayed because they had been told to concentrate their energies on employment outcomes, not eligibility verification. As one case manager said, "No more case management. We're going to verification now." Worker discretion to put maximum effort into the work-first goal had been a primary mechanism of solidifying their enthusiastic consent to neoliberal principles. This consent was threatened by the measures management took to avoid huge federal penalties. For workers, measures imposed from above to return to discarded eligibility rules made a mockery of "empowerment" and revealed the iron fist in the velvet glove of the new culture.

Operations managers, the supervisory personnel at the branch or local level, were key actors in the actual transformation of welfare culture, practices, and provisions. They actively interpreted and guided the process, linking the edicts of top managers to the everyday challenges facing workers as they responded to the (often) crisis needs of clients. While agency leaders communicated with frontline workers in occasional face-to-face meetings (as the example in the prologue about "Winter Priorities" exemplifies) and via memos and weekly e-mail "updates," most of the daily work of transmitting and overseeing the implementation of new policies and practices fell to district and branch-level managers. Here we explore the role and perspectives of branch managers, who did the difficult work of managing welfare reform on the ground.

In the early 1990s agency leaders effectively flattened the administrative hierarchy by reducing a considerable number of middle-management positions. (See chapter 3 for a more detailed account of this pre-TANF restructuring.) The former position of branch manager was replaced with management teams comprised of "operations managers" and a lower-level position known as HRS4 (Human Resource Specialist 4). In the reshuffling, some former management staff became operations managers, others were moved into other management positions, and some returned to frontline work or left the agency. These changes were consistent with the decision to devolve more responsibility to local braches and service providers. The vocabulary of organization change was consistently positive, emphasizing decentralization, innovation, local control, and worker empowerment.

We interviewed each of the eight operations managers at the three branch offices in which we did fieldwork in 1998. As a group they reflect the agency's effort to diversify management at this level: two were white men, three were white women, and three were women of color (one Asian American, one African American, and one Latina). Two of the women of color and one of the white men had less than two years as managers at AFS; the tenure of the others ranged from ten to twenty-four years. Their jobs involved responsibility for the day-to-day management of the branch, including program development, personnel, budget, maintaining relationships with partner agencies, and linkages with other branches and with district and state administrators.

Each of the operations managers (hereafter "ops managers," as they were called) articulated strong support for the agency's new mission, programs, and policies. One defined "the whole welfare reform…as a real positive move for the state," comparing Oregon's program favorably with programs in other states, which she thought were "stricter" and made it "harder for people to get on." But Oregon's program, she claimed, had "taken a real humanistic approach to this and just really looked at what we can do to really help our clients, so that is one of the reasons why we have been so successful." Other ops managers spoke in similar terms, generally applauding the efforts of agency leaders as "progressive," "visionary," and "forward thinking."

The ops managers defined their own jobs as transmitting the "big vision" and the "goals and priorities" of agency leaders to frontline workers and working with frontline workers to find the best way to implement these goals locally. They emphasized teamwork, collaboration, and mutual respect among agency staff, although some were more successful than others in achieving such goals. They talked about the importance of agency "performance measures" in guiding their work. These performance measures were seen as an objective measure of the success of their work, of their local programs and of their staff. As one ops manager put it, "We go back to our performance measures, I think. We constantly look at where we are in our jobs placement, where we are in our caseloads versus expenditures, our child support performance measures..." These performance measures (discussed earlier in this chapter; see "Adult and Family Services Goals and Performance Measures," above) were an important way that agency leadership held district and branch managers and all agency workers accountable for implementing agency mission in the context of devolution.

Each month these managers received statewide, district, and branch-level data measuring their progress in meeting the agency's performance measures. In the three branches we studied, these data were posted prominently on bulletin boards, comparing that branch's data with others statewide. While frontline workers varied in the extent to which they felt that their work was governed by the performance measures, there was no such equivocating from ops managers.

On the other hand, not all performance measures appeared to be equally important in shaping the branch's work. Throughout the interviews, ops managers referred only to the measures of caseload reduction, job placement, and reducing the Food Stamp error rate. The relative importance of these particular measures was also evident in interviews with frontline staff as they talked about their own work, and this was true even among those case managers who said agency performance measures were not essential in how they thought about their jobs.

Nevertheless, the interviews with ops managers clearly showed that *they* were concerned about meeting agency goals and objectives defined, at least to a significant degree, by these performance measures. While Oregon had posted some of the highest caseload reduction figures in the nation in the mid-1990s, by 1998 many branches saw their caseload reduction numbers begin to plateau. As one ops manager admitted,

> For instance there was this note that came out today from [the district manager] about our caseload growth...in the last month and she was

saying that she was real unhappy with our performance. And not just, this was not to outline our branch solely, it was throughout the entire district.

Ops managers, concerned about this, explained that they were caught between continuing pressure to reduce the caseload and the changing nature of the TANF caseload. Ops managers explained that caseload reduction was now more difficult because so many of the more employable clients were already working and, as a result, a higher proportion of the caseload was now clients with "multiple barriers to work." The vocabulary of welfare restructuring defined this group as the "hard to serve," but they were commonly referred to colloquially as the "drawer people" (files that stayed in the case manager's drawer because they were difficult to manage). This changing caseload spurred ops managers at each of the branches we studied to do some rethinking of service provision and to exhort case managers to find ways to be more successful with this group.

Shrinking available resources made this task more challenging. One ops manager claimed that although her staff agreed with agency goals, they also feared that the declining caseloads could cost them their jobs, and they struggled to provide families with the help they needed because they were being asked to reduce their expenditures:

> I think for the most part [staff agree with agency goals]. However, recently, with our caseloads, a lot of our case managers have come in really confused as to what we are trying to accomplish. We are asking them to reduce their caseload; however we are asking them to reduce their expenditures and so a lot of them are really confused as to what we are doing. And I think maybe not so much in this branch, but I think overall there is this fear of working themselves out of a job.... But again we reaffirm the staff about what our missions are because I really don't think we'll work ourselves out of a job.

Another ops manager explained that the hardest part of the job is keeping staff motivated in the midst of all the changes and challenges:

> So I think that's the hardest part of being a manager is just keeping people motivated, too. I know when I was doing the caseload you do kind of hit the wall, especially with the cases that are left. When welfare reform first came about, I think, the people that could got jobs almost immediately. Now you're sort of dealing with people who have lots of barriers and just working through those barriers with clients and keeping staff motivated so they can motivate clients, I think that is one of the hardest parts, especially when you are dealing with a lot of 1:90

> [shorthand for referring to each case manager's caseload of up to ninety clients] issues and expenditures.

She echoed the sentiments of other managers here that the combination of more difficult cases, the sheer number of cases (on average 90) held by each case manager, and decreasing dollars available for providing assistance to clients meant the work of welfare reform was even more challenging now than it had been in the first few years of the new program.

Despite the undeniable pressure they felt, the ops managers believed this new way, as one of them put it, "of doing business" was good for the agency. One ops manager appreciated the clarity the performance measures introduced to her work, saying that they promote a "clear vision, a clear set of expectations," compared to the "old days," when everything was "subjective," merely a matter of "perception." Another long-time manager, who had initially distrusted the performance measure system, stated that she was now a fan:

> I can recall that when we first went to the performance measure system and how awkward it felt and how weird it felt and how I didn't trust it, and I just want to reflect that I've changed, and I totally trust it and it's a very creative and constructive way to do business in social service.

She credits agency leaders with doing what was necessary to achieve the particular results being demanded by the state legislature, but doing so in a way that empowered frontline staff. Agency leaders, she said, were

> anxious to get the performance outcomes that the legislature and the people of Oregon expect of our agency. They were hearing consistently from staff that unless certain policies and procedures changed, they did not see how they would ever meet the caseload reduction goals being set by the legislature.... [T]hey recognized that one way to get results in a large organization is to empower staff and to take their thinking very seriously.

In two of the three branches we studied, both managers and many staff described a process in which teams of managers and frontline workers redesigned programs, services, and even the physical layout of their offices to achieve the agency goals. In the third branch, management favored a more "top down" management style, although even in that branch workers were involved to some degree in shaping branch services and practices. But all the managers echoed the rhetoric used by agency leaders who claimed that the agency's effectiveness was linked to the greater discretion local managers and individual case managers now had. While the state legislature, the governor, and agency leaders set outcome-based measures to which managers and staff were accountable, midlevel managers and frontline workers were encouraged to be innovative and to use discretion wisely as long as they were directed at meeting the performance measures that defined the agency's priorities. As one ops manager concluded,

> I would say we definitely get the vision and the budget picture from the state level, the coordination at the district level, and then at the branch level we take the programs and we make them our own.

Two of the eight ops managers we interviewed expressed a concern in their interviews that they might sound too much like organizational cheerleaders. One expressed her concern that she might seem to be a "mouthpiece" for agency leadership. Another thought we might see him as a "brainwashed flunky":

> I know this is going to sound like some kind of brainwashed flunky here, but I really do believe Oregon's approach is a much healthier one and I really believe that strongly.

Their zeal was an important aspect of the agency's organizational culture. Clearly reinforcing a positive assessment of the agency mission and organizational changes was essential in eliciting the support, enthusiasm, and cooperation of the frontline staff for the agency's new direction and practices.

Managers actively encouraged workers to see the new policies as designed to promote self-sufficiency, accountability, and choice on the part of clients. In this way the withdrawal or limitation of state support was not seen as an attenuation of social responsibility (of the state or society) but as the production of personal responsibility. The changing meanings of *welfare reform* were embedded deeply in the new bureaucratic language that was promoted by agency leaders and interpreted and attached to specific practices by ops managers at the local level. Thus, the work of ops managers was essential in reiterating and sustaining the neoliberal assumptions, values, and beliefs that were foundational in the agency's organizational culture.

For example, key words bore hefty ideological burdens, animating organizational discourse and helping to shape shared understandings of the practice of welfare restructuring. Two highly controversial aspects of welfare restructuring were the practices of *diversion* and allowing states to *sanction* clients off assistance. Both contributed to welfare caseload reduction, either by keeping clients from ever getting on assistance or by penalizing and then removing clients who were deemed noncompliant with welfare-to-work rules. Yet one rarely, if ever, heard agency leaders or workers in Oregon refer to the practices of diversion or sanctions explicitly.

Oregon did have a strong diversion policy, and agency leaders, including many ops managers, understood that diversion was one of the most effective ways of reducing caseloads. The practice of diversion in Oregon included hefty work search requirements of (almost) all applicants for TANF before a cash grant could begin. This practice was called "assessment," a term that implies a period of evaluation with an almost clinical connotation. During "assessment," most clients were also required to attend one or more weekly mandated employment-related workshops.

Case managers had at their disposal "assessment" payments to help "stabilize" the family and provide the potential breadwinner with what she/he needed to search for a job. Assessment payments ranged from helping to pay rent or past due utility bills to support for transportation, clothing or dental repair work, or anything else the case manager determined to be necessary or wise in supporting work search. Clients were also put on Food Stamps and helped to apply for the Oregon Health Plan during assessment. All this was left purely to the discretion of the case manager.

Of course, hefty work search requirements with potentially unachievable targets for job contacts discouraged clients from applying for cash assistance or returning to case managers for help if they had not met the work search targets. Not putting clients who were income eligible for TANF on assistance immediately reinforced the message that there was no longer an entitlement to receive cash assistance, that the agency's goal was to keep them off assistance. Calling this practice "assessment" cloaked the goal and effect of diversion and helped case managers think of themselves as evaluating and helping clients, rather than as deflecting them from public assistance.

Another example of how the language of the agency masked the more coercive or hardship-inducing effects of welfare restructuring on clients was the vocabulary used to describe sanctions in Oregon. For example, in an interview when asked about how the sanctions policy was used in her office, one ops manager explained that in Oregon these are called "disqualifications" and that they are used as "an opportunity to [get the client] to participate" in the program:

> Well, we call them *disqualifications*. We kind of got rid of that word *sanctions*. But the disqualification process is one that if for some reason we cannot get the client to participate in JOBS activities then there is a negative impact on their case. And the intent is to get the client to want to participate, to get them involved, help move through their issues....And through the whole process it gives the client the opportunity to participate, and we are always asking, do you want to participate?

And if not, then we move to the next step. Usually what happens is that we don't get their attention until the very end.

She goes on to frame this whole process even more explicitly as a matter of client choice:

> [The disqualification process is about] helping the client to understand where we are now, what's expected of them. But also what I usually do is just say, "You have a choice. You really don't have to do anything if you don't want to. But if you don't then this is where we have to go. But we would really rather help you." So it's sort of giving them that, that it's their responsibility and their choice.

Another ops manager from a different branch also defined the disqualification and conciliation process (i.e., the process of reengagement) as positive, though he admits that he was cynical at first and questioned the role of punishment in the process. But in the following quote, it is apparent that he tacks back and forth between conceiving of disqualifications as punishment (sanctions) and as a tool to foster client accountability:

> I think one of the things that Sandie [the agency leader] pushed really hard is that this [disqualification] is supposed to be a reengagement, not a disengagement process. Initially this was a real hard policy. Everybody looked at it cynically, you know, how can you reengage by punishing, all of us, including myself. *It seemed like it was just a play on words.* But in reality I think the Conciliation Board [a structure developed in this branch for processing most of the disqualifications] incorporates that concept because this is an opportunity to get that person back on track again....So we look at it basically as here is a contract we sat down and developed. (our emphasis)

He admits that it might seem like calling *sanctions disqualifications* is simply a "play on words," but he defends the process and suggests that it is actually a contractual arrangement the agency can now implement between itself and the client. He recognizes there is coercion involved, but believes the end—reengagement of the client—justifies the means. He believes it is fair:

> The client may feel pressured into having to sign it. I wouldn't want to try and fool anybody into thinking they all know what it says at the bottom, you know, I willingly sign this and I willingly agree to this myself and all that kind of stuff. To think otherwise is silly...I think the critical thing about disqualification in Oregon and I'm sure everyone has got a clear sense of this in this office is that you need to try to get people back

on track again. We are not using this as punishment....So I believe the process...is about as fair as you can make it and still have a program in which you are holding people accountable for their behavior. I don't know how you could make it more fair than we have it set up here.

From the agency head to the ops manager and from the ops manager to the case manager, coercive policies were discursively framed in positive terms, with the goal of disqualifications being to get clients "back on track." Despite his equivocation about the degree to which clients willingly enter into the contract that requires their accountability and about whether not using the term sanction is simply "word play," it is clear that he has come to define the disqualification process as a constructive tool to help people and as a process that is fair. This reframing quelled his initial cynicism and allow him to think of and encourage the staff he manages to think of sanctions not as coercive but as constructive.

Agency leaders and managers believed that welfare restructuring in Oregon was successful; that the program was better than the one it replaced; and that agency workers, clients, and the general public were now being better served by work-first policies. While agency leaders were far from immune from political pressures exerted both nationally and at the state level, their relative positions of power in the welfare state enabled them to exert considerable power in shaping welfare restructuring in Oregon. Moreover, their distance from the more negative effects of these policies—a distance made possible both because they were not frontline workers and because of class and, often, racial and gender differences from those whose lives were most directly affected by changing public assistance policies—inoculated them from some of the contradictions faced by the front-line workers who implemented these policies.

There is some truth in the statements of agency leaders that welfare restructuring in Oregon was perhaps more "humane" than in some other states. Not only did the bold health policy known as the Oregon Health Plan expand subsidized health coverage to a greater proportion of low-income families than was available to families in many other states,[13] but Oregon used a combination of carrots and sticks in their program (see chapter 3). Work supports, including subsidized child care, became more widely available than they had been under the previous AFDC program, assisting the many public assistance clients that would have sought employment without the work-first mandates (as they always have) as well as others who may have been pressured to seek employment but did so with significant work supports. Oregon was exempt (at least until 2003) from the five-year federal time limit because it operated under a waiver secured just weeks before PRWORA was passed. And Oregon had a higher minimum wage than in many other states, a minimum wage that was increased twice during the period of our study. The fact that many managers and workers spoke so highly of agency leaders, and that few spoke negatively, also suggests that for many (though not all) workers welfare restructuring, while challenging, did improve their own sense of efficacy and worth in their jobs.

Nevertheless, rhetoric only goes so far in influencing how workers experienced and implemented and how clients interpreted and lived with the consequences of welfare restructuring. Administrators' efforts to frame the new policies as empowering, for example, obscures the ways the new welfare regime functions much like the proverbial iron fist in the velvet glove. The welfare-to-work mandate compels clients to conform to neoliberal expectations of self-support and significantly constrains choices clients formerly had to determine the best balance of paid and care work at different periods in their children's lives. For workers, enhanced discretion to "really help" their clients requires them, for the most part, to assist as their clients find and keep jobs but otherwise to communicate the message that clients cannot expect much help from the agency. Everyone—administrators, workers, and clients—was subject to mandates, and everyone's performance was measured against those mandates. But the degree to which any particular individual or group had a say in what those mandates were, what was measured and monitored, and what the consequences of noncompliance were varied significantly depending on gendered and racialized class relations that position different groups to have more or less power and control within the welfare state.

The official story of welfare restructuring is the narrative the public has had the most opportunity to hear. It is not, however, the only story. As we show in the following chapters, some workers and many clients understood and evaluated welfare restructuring very differently, from their different positions in the welfare state and as race, class, and gender exposed them to the contradictions and hardships generated by the neoliberal contraction of the social contract. Understanding the multiple interpretations and different experiences of welfare restructuring reveals that neoliberal hegemony is neither as seamless nor as uncontested as the public proclamations of welfare reform as success would have us believe.

DOING THE WORK OF WELFARE

Enforcing "Self-Sufficiency" on the Front Lines

Like a majority of case managers at the three branches we studied, Adult and Family Services (AFS) case managers Elena Lopez and Donald Henderson embraced the ideology of welfare "reform." All the while, however, they were experiencing a dramatic shift in their own work of welfare provision. Like all case managers in the Oregon system, they were required to navigate a multidimensional process of transforming beliefs in individual responsibility and the primacy of paid work into daily practices that are geared to produce caseload reduction, employment, and self-sufficiency among this country's most economically vulnerable families. As Elena's and Donald's comments make clear, they had complex ideas about the meaning of self-sufficiency and "reform success."

> There was [at first] grumbling about having to change and having to have new training and new experience or whatever; but it worked. I would never have believed we could get away from bureaucracy, really do our job and that our job could be effective in people's lives and the culture as a whole....It's been excellent, I believe, for my clients and I think for us it has been satisfying....We haven't just pushed paper...we really helped somebody in their lives to hope that they will have a good life....That you made some kind of intervention, a point of impact, a positive thing in people's lives, and in our whole culture as a result of it.[1]

> (We) move people toward self-sufficiency with the idea of getting them off in a manner that they will be able to sustain or maintain themselves with a minimum amount of help from the state...it is to help

families achieve self-sufficiency and that is from A to Z in the spectrum....Somebody's self-sufficiency might be just getting in here to
keep an appointment where [for] somebody else it may be getting a job
and not requiring anything, no day care, no food stamps, no medical, no
zip. And all those areas in between are what it is about.[2]

Workers in welfare offices have more power than their clients. Over twenty
years ago Michael Lipsky argued that "street-level bureaucrats," including public
welfare workers, are integral to the policy process, that policy implementation is
an integral part of policy making (1980). But that power and authority is con-
toured and sharply limited by the welfare administrators and policy makers who
legislate, fund, and monitor the work they do. What is the daily work of welfare
"reform," the tasks agency employees must carry out in the name of producing
"success?" We look at the organizational demands and realities of welfare restructuring and the ways it was experienced by welfare workers as they interpreted,
implemented, enforced, and, sometimes, challenged the new policy regime. We
recognize that welfare restructuring impacts these workers *as* public employees.
Their jobs, daily work, wages, and benefits are subject to political contestation
and are the target of "limited government," antitax politicians and advocates who
favor welfare state retrenchment and privatization.

Frontline workers and their immediate supervisors mediate between top-
level state administrators and the clients who seek public assistance. Through
their actions, they bring to clients the neoliberal ideologies about the efficacy of
markets and the potent discursive messages about individual responsibility, self-
sufficiency, universal dependence on wage work, and conservative family values.
The introduction of these ideas reshaped everyday practices in the local branch
offices in Oregon, often in complex ways. One thing that did not change with
the changes in welfare policies, though, was a view of clients as the material to be
processed, excluded, or changed—with clients' problems being the often unsolv-
able conundrums that fill the working day.[3]

As Donald Henderson asserts above, the worker's role, as defined by AFS, is
to minimize, if not eliminate, state assistance. But, minimizing assistance may
contradict the view of Elena Lopez, quoted above, that now welfare "really helps
somebody." Case management involves managing such contradictions. A sec-
ondary and usually unstated goal of welfare reform is to reduce or remove non-
market, especially public, supports for wages, so that wages can be fully set by
the market—what Frances Fox Piven and Richard Cloward ([1971] 1993), Karl
Polanyi (1957), and Gösta Esping-Andersen (1990) contend is part of the process
of enforcing the commodification of labor. One consequence of these two goals
is that the practices carried out day to day by workers in welfare offices have the

net result of reproducing the race, class, and gender inequities of the low-wage labor force and of the larger society. Needless to say, contradictions arise between neoliberalism as an ideology that reshaped welfare policy and neoliberalism on the ground, where that ideology runs into obdurate reality. In chapter 4, we focus more closely on these contradictions and the complex processes through which workers come to accept and, in some cases, to question or reject policies that sometimes deny financial assistance to people in urgent need.

In addition to relying on ethnographic fieldwork observations in three local welfare offices, we interviewed 126 workers representing 95 percent of the agency staff at all levels in these branches. We also collected and reviewed agency documents and discussed agency policies and procedures with other agency personnel. When we refer to *workers*, we mean all personnel who are charged with the everyday work of ushering (or assisting with the ushering of) clients through the process of applying for and maintaining assistance through the agency, including clerical workers, case aides, case managers, family resource managers, employment specialists (JOBS staff), and operations managers. However, given the pivotal role of case managers in the implementation of welfare "reform," we emphasize their experiences and actions.[4]

Although we underscore the "welfare to work" responsibilities of case managers, they and other agency staff administered an array of programs. These included (during most of the period of our fieldwork) case management, employment and self-sufficiency services, assessment, TANF, Emergency Assistance,[5] Food Stamps, child care assistance, Medical Assistance programs, and the Child Support Program.[6]

Who Are the Workers?

U.S. social welfare workers, particularly those who provide direct services, are, and have been, since the early twentieth century, disproportionately white women (Dressel 1992). This is true in Oregon where both the majority of welfare clients (84%) and workers (50%) who were participants in our study were white women.[7] Also replicating national trends, women and men of color, although numerical minorities, were better represented within the AFS workforce than in the population at large or in most other public agencies,[8] although more often as direct service providers than administrators. White men, on the other hand, disproportionately occupied positions of authority within the welfare state as administrators and supervisors.

Of the total number of managers and workers that we interviewed in the three branches, 75 percent were women and 66 percent white. Women represented particularly high proportions of both managerial (75 percent) and clerical (90 percent) staff; men and women of color were also disproportionately well represented in managerial and clerical jobs. Among direct service providers, women constituted about 70 percent of case managers, 90 percent of JOBS staff, and 65 percent of family resource managers (FRMs). Men and women of color represented 24 percent of case managers and 45 percent of FRMs; there were no men or women of color in any of the JOBS positions. Among the forty-two case managers—the staff most directly responsible for enforcing welfare-to-work policies—twenty-four were white women, eight were white men, four were mixed-race women, two were Latino men, two were Latinas, one was an African American man, and one a mixed-race woman; no African American women worked as case managers.

Although AFS workers mirrored, demographically, the client population in terms of gender (mostly women) and race (mostly white), class differences between workers and clients were more pronounced. Clients were, with rare exceptions, working-class women with high school educations or less, who had worked primarily in low-wage jobs. The AFS workers in our study were more financially secure, with state jobs that provided good benefits and some job ladders for promotion. Nevertheless, the earnings of those AFS workers who provided direct services were modest and, depending on the size of their families, did not necessarily provide them with a middle class income, or even a living wage (see below). One-third of workers identified themselves as working class during the interviews, and an even higher percentage described backgrounds that social scientists would classify as working class. Over half of all workers had received some form of public assistance either as children or adults,[9] although the percentage varied among the branches we studied. While 45 percent of Woodside staff said they had ever received public assistance, 57 percent of Bridgetown and 64 percent of Coastal staff said they had done so. Many (55%) agency workers we interviewed had also been single parents at some time in their lives.

As a group, AFS workers—both case managers and FRMs—had more education than clients, higher incomes, and stable jobs. Most case managers, for example, had at least some college training; approximately 40 percent had graduated from college, while 25 percent of FRMs had graduated from college. A few workers (about 2%) had graduate education in a discipline related to human services. Most welfare workers learned their work on the job, through agency courses and workshops, coaching from supervisors, advice from colleagues, and their own trial and error dealing with clients and managing demanding workloads.

The vast majority of them ended up with jobs at AFS because a position in the agency was open when they were seeking work, and the position offered them job stability, benefits, and decent pay. A minority volunteered that they specifically wanted a job "helping people." Elena Lopez, the Latina worker quoted at the beginning of the chapter, noted that the pay, benefits, and hours matched her needs as a single mother:

> It's a job that paid better than other jobs for women. And as a single mama, I had to make better money for my kids, and medical, and Saturdays and Sundays off and home at 5:00. That's why I took the job. But mostly because it paid better.

The average length of time the staff had worked for the agency was about ten years, although the average length of job tenure was much lower among clerical workers. Among case managers, job tenure with the agency ranged from less than a year to thirty years. Two-thirds of case managers had worked for the agency more than five years; this means they were AFS employees before the current welfare-to-work regime went into high gear. Indeed almost half of case managers had worked for the agency for more than a decade.

Nonmanagerial workers employed by AFS were members of the Oregon Public Employees Union (OPEU), the largest union in the state. These unionized state jobs offered benefits and incomes that were modest, but secure. In 1998, when we were doing the fieldwork, annual gross salaries for case managers ranged from $25,464 to $33,768, and those for FRMs ranged from $23,364 to $31,068. Compare this to what a nonprofit research group estimated, only two years later, as a *living wage* in Oregon for a single mother and two children—$34,020 (Northwest Job Gap Study 2001), a salary above those of most AFS nonmanagerial or administrative workers. Though workers profited from a host of benefits, including health insurance and retirement pensions, the salaries alone would not have placed them solidly in the middle class, as we pointed out above, unless it was a second income in their family. The relatively low wages, as well as the nature and relatively low status of the work, helps explain why such a high proportion of welfare workers are men of color or women.[10] This grated on a number of the men we interviewed. More than women, men complained about their salary levels, claimed they had never expected to stay in this job, and were more likely to say they felt uneasy with the mandate of grappling with clients and their families' real problems.

A small but significant number of welfare workers we interviewed, especially in positions below the level of case manager, were former clients who either sought positions in the agency or who ended up in permanent positions after being successful in "work experience" jobs with the agency.[11] Upward mobility within the branches seemed to be common; the typical branch employee began her tenure with AFS in a clerical position and was later promoted to case manager or family resource manager. However, having been a former client of the agency did not guarantee that a worker could be counted on to be more sympathetic to clients.

While some former clients, now AFS employees, explicitly said that their own experiences of poverty and welfare receipt made them more empathetic than their coworkers, others, arguing that *they* had managed to pull themselves up by their bootstraps, had little sympathy for clients who could not or did not do the same.

Social location is, by itself, an unreliable predictor of points of view. Social location was among a number of factors that shaped workers' perspectives on their work and their clients and helped to determine the ways in which they implemented the newfound discretion welfare reform brought. Linkages between work practices and broad indicators of social location are complex and difficult to unravel; it is not possible to simply delineate certain points of view or practices from a listing of class, race, and gender identifiers. However, we were able to see broad patterns that, we contend, reflected some of the ways that workers' racial and class privilege played out.

The Welfare Office as a Workplace

As we discussed in detail in 1, welfare reform in Oregon was not the result of a single piece of legislation or the vision of a single political or administrative leader. Welfare restructuring spanned the entire decade of the 1990s, shaping an agency, and by extension, workplaces, where changes in policies, organizational structures, and daily work, were endemic. Spurred by the growing influence of conservative policy makers pushing for reductions in the welfare rolls and a recurrent state fiscal crisis resulting from economic restructuring in the state and regressive tax-related ballot initiatives, the agency experimented with programs to shrink their expenditures. Like many in the private sector, they shrank the organization (what management gurus at the time called "downsizing") through the drastic reduction of middle management, the introduction of teamwork, implementation of measurable outcomes, and devolution of decision-making to lower levels of the organizational hierarchy. The branches were restructured. Former management positions were eliminated and replaced by a new management team made up of operations managers (known as "ops managers") and human resource specialists (known as "HRS4s"). During the mid- to late 1990s, over two hundred positions were cut agencywide, or 10.4 percent of the workforce. The biggest cuts were in managerial positions, which were reduced 45.8 percent (these had been targeted for 68% of the cuts).[12]

In 1996, when Oregon was granted waivers to the AFDC program allowing them to fully implement the Oregon Option (Oregon's welfare-to-work program), a new job category was created—the "case manager." Case managers were assigned primary responsibility for carrying out the frontline work of welfare "reform," administering Temporary Assistance for Needy Families (TANF) and the new, more intensive work-attachment services that required almost all applicants for aid to search for a job before they could qualify for any cash assistance and required most of those receiving a cash grant to continue job-related activities.[13] The other major category of direct service provider (formerly "eligibility worker") was renamed "family resource manager" (FRM). These workers, who had much higher caseloads, were not responsible for case management. They continued to do most of the work most welfare workers had done for decades in the agency: determining eligibility for and processing benefits such as Food Stamps and the Oregon Health Plan (Medicaid), but not TANF, the cash benefits for children and families.

This organizational restructuring required that all workers be "reclassified," competing, if they chose to, for the new case manager positions. Those who were not selected to become case managers generally served as FRMs. As we will discuss, in Bridgetown, people of color were concentrated in the FRM positions, though, by the time we ended our observations nearly a year later, the branch seemed to be in the process of addressing these inequities by hiring and, in a few cases, promoting workers of color.

Although some workers reportedly preferred eligibility work over case management and opted to stay on as FRMs, we were told that the transition resulted in diminished morale for many. Anna Borelli, an ops manager with over ten years in the agency told us, "[Y]ou want an issue that will divide everybody? That was one! We got through it okay, but there are still open wounds from that time." Frustrations over the transitions combined with discomfort with new case management responsibilities and favorable offers from the state retirement system led to a high number of resignations in 1996. Though resentments persisted, workers who became case managers were generally enthusiastic about welfare reform and their amplified helping responsibilities. As one ops manager observed, "The staff went from old and cynical to young and enthusiastic."

Although the managerial hierarchy was flattened, new status distinctions emerged among frontline workers. Case manager work was considered to be more professional, skilled, and complex than that of FRMs, whose work was seen as being only a brief step above clerical work, though many FRMs informally case managed their clients. Case managers carried caseloads of approximately 90 cash assistance (TANF) clients and Food Stamp clients, while FRMs handled caseloads of up to 250 Food Stamp, Oregon Health Plan, and Employment Related Day Care clients who were not receiving cash assistance. Despite these differences in status, work, and caseloads, salary differentials were not large; for case managers the salary range was from $2,122 to $2,814 monthly, and for FRMs from $1,947 to $2,589 monthly.

Welfare reform involved much more than organizational restructuring. The daily work of welfare changed significantly over the course of the 1990s. Local branches were allowed to design many facets of their welfare-to-work programs as long as they achieved the mandated outcomes. As a result, there were some differences among branches in the ways that both workers and clients were confronted by and involved in welfare "reform."

Three Branches, Three Realities

Each of the three branch offices we studied offered a unique perspective on how neoliberal welfare policies were enacted along a continuum of—simply put— punitive pushing to supportive pushing into the labor market. How each branch interpreted and designed their welfare-to-work program depended on local leadership, the size and prosperity of the community, and the particular historical, racial, economic, and social relations in which they were embedded. Here we briefly trace those conditions and introduce the contours of the work of welfare in each branch.

Bridgetown

Bridgetown served a racially segregated, high-poverty, high-unemployment enclave within a prosperous white metropolis that was home to a number of successful high-tech companies and giants of globalization, such as Nike. During the time of our study, the city experienced a high rate of economic growth. The area in which the Bridgetown branch was located had a large African-American population (34.5%), compared to Oregon as a whole (1.6%) and the city in which the branch was located (8.7%).[14] Unemployment was very low in the city as a whole (4.4%), while it was slightly higher in Bridgetown's neighborhood (6.0%). The poverty rate in the branch district was also high, at 21.5 percent, compared with the city as a whole in which the poverty rate was 15.1 percent. The Bridgetown branch was one of the largest branches in the state. The staff in Bridgetown was relatively diverse, with a substantial representation of African Americans (26%), while people of color as a whole, including Latinos, native and Asian Americans, and those of mixed heritage, represented 52 percent of the staff.

Woodside

The Woodside branch served a partly urban and partly semirural population within and on the fringes of a smaller prosperous city, which was the location of a major state university. The city enjoyed considerable wealth as well as the fruits of globalization during the boom of the late 1990s. The county, which included the city and the nearby rural area, had an unemployment rate of 5.6 percent and a poverty rate of 13.7 percent[15] during the period of the study. In all likelihood, the city itself had a relatively low unemployment rate and poverty rate, in comparison with the rural area around the city, but employment and poverty rates are not available for these geographical areas. The community was predominantly white, with small and growing Latino and Asian American populations, but very few blacks. The racial composition of the staff reflected the makeup of the community: 25 percent of the workers were people of color, but none were African American.

Coastal

In contrast, the Coastal office served a sprawling, mostly rural working-class county that had been historically dependent on timber, fishing, and agriculture and was experiencing serious economic troubles linked to globalization-related industry restructuring during our study period. The county was also predominantly white, as was the branch that served it. In Coastal, 81 percent of the workers were white, 12 percent were Latino, and 7 percent identified as mixed race. The unemployment rate was much higher than in the other two sites, climbing to between 10 and 11 percent during the period of our study. The poverty rate reached 17.5 percent in 1998.[16] The county where Coastal was located was designated as having a "surplus labor supply," defined by the federal government as an unemployment rate exceeding the national average by 20 percent over a two-year period. Coastal had a higher number of two-parent family welfare cases than the other two branches, reflecting the high unemployment rate and the seasonal nature of many men's jobs in the county.

The varying approaches to welfare reform in these three branches were evident even in the physical design of each office. The design and appearance of the offices conveyed a series of messages to both workers and clients and reflected the class and racial hierarchies of each community. Internally, all three branches were arranged similarly, with cubicles for individual workers separated by five-foot-high dividers in large open spaces. This open arrangement afforded workers and clients little privacy in which to discuss often very confidential matters. As one black female worker observed, "I think it [the configuration of the cubicles] keeps clients from talking about their problems…privacy is a problem here." The bureaucratic hierarchy was preserved in the allocation of private offices to ops managers.

Although office arrangements were similar, there was a marked contrast between the Coastal branch and the other two branches in their public entrances and waiting spaces. In Coastal, AFS was housed in the Coastal Center, one of the first of a group of "one-stop" centers created around the state. One-stop centers gathered a variety of service providers in one location to make it easier for clients to access services. It also meant that "the welfare office" was not just a welfare office, but part of a suite of agencies that shared work and service space. The Coastal Center was a new building with an inviting entrance under a small portico. The building looked like a prosperous professional building. There were no glass-enclosed counters, no barriers, no posters informing people that they were in an AFS office. A receptionist welcomed clients from a desk at the edge of a well-appointed lobby that rarely seemed crowded.

The Woodside and Bridgetown offices were less inviting, with physical arrangements suggesting that the agency was suspicious of clients. Both Woodside and Bridgetown had a glassed-in counter to which clients took their requests for service. The office areas were behind locked doors, opened by staff when a client needed to enter. The waiting rooms were sparsely furnished, dreary, and, often, crowded. A uniformed guard was on duty in the Bridgetown office, a signal that the staff needed protection from clients. His presence added to the aura of surveillance and criminalization. The Woodside office was in a large, formerly industrial space in an asphalted shopping area, while the Bridgetown office was in a one-story cement building in a mixed residential and commercial neighborhood. At busy times in both Woodside and Bridgetown, long lines of clients waited to speak to a receptionist. At such times, it was not unusual for tensions to rise for both reception staff and clients.

Work relations were, on the whole, harmonious in Woodside and Coastal, while tensions and suspicions were acute in the Bridgetown office. Although these differences had many causes, varying leadership strengths helped to set the branch climates. Operations managers were particularly important in this process. Most of the daily work of transmitting and overseeing the implementation of the new policies and practices fell to the ops managers, as well as the HRS4s (human resource specialists). They were the key link between frontline workers and the goals and priorities determined by agency leaders. Woodside, in particular, had strong leaders who were generally liked and respected by workers. The ops managers were deeply committed to the new mission of the agency, approaching it as a mandate for highly constructive and humane work with clients. This enthusiasm, along with the ops managers' skillful approach to problem and crisis management, seemed to motivate and inspire many of the workers to follow their leadership. Most Coastal workers were satisfied with their workplace, although workers spoke of personnel problems in the past. Agency restructuring resulted in the resignation of many long-time workers and ushered in new leadership who were, reportedly, easier to work with than previous supervisors. This contributed a great deal to the new and improved worker satisfaction, which seemed to carry over to other workplace relationships. Workers in Bridgetown frequently voiced a sense of friction and mistrust between management and staff, but, as we will see, it is difficult to tease this tension out from long-standing race dynamics in the branch. Nevertheless, on the whole, the ops managers were not able to move the branch onto a more positive course during our study period.

Resource allocation, especially influencing the number of case managers available to deal with clients applying for and receiving cash assistance, also influenced the differences we observed among the branches. For most of the study period, Bridgetown was short *eight* case managers. To put this in stark comparative perspective,[17] Bridgetown served approximately 88 TANF cases per case manager, while the Woodside and Coastal branches assisted 36 and 49 TANF cases per case manager, respectively. Thus, on average, the Bridgetown branch was responsible for juggling the needs of *two-and-a-half times* the number of TANF cases per case manager as Woodside and *nearly twice* as many as Coastal. The actual number of TANF cases each case manager carried varied greatly and was supplemented by clients who had left TANF but were receiving the Oregon Health Plan, child care subsidies, and/or Food Stamps. More active TANF cases meant the need for more intensive and time-consuming case management. These vastly different numbers speak to the greater stress and more demanding workload Bridgetown case managers dealt with as well as the greater potential for clients' needs to fall through the cracks.

A complex collection of local and state histories, political-economic realities, and personalities mediated the work of welfare in each of the branches we studied. We will return to an examination of the differences among the branches in chapter 4, highlighting the racial dynamics in these offices—dynamics that helped shape experiences of welfare for workers and for clients. But first we discuss how overarching changes in the agency mission and the ways it "did business" shaped welfare provision practices and the experiences of the workers who provided direct services to a diverse clientele every day.

"Work Is Always Better Than Welfare": Caseload Reduction in Practice

At the heart of welfare "reform" in Oregon was the motto "work is always better than welfare." This slogan—plastered visibly on the walls of branch offices, threaded prominently through agency documents, and articulated repeatedly by agency leaders and managers—constitutes the shorthand version of the intertwined neoliberal goals of welfare restructuring: TANF caseload reduction and employment promotion. As the work-first ideology emerged as the foundation of agency practices, AFS changed its mission statement to reflect this change. At the start of our fieldwork in 1998 the agency mission read: "To help families become self-supporting while assisting them in meeting their basic needs" (AFS 1998). But within a year the mission statement was changed again, deleting the reference to helping meet basic needs. The new mission statement was "To help Oregonians become and remain self-supporting," a goal to be accomplished largely by "Helping people to find and keep jobs." This unambiguous statement of the "work attachment model" was unmodified by the realities of varying job availability, children's needs, or the complex issues facing many applicants for assistance or by the long-term agency mission of helping to stabilize or provide minimal economic security for families. The centrality of caseload reduction was enshrined in the "performance measures" we discussed in chapter 2. In addition to the measure of TANF cases per 1,000 Oregonians (the measure used to gauge caseload reduction) the other performance measures that most directly shaped frontline work were "total job placements" and "average cost per job."

By the time we began our study, the agency and its case managers had achieved great success in reducing the numbers of TANF recipients, as had state welfare departments nationwide. Between January 1995 and January 1999, Bridgetown TANF rolls dropped by 55 percent, Woodside by 66 percent, and Coastal by 40 percent, reflecting the varying local economic conditions and racial barriers faced by clients in each branch.[18] These reductions were not solely due to the work carried out on the front lines. State policies and economic conditions, over which workers and local branch offices had no control, contributed to reducing the numbers of people receiving TANF. The expanding economy of the late 1990s meant increased employment and new job opportunities for TANF recipients and applicants that contributed to some proportion of the caseload reductions (Mishel, Bernstein, and Boushey 2003).

Caseload reduction also resulted from bureaucratic tools specifically constructed for that purpose. Caseloads were kept in check by Oregon state TANF eligibility policies that steadily reduced the pool of eligible clients. In 1999, a single mother with two children could qualify for cash assistance only if her income fell below $616 per month—the same income eligibility limit in place in 1991. Needless to say $616 in 1999 contributed much less to household budgets than it did in 1991 because of both inflation and rising costs for basic necessities. Thus, to qualify for assistance, a single mother had to be poorer in 1999 than she was in 1991. Stagnant eligibility limits thus diminished welfare caseloads over the years.

However, none of the workers or administrators whom we interviewed linked eligibility levels to declining caseloads.

On the other hand, case managers were quite aware that declining caseloads were also changing caseloads because a growing portion of the TANF caseload was comprised of clients called the "hard to serve," otherwise known as those for whom labor market–based solutions were not easily accomplished. Case managers believed that many of the "hard-to-serve" had severe or multiple impediments to employment, such as drug and alcohol addictions, domestic violence, homelessness, learning disabilities, and chronic illness. For these clients, the available policy tools were often sorely inadequate. People with addiction issues were offered, and sometimes required to seek, treatment, though treatment options were often limited. Women who had experienced domestic violence were routinely exempted from immediate work requirements, eligible for additional financial resources (up to $1,200), and referred to women's shelters. Case managers occasionally referred clients with learning disabilities to vocation rehabilitation services or put them in courses to boost their basic skills or in volunteer positions, but their options for dealing with these issues were not adequate. Clients with chronic illness might qualify for Supplemental Security Income (SSI), but the application process was difficult and lengthy.[19]

Treatment services for those with physical and mental health issues were similarly limited. As Anna Borelli, the white ops manager quoted earlier, explained, in the past, clients with mental health issues were often left to "rot on the caseload for eighteen years and then become bag ladies." Now, she said proudly, case managers work with clients to figure out

> how could they be successful in a job given their mental illness. It's a whole different way of looking at clients as people with capabilities, not people just to be shoved off in the back of your file cabinet.

Her comments reflect how, with agency goals geared toward employment, even the "hard-to-serve" became redefined as potentially capable workers. Another group of clients are "non-needy caretakers," often grandparents or other relatives caring for children whose parents were absent. But this group, now nearly a third of the caseload, are not subject to "work first" rules, and thus not cases that can contribute to the goal of caseload reduction.

With the change in the composition of the rolls, the primary strategies for keeping caseloads down involved moving new recipients off of TANF as quickly as possible or, as an increasingly important strategy, *diversion;* that is, preventing applicants from going on the rolls in the first place. Though Oregon's policies in general were geared to discourage, if not phase out, welfare use over the long term, Bridgetown policies and practices exemplified particularly strict diversion tactics. Compared with the other two offices, the process of applying for and being on welfare in Bridgetown was more time consuming, more laden with inconveniences and hassles, and potentially more humiliating. The process seemed designed to frustrate clients into leaving—whether they had secured employment or not. Indeed, one white worker explicitly asserted this objective: "That's one of our jobs, to make you tired of welfare." We did observe evidence of client fatigue with the system—head shaking, heavy sighs, and open declarations such as "[I]t's so frustrating to come here" and "This is a stupid thing to go through."

On the other hand, Woodside ops manager Christy Kahoe fretted about the possibility that establishing too many hoops could discourage needy families from getting through the assessment process. In discussing her branch's nascent efforts to track clients who opt out of the assessment program, she said:

> If it is our assessment program [discouraging clients], then maybe we need to relook at what information is being given to the clients at that point. If it's being presented as you're going to jump through all of these hoops, then obviously we are going to need to change our presentation.

Hoops, however, *were* the norm in all three branches. The very process of applying and getting a case manager to "assess" one's application was an arduous task, involving multiple trips to the office that could take up to a week, or more, to complete.

Diversion: The Pre-Assessment Process and "Assessment"

Some prospective applicants diverted themselves by walking away from the branches without completing an application. However, the first *formal* application/diversion tool was a fourteen-page form, to be filled out by the applicant, documenting the applicant's financial, work, and family situations. In the applicant's first contact with the agency, receptionists or case aides in local offices distributed these forms to prospective applicants along with information about next steps. Clients who were clearly in crisis might be referred to other community resources, such as food banks.[20] At each of these local offices, if a client was experiencing domestic violence or was in the late stages of pregnancy, she was likely fast-tracked to an assessment appointment with a case manager.

The next step for most applicants was a required group meeting designed to introduce them to the services and expectations of the agency and changes in policy. During this meeting, prospective clients in Woodside viewed a motivational video emphasizing the merits of work and challenging many of the common reasons clients might "not want" to work, especially at low-wage jobs, at that point in their lives. We observed that the video appeared to put off, even insult, some applicants, many of whom were already experienced workers. In Bridgetown, testimony from an employee who was a former AFS client replaced the video, but the focus on work motivation was similar to Woodside's meeting. At Coastal, the group meeting focused on information about community resources provided by representatives from a number of community agencies. Work motivation was less central, perhaps reflecting recognition that unemployment was so high in the community. In all three meetings, workers explained the procedures for application and receipt of welfare, heavily peppered with what one worker called the "expectations for self-sufficiency," and the employment-oriented services the agency now offered. At the end of the group meeting, applicants in Coastal and Woodside could sign up for appointments with case managers to have their cases "assessed," eligibility determined, and case plans developed. The process was more difficult in Bridgetown. Assessment appointments were available every day except Wednesday from 7:30 a.m. to 8:30 a.m. on a first-come, first-serve basis, with only nine slots available each day. Clients did not have the opportunity to set up appointments at the group meeting for most of our observation period.

Next the client had her "assessment" meeting with a case manager, a meeting managers defined primarily as an assessment of "work readiness." Clients would find out if they were definitively (financially) eligible for TANF, and, therefore, the "JOBS program." The information given on the fourteen-page application form the applicant had filled out was considered as part of this eligibility determination. If they were not eligible, their applications were denied, but they might be given counseling, given a small amount of cash assistance to meet immediate needs, or enrolled in another program for which they were eligible, such as Food Stamps. Nearly all of the "over-income" diverted applicants whom we interviewed did receive some other assistance, such as the Oregon Health Plan, Food Stamps, day care assistance, and, for some, other limited financial help, such as money for car repairs.

During the formal assessment phase, almost all new applicants, with the exception of those with serious impediments to immediate employment, spent thirty days (extended to forty-five days in 1998) engaged in job search and JOBS classes before their cash grant was opened. John Alpert, a white Bridgetown case manager, made explicit the point of the assessment period: "Everyone goes through this [assessment], and the whole purpose is to divert you from getting cash assistance." Assessment served as a "labor market test" to determine clients' employability, with support from the agency in terms of mandated classes and, at the discretion of the case manager, possibly some financial assistance ("assessment payments") to avert financial crises that might interfere with the job search.

After the initial information-gathering part of the interview, the worker was obligated to formulate an employment development plan (EDP) that detailed the steps the client would take to get a job. The case manager accomplished this primarily through talking with the potential client, probing the situation, and uncovering what small steps might be taken toward stabilizing the family. This discussion was, hypothetically, in collaboration with the client, and always within the framework of moving her toward employment. The typical EDP required the client to devote forty hours a week to JOBS activities, including completing thirty verifiable job applications in the first two weeks and forty verifiable applications during the second two weeks; attending approximately ten to twenty hours a week of employment-related workshops; searching for child care; perhaps taking basic skills and drug and alcohol tests (if required); turning in documentation for all JOBS activities; and following up with their case manager.

These seventy verifiable job applications in a month combined with the workshops constituted another bureaucratic means of diverting clients and reducing caseloads; such an onerous task was strong "encouragement" to take the first job available. In Bridgetown, clients were routinely told that they could not turn down jobs, if one was offered, no matter the pay, hours, or conditions; we did not observe this explicit rigidity in the other offices. Moreover, Bridgetown's stated policy allowed AFS employees to call and corroborate clients' applications with potential employers, which they told us they did, not infrequently, if they questioned a client's activity log. John Alpert, a white case manager quoted above, told us that if he doubted an entry on a client's weekly activity log, he would call the client on the mat about it at employment workshops, a practice he referred to as a "shaming technique."

Each branch contracted with partner agencies (e.g., JOBS contractors, community colleges offering work readiness classes) who had been awarded subcontracts to provide employment-related workshops and activities.[21] Typically, the "training" entailed basic activities such as resume writing, interviewing, dressing appropriately, and communicating effectively with employers. Clients were also often required to attend job search support groups and agency-sponsored job fairs. The partner agencies tracked client participation and reported on client performance to case managers. At all mandatory workshops and activities in Bridgetown, the doors were locked promptly at 8 a.m. in an effort, we were told, to mirror workplace expectations in "the real world." According to the JOBS contractor who coordinated these trainings, a "no show" was considered a withdrawal of one's application; moreover, he estimated the "no show" rate to be approximately 80 percent, suggesting a high degree of diversion very early in the process. In Coastal and Woodside, a "no show" merited contact with one's case manager who would then work toward "reengaging" the client into the process of assessment.

New discretionary tools available to agency workers represented both carrots and sticks. Case managers generally offered immediate help to those who were eligible for TANF, but who might be diverted from TANF if the agency could address their immediate crisis and support employment seeking. The "assessment payments" workers had at their disposal could also help clients financially while they searched for jobs by paying for rent, gas, or auto repair, for example. Some case managers (and this was echoed by many of the clients we interviewed) believed that these financial resources, available because the state and the agency decided to invest in the principle of "making work pay" (at least in the program's early years), were the most valuable component of the JOBS program. For example, Oregon increased the subsidies available for child care (for clients in assessment, but also on TANF and in the JOBS program) from $12.1 million to $46.2 million between 1991 and 1998 (Tapogna 1998). Donald Henderson, a white case manager with fourteen years experience with the agency, compared the current version of the JOBS program to previous ones favorably because of the resources now available:

> Number one, you have the ability as a worker to do things you could not do [before]. Number two, you have the funds at your disposal to help individuals where you never had that before... [T]his is one thousand times the program the JOBS program ever was in the past.

However, case managers varied in the strategies they used to provide financial resources (discussed below), so receipt of monetary assistance was not an entitlement, and case manager practices ran the gamut from generous to stingy. Moreover, "assessment payments" could also be given as an incentive for compliance or withheld as a punishment for noncompliance during the tough thirty- to forty-five-day period without TANF.

Case manager discretion was codified in the practice of "principle-based decision making," meaning that decisions were to be made according to these broad goals of the agency but not limited by rigid rules. This was a highly individualized process; the resources they offered depended a great deal on the philosophy and experience of individual case managers. The relaxation of eligibility rules and the provision of discretionary funds to help clients were deliberate parts of policy, intended to free up time to work more intensively with clients and other agencies, to monitor clients' progress, and to provide immediate and tangible help. Case managers were extremely positive about these aspects of the program change:

> Of course, there's much more freedom in that [case manager discretion] but also much more responsibility, and you become much more

conscientious when you make those decisions, and I think it is wonderful. AFS has, in my opinion, empowered their staff beyond belief. (Danielle Olson, white female case manager, eight years with the agency, Coastal)

Workers were empowered to use, admittedly limited, funds to provide immediate supports to prevent families from even worse economic disaster. However, the amount of these funds began to decrease during the period of our study. Temporarily, then, such discretionary interventions attenuated neoliberal principles by acknowledging and responding to the fact that the labor market cannot solve all income problems.

The JOBS Program

Clients who complied with their EDPs but failed to find a job within forty-five days had their cash grants opened at the end of this period, but efforts at moving them off TANF continued. To keep their cash grant, clients had to meet the requirements of their EDPs and to be monitored by their case managers. Given that they had "failed" the "labor market test" during assessment (i.e., were not diverted from TANF), the goal now shifted to reducing the length of time they would be on assistance. Often their EDP, which generally still included required job searches and JOBS classes, also mandated activities designed to address their case worker's assessment of their "barriers" to employment; for example, mental health or drug and alcohol treatment, basic skills classes, or lack of work experience (by mandating they take "work experience" jobs—unpaid jobs for which they received their cash grant). Some clients entered the JOBS Plus program where they received wages for temporary jobs subsidized by AFS. Case managers, hypothetically, checked up on their clients on a regular basis, calling them in for discussions if they failed to follow their plans, and initiating a "conciliation" process in which case managers tried to "re-engage" the client in activities that might result in employment.

The definition of *lack of compliance* was a matter of local and even individual case manager decisions. Case managers recognized that most clients did not comply fully with their EDPs. But they had discretion in how they responded to noncompliance. For example, at Coastal, the local partner mandated that clients must check in at the partner agency office every day at 8:00 a.m. and again at 4:00 p.m., ostensibly to give clients encouragement and support in their job searches. Compliance with this requirement, however, was difficult for some clients. Many lived in surrounding rural areas; some did not have cars, nor was public transportation available. Compliance was almost impossible if they were to drop off and pick up children from school or day care. Case managers cut corners for some clients, and some were quite aware of the contradictions between helping and coercing them to do as they are told. As Toni Schlosser, a white female case manager who had been with the agency and at Coastal nearly eight years, said:

> The work search plan that the JOBS agency has set up right now is specifically set up to cause people to fail. You ask a client who's got child care issues and this issue and that issue to check in at 8:00 in the morning and 4:00 in the afternoon…and so a lot of times I make allowances.

Although the Oregon Option plan had a two-year time limit on benefit receipt (the federal limit was five years), the clock did not start "ticking" if a TANF client fulfilled their EDP. If the client failed to participate and to respond adequately to attempts to reengage them in work activities, the case manager had the option of initiating the process of disqualification.

Full disqualification, or case closure, could hypothetically be accomplished in three months, but the process involved a series of six steps, with incremental financial penalties. Case managers tended to describe the disqualification process not as punishment but as a key tool designed to "get the client's attention." Anna Borelli, the ops manager quoted above, described it in this way:

> The use of disqualification is one of many tools to see what's happening in somebody's life that they would make the choice to remain at 75 percent of the poverty level versus someplace better.…With some people, you need the shock of the fact of reducing the money to get the discussion [about what's keeping them from moving forward] started…I think it's just one of many tools, and in Oregon it's a fairly lenient tool where you can just be given something within a day to do to get back on the grant, and we have multiple stopgap measures to prevent anybody from being punitive in the process.

From this perspective, disqualification is understood as a more or less gentle nudge. Cases could be closed only after a final review process during which the client would be asked to explain to a committee why she/he should not be disqualified. The procedure was different in each of the branches, but they all followed the agency policy of review of the final stage, the "full family sanction," so that children in families vulnerable to that sanction would not be "endangered" if the agency took that action. A small proportion of clients, 5 to 7 percent, reached the sixth and final stage of disqualification. Most clients in danger of disqualification threw up their hands and closed their cases before this point. A client may reach a particular stage in the disqualification process and leave the program, but then, later, attempt to reopen the case. When that happens, the client reenters at her/his previous disqualification stage. Case managers, on the whole, believed that clients who stayed on grants decreased by disqualifications had already found alternative sources of support.

Caseload reduction was embedded in every stage of welfare receipt, though each branch accomplished this differently. The agency apparently intended to pursue this goal at various levels of client contact. If clients could not be moved into employment through the basic steps of assessment and the JOBS program, the hassle, stigma, and/or long wait for benefits might motivate them to find jobs or to leave the agency. Case managers reported that they concentrated on motivating people to work, "giving quality time to folks," brokering resources, removing barriers, and advocating for clients, all with the goal of moving people toward employment and self-sufficiency. In the late 1990s, the capacity to provide clients with financial help and services during job searches constituted an important factor in the agency's considerable success at caseload reduction, as did the strong economy and expanding job market. In later years, when money for the JOBS program was reduced and the economy weakened, caseload reduction was less successful.

Through the numerous practical actions of caseload reduction and the promotion of employment en route to "self-sufficiency," workers carried out welfare restructuring in ways that varied by case manager, by the policies of different branches, and by both local labor market conditions and the mixture of other human services resources available in different communities. In chapter 4, we trace the interpretations of workers as they grappled with the contradictions arising out of the work of welfare. Neoliberal ideology did not always fit neatly with the everyday realities faced by either clients or workers. These incongruities lay bare the ways "success" was framed and maintained by agency workers and the ways they accepted and contested the hegemony of neoliberalism.

4

NEGOTIATING NEOLIBERAL IDEOLOGY AND "ON THE GROUND" REALITY IN WELFARE WORK

Welfare restructuring is not simply the straightforward implementation of policies and practices, but a continual negotiation, an active (if not always intentional) navigation between the principles embodied in welfare "reform" and the on-the-ground realities of workers' and clients' circumstances. In navigating the difficult terrain of helping clients within the constraining network of "work-first" bureaucratic rules and political-economic realities, workers faced a number of contradictions: self-sufficiency versus low-wage work, choice versus coercion, helping versus enabling, work versus family and unpaid care work, diversity versus inequity, and empowerment versus regulation. Workers openly recognized some of these contradictions while others remained implicit. Moreover, workers varied in their interpretations of these inconsistencies. In this chapter we examine these contradictions, analyzing how workers reconcile the contradictions and how they use welfare program tools to implement welfare "reform." These contradictions also reveal localized fissures in the seemingly solid foundation of neoliberal ideas and policies and point to the potential, and sometimes actual, points of resistance to these new policies.

Self-Sufficiency versus Low-Wage Work

Workers faced a discrepancy between the agency goal of promoting self-sufficiency and the realities of low-wage work and constraints some clients faced. As we detail in chapter 5, a majority of those leaving welfare in our study (about 55% in 1999) ended up taking jobs that paid wages at or below the poverty line (Acker et al. 2001) with 98 percent having incomes at or below the figure calculated as a living wage for Oregon (approximately $2,835 a month for a single parent with two children) (Morgen et al. 2006). Moreover, almost all the clients we interviewed continued to use public assistance benefits such as Food Stamps, the Oregon Health Plan (OHP), and Employment Related Day Care (ERDC) after they left or were diverted from TANF. Some clients also relied on housing and other subsidies. Thus, many were "self-sufficient" only in the technical sense of not receiving TANF (cash assistance), and many of those diverted from TANF during our study later reapplied for, and sometimes ultimately got on, TANF if they lost their jobs or their incomes dipped below eligibility levels (Gonzales, Hudson, and Acker 2007).

Administrators rationalized away this seeming contradiction between self-sufficiency and low-wage employment with the argument that the agency's key objective was not self-sufficiency per se but the movement toward self-support, even if that did not result in poverty reduction. As we mentioned in chapter 2, administrators viewed poverty as a complex societal problem beyond the scope of what the agency could address. Thus moving clients into jobs, even a minimum- or low-wage job, was viewed as the goal, one presumably serving as a first step out of dire economic distress. The concept of *self-sufficiency* served as an important touchstone for case managers, and they used it in specific ways that served to temper the contradictions between the mandate of caseload reduction and the realities of the low-wage labor market.

Many times, workers equated self-sufficiency with self-support (implicitly defined as leaving welfare and no longer receiving TANF). Thomas Dennison, a white male case manager from Woodside who had three years on the job, told us, "[Y]ou are basically trying to find out what are their barriers to becoming self-sufficient. Some people it's not going to be employment that makes them self-sufficient, some people it's going to be finding money from sources like Social Security Disability and those things." Interpreting self-sufficiency as self-support, with its connotations of financial adequacy, served as one means of rationalizing the realities of working and living in poverty. Similarly, workers tended to focus on the positive but incremental process of self-sufficiency. Even small steps, such as keeping an appointment, were sometimes counted as a client being on the path toward self-sufficiency.

In the agency, the term *self-sufficiency* was imbued with unquestionable value. Workers tied self-sufficiency and leaving welfare to enhanced self-esteem, greater choice and hope for clients, and serving as better role models for their children. For example, Terri O'Reilly, a white female case manager with over ten years experience with AFS, defined her primary goal as helping families to have a "better life" by "working with people, just working very closely with clients who receive TANF and assisting them in making progress, *moving forward and slowly getting off public assistance and having better lives for their families*" (emphasis added). Though she recognized that self-sufficiency might not be achieved quickly, she had no doubt that leaving welfare would improve clients' lives.

When asked what she thought was the most positive aspect of welfare reform, Amber Suarez, a mixed-race case manager with under five years experience with AFS, clustered self-sufficiency with accountability, "getting people off welfare," and enhanced quality of life. She too conflates self-sufficiency and caseload reduction:

> The self-sufficiency focus. The fact that we are making clients account-able. That is huge. We are doing what needs to be done to get folks off welfare....And let's talk quality of life, that's what we are doing, that's what needs to be done.

Many workers valorized self-sufficiency and linked it to ideals associated with individualism in U.S. mainstream culture: self-respect, choice, accountability, and responsibility. An unspoken neoliberal assumption underlies these values: that the individual is solely responsible for her- or himself in a world of self-interested choice-making others. Implicitly, a responsible adult makes responsible choices, and the ultimate responsible choice is portrayed as getting a job and going to work for pay.

Some workers, however, recognized that some clients were limited in their capacities and/or that economic opportunities in the low-wage labor market were restricted. These realities moderated workers' expectations for client self-sufficiency. As Todd Eitzen, a white male worker from Bridgetown with over twenty-five years with the agency, said:

> You are going to find some people who are going to be chronically unemployable...no matter how hard they try they cannot hold a job. And I will reserve judgment on the whole thing until I see what happens when we start hitting a recession or depression, which is going to happen...[Welfare reform] hasn't decreased the need; it has just made people have to get more things out of the food bank.

Allen Taylor, a white male worker who had worked for the agency for less than five years, reported that he felt the need to introduce a "liberal" view into Bridgetown, his branch office, and refuted the idea that clients were necessarily headed for self-sufficiency:

> Real reform isn't going to happen until the minimum wage hits ten to fifteen dollars an hour. This is a wonderful little joke that they're going to be self-sufficient at six dollars an hour.

Some case managers also worried about clients and former clients "falling through the cracks," suggesting that the operational equivalence of self-sufficiency as caseload reduction in everyday implementation obscured the reality of poverty, low-wage work, and unemployment. In the introduction, we quoted case manager Thomas Dennison's concern that deserving people in need are being denied help. He worries that

> [T]here are people out there that deserve help but don't know how to go about getting the waivers required to get the help. . . . We can't say that it is all positive, that everybody that needs help is getting help and that everybody that has been disqualified deserved to be disqualified. You know there are people out there that are legitimately hurting who can't get help now or feel they can't get help now.

Self-sufficiency was flexibly defined and understood as encompassing a range of sometimes contradictory experiences. Its inconsistent, but positive, associations allowed it to serve as a useful tool for making the job of caseload reduction a more palatable task. Small steps toward self-sufficiency kept workers focused on positive action in the present rather than on the reality that not everyone can become self-sufficient in the long term, particularly if they are being steered into jobs that do not pay a living wage. If workers believed that leaving welfare and thus, achieving "self-sufficiency," was an important and necessary first step toward a "better life," self-respect, and responsible adulthood, then it became easier to overlook the poverty and hardship many clients were facing in the process. In these ways, the changing role of welfare and the neoliberal ideology that informed the change was manifest in both welfare workers' and recipients' perspectives and expectations.

Choice versus Coercion

One of the first messages clients encountered on entering many AFS offices during our fieldwork was a lobby sign proclaiming, "The *choice* to request assistance in Oregon is a request for JOBS and self-sufficiency services (emphasis added)."[1] The language of "choice" saturated agency documents and interactions. Administrators, managers, and workers frequently used the vocabulary of choice to explain or justify decisions; for example, presuming that clients made explicit choices when they decided to seek public assistance or that "choice" was involved in actions that led to their disqualification for noncooperation. And yet, as we have detailed in this and the preceding chapters, clients actually have highly constrained choices in their dealings with the agency. They can comply with the rules and the EDPs that case managers construct, withdraw from the process, or risk sanctioning.

How do workers manage to maintain that clients have choices given a system of rules that, for example, obligates clients to participate with the rigorous job search requirements, mandates participation in employment activities, denies most clients the choice to go to college or get job training instead of working for pay, and requires new mothers with infants over three months of age to look for work? For most case managers, the contradictions between the rhetoric of choice and the reality of limited choice appeared to lurk below the surface, something they tacitly dealt with, mainly by defining what they were doing as fostering self-sufficiency, responsibility, and accountability. This emphasis on choice worked in two ways: It portrayed the agency as fostering highly cherished values associated with freedom and social citizenship, while simultaneously cloaking the coercive nature of the process and their own greater power in interactions with clients.

The rhetoric of choice was built into the design of welfare reform in two key ways: the formulation of the employment development plan (EDP) and the new-found discretion case managers held. Case managers convinced themselves that clients have choices in part by defining the process of developing an EDP as a mutual process or a partnership. That clients have to sign the EDP, which is defined as a "contract," makes it appear to be a volitional act, even though failure to sign the plan would halt the process of applying for benefits or receiving resources. The vocabulary and practices of welfare reform thus defined the relationship between public assistance clients and the agency as premised on mutual obligation.

Our observations of worker-client interactions made clear that case managers differed significantly in the degree to which they actively involved their clients in developing EDPs. Moreover, the vast majority of the EDPs we saw developed contained essentially similar obligations (i.e., work search, JOBS classes), with only limited variations on the basic themes. The agency mission and performance measures framed the process as being ultimately about promoting employment and caseload reduction. Nevertheless, case managers struggled against seeing what they did as coercive, as imposing their will on clients. For example, Toni Schlosser, a white female case manager from Coastal with nearly ten years experience with the agency, defined the development of the EDP as a partnership:

> I look at each family and each situation and what's brought them here and what strengths they have, what weaknesses. And just figure out with them, really, what the best way is to get them on their way and off cash assistance and bringing in income. . . . I really try and let them feel like this is something that we are going to do together. I am not going to sit there and write a plan for them, and say well this is what I think you should do.

When clients don't (or are unable to) comply with the EDP, workers are encouraged to define noncompliance as resulting from clients' choice. The agency then defines the sanctions or "disqualification" process as being about fostering client accountability and "re-engagement," masking both the coercive and punitive dimensions of sanctions. Agency leaders explicitly framed the tool of sanctioning as a constructive means to the end of "re-engaging" clients in welfare-to-work policies and practices, as discussed in chapter 3. But in practice, case managers often had to work out the tension between the rhetoric about choice and empowerment for clients with the reality that clients often had very limited choices and were subject to coercive practices. Their main strategy for resolving this contradiction was to justify restricted choices as "good for" clients.

To make coercion more palatable, case managers frequently invoked the value of accountability. Tim Berg, a white male case manager with three years experience in the agency, argued that some clients ultimately appreciated the "kick" that comes with accountability: "I've heard clients say that before they could do whatever they wanted. We never held them accountable for anything....And I've also heard them say that they were glad someone gave them a kick and said, you need to do something." Alice Cobain, a white case manager with over fifteen years experience at AFS, told us she tries to give clients the impression that they have choices, but, ultimately, she supported the notion that the agency should be able to set the conditions under which aid is received. She described her work this way:

> How to meddle without meddling. I don't know a better way of phrasing it. How can I meddle in someone's life and try to convince them that the way I see their life is the way they should see their life...I don't want to feel like I am imposing my values on somebody else....But yet that is what I am doing a lot, imposing my values...I try to...turn it around so that I am not imposing my values but simply say that you have your values, you have a choice to live with them, but if you choose to get this assistance, these are some of the things that you are going to have to live with. So you have the choice.

Though Cobain recognized that clients are restricted by the rules governing welfare, she frames obligatory compliance in terms that purport to respect individual volition.

The focus on choice also draws on and reproduces the assumption that poverty is the result of individuals' failings and actions rather than a systemic problem embedded in the economy and the limited power of low-wage workers. This focus on individuals reinforces the dominant ideologies of poverty and welfare associated with the new welfare paradigm. The idea of choice represented an important double-edged tool in the work of welfare. On one hand, it helped to portray the agency as respectful and sensitive to clients' needs. On the other hand, it conveyed to clients that they would bear the consequences of their "choices." In this way, it absolved the agency of responsibility for clients' choices. The rhetoric of choice, then, helped to mask the absence of actual choice in clients' lives and to veil their loss of entitlement to welfare. The ideology of choice maintained a tight hold on the minds of case managers and permeated every level of the work of welfare.

Indeed, clients may have unwittingly reinforced workers' abilities to define the program as noncoercive. As Catherine Kingfisher (1996) notes, savvy clients understand that they have more to gain from their workers if they appear cooperative. Appearing to "buy in" helps position them as more, rather than less, deserving clients while creating the opportunity for workers to reinforce their belief that working toward self-sufficiency is good for the client and her family.

Helping versus Enabling

Case managers almost to a person expressed the belief that they saw themselves as "helping" people work toward a "better life." But over and over they qualified the definition of help, counterposing it to a discourse about "enabling" that was rampant in the agency:

> I think everybody has really the best interest for their clients. They may not know how to do it, but that's what they're funded for. I think they want to do it, and *I find people really want to help people.* I mean, *not just enable them,* but really would like to see people get a better life. (Elena Lopez, Latina case manager with twenty-four years in the agency [emphasis added])

Helping was defined in multiple circumscribed ways consistent with agency goals of reducing caseloads and moving clients toward employment. Though many clients told us that the kind of help that really needed was assistance that would help them get stable, well-paying jobs that would allow them to escape poverty, welfare "reform" practices in Oregon (and nationally) were more circumscribed, defining employment per se, not "good jobs," as the objective of "work first," as we discussed above.

AFS case managers often defined *helping* as encouraging steps toward self-sufficiency, but almost always against the backdrop of fostering responsibility, as the words of Angela Orozco, a Latina case manager with three years work experience at AFS, indicated. She sees herself as a client advocate:

> I'm a client advocate in the sense that I try as hard as I can to help the client…I think by helping that client it means you encourage their self-sufficiency. So I am not a person to throw money at them. Probably I spend less money than a lot of people. I really want them to explore other resources. I really do. I think it is important for them to feel self-sufficient, that they can take care of themselves as much as possible.

Helping, in her estimation, is less about providing monetary resources and more about promoting feelings of independence (rather than enabling dependency) to "encourage their self-sufficiency." She sees cash resources as potentially counterproductive to the goal of self-sufficiency. Absent in her discussion is any acknowledgment of what clients typically wanted (a good job) and what the agency offered and insisted on. This disconnect was rarely addressed in discussions of helping.

While case managers frequently differed in their approaches to helping clients, they generally agreed that teaching independence was at the core of helping. Estelle Sharff, a white case manager at Coastal with five years agency experience, identified a more resource-generous method of helping clients than the case manager cited above, but still asserted that clients need to take initiative:

> My husband always says I'm an enabler and I now get paid for it!…I mean I'm not an enabler in the sense, in a negative sense. I expect a lot, and I don't do it for them. I will give them every resource until they accomplish whatever they want to accomplish. But they've got to do it, you know. I'm not going to do it for them.…But I really like what the agency stands for, in moving people out of welfare. So they feel better.

Sharff took on the negative agency rhetoric about enabling, but she redefined it, seeing her way of enabling as positive, albeit likely skating a fine line in terms of agency practices. She clearly supports the agency's goals, but organizes her practices to provide resources to clients to act for themselves and in the context of her own high expectations of them. But the fine line between "helping" and enabling often creates difficult decisions for workers. Angela Orozco, a case manager quoted above, identified this "balancing" as her biggest challenge: "balancing between my natural…propensity to want to be a giving and caring and helpful person, and me wanting people to feel like they can do it themselves." She perceived typical "giving and caring and helpful" behavior as potentially at odds with encouraging independence.

The term *enabling* reveals how the vocabulary of substance abuse treatment, especially "twelve-step" programs, has infiltrated social welfare policy and institutions over the past two decades, signaling what Sanford Schram (1995) has termed the "economistic-therapeutic-managerial" discourse of welfare reform. This discourse is preoccupied with the condition of *dependency,* a term imbued with negative moral and psychological connotations and used in ways that blur the differences between welfare reliance and drug or alcohol addiction (Fraser and Gordon 1994). Warnings about the dangers of enabling clients to maintain unhealthy and unproductive lifestyles circulated frequently in the welfare offices we observed, transmitted through trainings and everyday exchanges among workers, their supervisors, and social service contractors. For example, Anna Borelli, one of the ops manager we interviewed, said: "[L]et's offer help and if people don't want help, be there when they are ready to accept it, but don't enable people with bad habits such as drug and alcohol abuse…I don't think it's good for our society."

Even though workers may not have always overtly referenced this larger discourse when using the term *enabling,* these connotations traveled along with the term, restigmatizing clients and contributing to their construction as flawed, dependent, and not wholly adult. In workers' conceptions of helping/not enabling, twelve-step discourse merges with the rhetoric of choice and overcoming dependency in order to achieve self-sufficiency. Danielle Olson, a white case manager at Coastal with nearly ten years experience at the agency, illustrates this view of helping/not enabling:

> [A]nd the first thing I say [to a client] is, who would you call if you couldn't call me? Because, not because you [the worker] don't want to help, but you don't want to enable them, and you don't want to take all of the responsibility away from the client, because you want to wean them away from us. It's just like being a mother. But anyway, so, yes, you do have to make choices.

According to Olson, helping/not enabling clients involved getting them to "take responsibility," make choices, and act like adults. While she uses a discourse common in the agency, she was unusual in comparing the role of case manager to the role of mother, a highly gendered conception and one that connotes the struggle between intimacy and care, on the one hand, and encouraging independence, on the other.

Helping was implicitly at the crux of the agency's charge and, in case managers' eyes, could entail a broad array of resource offerings for clients. Workers reconciled the contradiction they perceived between helping and enabling clients by defining helping in specific, circumscribed ways. The edge of helping meant avoiding the enabling of client dependency on the system, an objective that meshed with agency missions of caseload reduction and job placement. The ideology of enabling helped to buffer the limitations of these objectives for clients by drawing attention to the dangers of allowing clients to be "dependent" on safety nets (i.e., to use safety net resources to help ameliorate need). In this way, it diverted attention away from the agency's inability to truly foster self-sufficiency for clients. Examining the relationship between helping and not enabling highlights important discursive connections—choice, dependency, enabling, and self-sufficiency—that work in conjunction and interdependently to support neoliberal values and policies emerging from those values.

Workers' positions within the welfare state required them to negotiate the boundaries between agency-defined goals and the realities of need and client circumstances. This they did, partly through striving for an uneasy balance between helping and enabling. Their clients interpreted and experienced these balancing acts very differently, as we discuss in chapter 5. But, of course, workers had greater power than clients; workers' understandings of good welfare practices (e.g. not enabling) were those that usually prevailed.

"Work" versus Family and Unpaid Care Work

The potential conflict between the demands of low-wage work and family responsibilities, which we explore in greater detail in chapters 5 and 6, constituted another contradiction that had to be confronted in the work of case management. Working for pay was highly valorized in branch offices with little attention to the realities of the jobs clients could get and the problems that combining paid and unpaid work created for female-headed households with very limited means. When (some) workers did question how clients would reconcile work and family demands, they lamented the lack of time parents would have with children and usually couched their concerns in terms of traditional familial expectations. To varying degrees, workers grappled with the perceived advantages and disadvantages of working, but the negative aspects, though observed and commented on, tended to be swept under the discursive rug of the positive benefits of working.

Some case managers acknowledged the difficulties in maneuvering low-wage work and caring for dependents under conditions of inflexible schedules, paltry pay, and irregular hours. They also worried about what it meant that mothers had much less time to spend with their children. Some recognized that clients faced different conditions than many other working parents. When asked about the work mandate of welfare reform, for example, Tammy Hill, a white woman employed as a case manager at Woodside with over two decades experience at AFS, expressed ambivalence:

> It's realistic in terms of what happens for other people. So I think that is good. I think it's hard for families where the parents are of lower ability because even a person that's functioning real well or average has a hard time working and raising children. Somebody who has lower ability and has a lot of different issues…the kids are definitely not going to get as much attention, although they may get a more positive role model [from] mothers that work as opposed to staying home. So it's six of one, half dozen of another. For some people it's a very positive thing, for others it's not. And I would think more in terms of children. I really am a proponent of families trying somehow to be with their kids more often.

Hill's response reveals assumptions common among those working in the three welfare branches we studied: (1) employment is inevitable, (2) it provides an opportunity to model productive behavior to children, and (3) many clients have *individual* problems that impair their functioning. She voices her concern that children may lack attention from their parents but notes that employment is necessary in this day and age. By concentrating on individual-level problems, however, larger-scale issues, such as the conditions and remuneration of low-wage jobs or lack of family-supportive policies, are overlooked.

The most consistent (though still relatively uncommon) concern case managers articulated with the strict welfare-to-work mandate they enforced had to do with Oregon's rule that mothers were subject to work requirements when their babies reached three months of age. Christy Kahoe, an ops manager in the Woodside branch, said:

> If I had to choose one thing that I didn't like about [the work mandate], it's probably the fact that we have mothers going to work after their children are three months old. Before it used to be a year…I really believe that first year is important…I just wish there were some way we could sort of accommodate that or at least give a bit more support to those mothers. I mean most of them are single mothers having to deal with everyday issues of being a single mother, as well as the anxieties of leaving their child, a three month old, with a baby-sitter or whatever.

Workers reconciled the potential contradiction between work and family in multiple ways. Key to this reconciliation was the veneration bestowed on employment by the agency and agency workers. As we have documented in previous sections, work was held up by welfare workers as a positive, redeeming force.

As Beatrice Jacques, a white case manager with twenty-five years in the agency, responded when asked what she saw as the most positive aspect of reform,

> The positive is, we are getting *people* to work. It is totally helping their self-esteem. It is a good role model for the children. All that stuff in employment is wonderful...I think that whole idea of case management and getting *people* back to work is a wonderful idea. (emphasis added)

Interestingly, Jacques calls the almost exclusively female clients she mandates to work "people" twice in the above quote. In contrast, Kahoe, the ops manager above, expressed concern about "mothers" and more specifically "single mothers" having to leave young babies for jobs, but her recognition of clients' gender was an exception among agency staff. This speaks to a much larger pattern we witnessed among case managers (and the agency in general). By defining the subjects of agency practices in abstract, disembodied terms, usually *clients* or *people,* they contributed to making gender invisible, along with the racial and class situations that shape gender experiences and that powerfully affect the conditions of mothering (see chapter 6).

Economic and cultural changes have brought increasing numbers of women into the labor force over the past forty years, a reality that helps to prop up the expectation that everyone should be working. As noted above, case managers and other welfare workers are primarily working-class and middle-class women, most of whom have been employed throughout their adult lives, coping with the multiple problems of combining work and family. Thus, for them, the expectation that women should have paid jobs is unremarkable and should apply to TANF recipients as well as to everyone else. As Andrea Lovell, a white family resource manager (FRM) at Woodside with just over five years experience with the agency, said,

> I come from a long line of workers in my family and I have a real strong work ethic, and I feel...I was a two-parent family but I had to work while my kids were young. I still have to work, and if anybody is able, I think they should be working.

Beatrice Jacques, a white case manager quoted above concurs:

> Now wait a minute, it is nice to be home when they [children] are off to school and then when they are home. I forgot the fact that when *we* have children, *we* have our eight weeks off and *we* have to go back to work too. I have really gotten to realize that in the last couple of years. That is the way it is when people work. (emphasis added)

In Lovells' and Jacques' (and many others') opinions, it is only fair that clients should have to work when other mothers are obligated to work. But, as political scientist Gwendolyn Mink (1999) has pointed out, such a view conflates middle-class women's greater *choice* (albeit a diminishing choice) to work with poor and working-class women's *obligation* to work. Moreover, it presupposes that each group comes to employment with similar resources, life conditions, networks, and coping skills. Hence, the realities of poor women's lives are obscured in the effort to ensure "fairness." Though some workers (such as Kahoe, quoted above) are cognizant of class differences in family caring resources, many other workers reconcile the demands of work and family by glossing over them. For example, Amber Suarez, a young, mixed-race worker said,

> I can go right back at them [clients] and tell them, you know, [I] have an eight-month-old baby. I have not only a day care provider, a back-up provider, I had six back-up providers that I had went to visit, seen their home, checked their references, and I know who's OK. But that's what it takes to keep your day care stable.

Suarez operates from the assumption that if she can care for a baby and work, so too can her clients. The time required to find and investigate back-up child care providers becomes invisible, as does the effort to drag children around on the bus to visit potential providers or to make contact with possible providers or their references, perhaps, without the benefit of a home telephone. Suarez implicitly takes her own resources for granted.

In the course of discussing the pros and cons of mothers of infants staying home, Thomas Dennison, a white male worker from Woodside, similarly said this about working and finding time for children:

> I think that you need to take time in the evening. You can have all the time you need in the evening if you work that regular eight-hour job. You can have lots of time with your kids. You've got to get rid of your television okay? So, that's another choice we make.

He, too, fails to notice the realities that many employed women face—let alone women who work in low-wage jobs—and instead falls back on the rhetoric of choice. If mothers choose to "take time in the evening" with their kids (implying that this leisure time exists for everyone and that, perhaps, they have been using it for other things) and "get rid of the television," they can balance work and family in a way that allows them "lots of time" with their children. What are the realities he ignores? For many workers, "that regular eight-hour job" is an anomaly. Many jobs require nonstandard hours (Presser 2003), a condition that restricts time at home in the evening, making it difficult for mothers with school-aged children to spend time with children or to arrange care. Eight-hour-a-day jobs easily become ten-hour-a-day jobs when commutes and/or bus schedules are added on, leaving

little time for the necessities such as eating and preparing meals, shopping, or vis-
iting the laundromat to ensure everyone has clean clothes. Not everyone—due
to employer demands or the need to make ends meet—has the luxury of limiting
their work schedule to an eight-hour day. In reality, more than half of the welfare
leavers we interviewed worked forty hours a week or more. Both of the quotes
above illustrate the assumption by workers that their resources and those of clients are congruent.

Another way that workers reconciled the potential contradiction between
work and family was to draw on class- and race-based assumptions about the
parenting abilities of clients. For example, Beatrice Jacques, a white case manager
quoted above, admitted that she sometimes felt bad about forcing new mothers
of very young children to participate in the JOBS program, particularly those
whom she judges to be "wonderful mother(s)" which she claimed she doesn't
"see . . . a lot." However, she lives with the policy by reminding herself that so many
of these children are "better off in day care" because (she believes) their mothers
do not parent well, exemplified for her by their failure to read often enough to
their children or to pay sufficient attention to them.

The original intent of Aid to Families with Dependent Children (AFDC) was
to *enable* women to stay home to care for their children in the absence of a (male)
family breadwinner. But this possible reason for a mother's not wanting to work
has been lost in a discourse that incorporates the language of codependency and
that presumes reasons for not working are largely faulty work ethics or negative
barriers (e.g., substance abuse, mental or physical health problems, lack of child
care or transportation) rather than positive values, such as caretaking.

This reversal of goals reflects raced, gendered, and classed components of the
neoliberal restructuring of the political economy of the United States over the
past forty years. The expansion of the service sector has created new gender-
defined, often low-wage jobs for women, while the decline of high-wage male
working-class manufacturing jobs has increased the pressures for two incomes
in many families. Black men in particular have suffered from these changes, and
the racial gap in earnings for African American and Hispanics remains large
(Mishel, Bernstein, and Boushey 2003). Middle-class women have many more
work opportunities, but their families also often need two incomes. The women's
movement's support of equal opportunities and government affirmative action
provisions contributed to a changing culture in which women are now (sometimes unreasonably) expected to support themselves and their children, absent a
husband with a good income.

In most other wealthy industrial countries where similar trends have developed,
welfare state provisions for child care, paid parental leave, and income supports
for parents cushion the class and racial inequalities that severely disadvantage

working-class women, especially single mothers (Leira 1992). In the United States, however, the historical underdevelopment of welfare state programs and the neoliberal agenda of downsizing the state have obstructed the emergence of such supports. Work-family balance is a major public issue in the United States (Jacobs and Gerson 2004), an issue that can be much more difficult to resolve for families living on poverty-level incomes than for others (Garey 1999; Albelda and Tilly 1997). With welfare reform, poor women have lost what little flexibility they held in arranging the balance between paid work and unpaid care work. The choice to stay at home to provide unpaid care work is, in practice, now available primarily to women of relative affluence. Through their work, welfare workers help to maintain the supply of low-wage workers (Piven and Cloward 1993) in this highly stratified economy. Welfare staff also contribute to the transformation of caring for dependents into a class privilege. Yet the valorization of paid work is not universal among the welfare workers in our study. Some workers acknowledge the importance of mothers as caregivers and of the value of care work, even if, institutionally, they cannot currently support it.

Diversity/Equity versus Racial Inequity/Racism

Just as gender and gender inequity have become invisible in an agency that serves poor women, race and racism, too, are hardly visible, at least to whites. For many white workers the abstract language of "diversity" and "multiculturalism" displaces a concrete analysis of racism as it sometimes affects relationships among workers and between workers and clients. This means that at least some workers struggle with another contradiction: between the agency's stated commitments to diversity and equity and the realities of racial disparities and racism. Given the pervasiveness of racism in the society at large and, particularly, the racist undertones (and sometimes overtones) of discourses about poor women on welfare, it is hardly surprising that racist attitudes and practices would be widespread in welfare agencies. Indeed, researchers have documented differences both in how clients of different races are treated and have fared in the new welfare regime[2] and in the policies states adopt that are correlated with the racial composition of a state's TANF caseload and/or of the state.[3] As a state with a relatively small black population, Oregon compares favorably on a number of policies that have been defined, in these studies, as "stricter" or "harsher" and correlated with race, particularly with African Americans (Gooden and Douglas 2006).

However, the production of racial inequity also occurs at local levels in ways not captured by large comparative studies of state policies. Workers and managers engage among themselves and with each other in an organizational context that does not admit that racism colors relationships between and among workers and clients. Nor does organizational policy or ideology take into consideration that racial and gender discrimination is still a fact for clients subject to work mandates. Instead AFS leaders and management promoted the principle of "diversity" and took pride in the agency's comparatively good record on diversity. AFS received a state diversity award to recognize its success in recruiting and retaining a higher proportion of staff from ethnic and racial minorities than many other state agencies, as we detailed in chapter 3. This commitment was also encoded as one of the seven performance measures the agency adopted (see chapter 2, "Adult and Family Services Goals and Performance Measures"). The goal—"ensuring [that] AFS has a well trained, diverse workforce which understands the communities it serves" was to be measured by "diversity within AFS workforce."

However, diversity in action, in the everyday workplace was another matter. In our interviews it was apparent that white workers were far less likely than workers of color to believe that racism affected either workers' differential treatment of clients or workers' relationships with each other or management. Most white workers appeared to have adopted a "color-blind" stance, suggesting that race was not a factor in the way they worked or treated clients. As Stan Fellows, a white male worker in Bridgetown with nearly fifteen years with AFS, put it: "As far as clients are concerned, for the most part, they're color-blind and I'm color-blind. I give the same services to everyone, it doesn't matter." White AFS workers in these three offices shy away from discussing race, as if it is impolite, preferring instead to focus on "cultural differences." This is unsurprising given that the diversity trainings offered by the agency (two of which we observed) tended to conflate racial diversity with cultural diversity, circumscribing race to varying cultural and communication practices and largely overlooking historical, economic, and political forces that may have shaped racial inequities. When race issues were mentioned, these were often cast as a matter of interpersonal issues "between individuals," rather than as part of the workplace environment. Consider, for example, this quote by mixed-race case manager Amber Suarez:

> There's no racism in this office. You don't get any of that here. You might get petty arguments between individuals but I don't think it has anything to do with culture in any manner, form, or shape.

But some other staff of color in each branch did identify racism and tensions around how race and ethnic difference was experienced in their office. In an explicit statement, Elena Lopez, a Latina case manager at Woodside, differentiated the standard or hegemonic practices of other (white) case managers with her own, claiming that she doesn't do her work the way many others do; that is, she doesn't "do it white." She sees her branch operating in a "white" way, while she sees herself as

> Having that compassion. Wanting more education, more feeling. Going in there and having to fight for my clients because this is outrageous, the decisions they [white administrators and workers] made. If they want to help these people, then this is the dance we have to do.... They're making decisions without understanding the culture. And the only [thing] we have here is a very white culture ... [T]hey have a lack of understanding of diversity, a lack of understanding of a different culture, nor do they value it.

She is clear that her way of relating to clients puts her at odds with the "very white culture" that is her workplace so that she has to navigate carefully the "dance we have to do."

A growing body of literature has drawn attention to the normative, "unmarked" nature of whiteness in U.S. society,[4] which presupposes a particular set of resources and particular cultural understandings and is embedded in institutional settings (Piña and Canty-Swapp 1999). For example, Helan Page and R. Brooke Thomas use the concept of "white public space" to identify the ways racism is produced in organizational settings that "routinely, discursively, and, sometimes coercively, privilege Euro-Americans over nonwhites" (1994:111). At the same time, white-dominated organizations often engage in the process of "whitewashing" (i.e., covering up or glossing over) practices that deny the significance of race—whether in terms of racial politics, racial inequities, or racial experiences—so that white ways of being are normalized and existing racial dynamics are "naturalize(d)" (Reitman 2006, 268).

Though we observed and were told about examples of racism in each of the branches, the Bridgetown branch, with the higher percentage of workers and clients of color, was especially marked by significant racial inequity and attempts by white workers to justify the racial hierarchy. Workers and managers at Bridgetown acknowledged (and complained) that the branch had a negative reputation and was perceived, as different respondents put it, as the "hell hole" or the "punishment branch" or "training branch." And indeed the branch had a relatively high turnover of employees and was often, as during the period of our observations, "down" in its staffing, as discussed in chapter 3. Racial tensions were evident from the first day in the office when we met with the staff to explain our project. White employees sat in the center of the room at the table, while employees of color sat around the perimeter of the room in chairs pushed up against the walls.

Our observations and interviews confirmed that these separations extended far beyond where people sat at this meeting and had deep roots in branch culture. Black workers were then (and had been historically) concentrated in the lower rungs of the organizational hierarchy—as clerical workers and as family resource managers. When organizational restructuring created the position of case manager, whites claimed all of these higher paid and higher status jobs, giving them new control over clients and client resources. Limiting the employment of blacks in positions of power over clients is an old tactic in welfare work and has been part of strategies of keeping local racial hierarchies in place (Neubeck and Cazenave 2001). Nevertheless, one of the ops managers denied any racism in this racial staffing pattern, suggesting that African American staff "chose" not to apply to be case managers:

> [I]f somebody does not want to go there [be promoted to case manager], you cannot force them, it is their choice. I don't think that is about race, I think that is about the kind of people who have been here longer who want to do that more eligibility-driven work and they happen to be mostly black. I could be wrong about that, but that is my belief.

In an environment lacking a critical discourse on race as structural, inequities are explained by (white) hegemonic understandings that tie in cohesively to neoliberal conceptions: Individuals make free choices and are relatively unconstrained in making those choices. We heard no discussion of the fairness of the process by which whites were hired for these positions, of perceived risk of moving into new positions in a predominantly white institution, of conflicting loyalties, or of other considerations that might discourage black workers from applying for these jobs. The outcomes of institutionalized racism are attributed to individual choice because that is the lens available when race is erased as a legitimate analytical frame.

The racial tensions in this branch could not be ignored by whitewashing. In fact, one result of tensions was a backlash against the black workers by some white agency staff. One worker, speaking about a group of black family resource managers, claimed, "[This is the] most racist branch I've ever been in…[T]here are definite ethnic cliques who have attitudes and *they* are the ones who are racist." Another dimension of the backlash involved supposedly widely shared sentiments among white workers that some black workers were not working to standards expected of them, but, as one worker said, are being kept on "to maintain the diversity percent."

Vanessa Johnson, a mixed-race worker with over ten years in the agency, commented on the practice of superficially embracing diversity while overlooking inequities:

> Because you work in a population that is diverse does not mean that you don't have tensions and all kinds of things going on. I mean this whole place here is just a hotbed; it's just like a Mt. St. Helens in here.

The depth of the problems at Bridgetown finally received attention from a new management team, and by the end of our fieldwork, the branch had begun to redress the concentration of blacks in lower positions by promoting one black family resource manager and hiring two new black case managers. Whether and in what ways changes in the staff translated to changes in some of the comparatively harsh treatment of clients that we observed at the Bridgetown branch we do not know because the results would have been felt after we had stopped our observations. But during the period of our fieldwork, there was little question that Bridgetown, the most racially diverse branch, but also the one that exhibited relatively greater occupational segregation by race than the other two, was also the branch that engaged in the most rigid, punitive, and harsh treatment of clients.

Though we observed a wide range of worker empathy and engagement in each office, generally speaking, workers in Bridgetown tended to interact with and speak about clients differently than workers in Coastal and Woodside. At Coastal and Woodside, workers tended to talk about clients as suffering from "barriers" which kept them from working. Frequently, clients were portrayed as being psychologically damaged, presumably because of their backgrounds. Others were described as needing some help during a difficult time—periods of unemployment, family transitions, or bouts with illness. Most often, clients' problems were interpreted as external to them, perhaps of their own making, but not intrinsic to their nature.

In comparison, Bridgetown workers tended to see clients as having character flaws that prevented them from working or caused their poverty. Workers' assessments typically closely matched racialized stereotypes of welfare recipients in the United States: hyper-fecund, immoral, pathologically dependent welfare queens.[5] Clients were judged for not being sufficiently motivated, for being perceived as forceful or rude, and for not being sufficiently submissive—all of which represent code for the "inappropriate" (read: nonwhite) gender expressions of black women.

The varying perspectives on clients may, in part, reflect the socioeconomic and political particularities of each branch—the liberal attitude of Woodside or the economic realities of Coastal—but there is no denying that Bridgetown clients were not, at least not overtly, given a corresponding benefit of the doubt on the grounds that they faced complicated circumstances not entirely of their own making. In the eleven months that we observed in Bridgetown, we failed to hear anyone comment on the racial realities of the marketplace (the long-standing pervasive racism in the state, discrimination in the labor market and housing markets, wage differentials, etc.) and how they might play a part in clients' poverty or unemployment. In contrast, Coastal workers frequently identified clients' problems as linked to a restructuring of the labor market and mentioned the labor market realities of the community. Though the exact mechanisms may not be altogether clear, we can agree that the disparaging nature of the Bridgetown images coincided with inequitable policies and practices in Bridgetown when compared to Woodside and Coastal.

Empowerment versus Regulation

Agency leaders framed the devolution of greater authority to branches and discretion to case managers as a process that was to "empower" agency staff and marshal their collective efforts to achieve agency goals. In practice this meant a relaxation of the agency's former rule-bound, eligibility-governed process of "doing the work of welfare." "Principle-based" decision making on the part of case managers and "results-based" performance measures for the agency and its branches constituted a significant departure from the agency's older culture. Case managers were permitted to spend less time and effort on collecting financial documents and verifying their accuracy and more time and effort on helping people attain "self-sufficiency." The change from eligibility work to case management was crucial in fostering the feeling among case managers that they were, indeed, *empowered* by the changes to work with clients in ways that were not possible or encouraged by the former system.

Nevertheless, on the ground, workers often felt far from empowered. Work overload, and toward the end of our research, declining resources, obstructed the ambitions of agency leaders, managers, and workers to provide intensive individualized help in moving people toward self-sufficiency. Work overload resulted from the mandated size of caseloads, the necessity of documenting all contacts and decisions, the requirement to monitor client compliance and progress, frequent crises in clients' lives that necessitated responses, the incessant pressure to respond to twenty to thirty telephone calls per day, and the necessity of working closely with other agencies. As a result, almost all case managers described their jobs as high stress, entailing more than they could possibly accomplish. Across the three branches, workers routinely used words such as *very stressful, extreme, awful,* or *intense* to characterize their workloads.

A primary reason for stress was the numbers of people workers were expected to manage. AFS set caseloads for case managers at 90 clients[6] (except workers assigned exclusively or primarily to work with teens, whose caseloads were lower) and family resource managers at 250; the ratio of intensive case managed TANF or assessment clients to less intensive Food Stamp, Oregon Health Plan, or child care subsidy clients differed among the three branches (as discussed in chapter 3).

These numbers made it impossible for workers to stay "on top" of the caseloads. Two case managers exemplify what we heard repeatedly from others:

> There is no way someone can manage ninety cases. And you are supposed to see each person at least once a month....Just using common sense and breaking it down, how much time you would have with each person would be minutes....There is no way we can do it. (Tim Berg, white case manager with three years experience in the agency)
>
> It's just impossible to case manage ninety cases. They are just asking too much. I think my job...has become more tough, more stressful, more challenging. I don't mind the challenging part as long as I have the needed resources to do it. I think we need more resources to do our jobs. (Marc Mendez, Latino case manager with five years experience in the agency)

Neither worker sounds empowered; both recognize significant constraints on achieving agency goals because of resource-related issues such as high caseloads. Moreover, case managers in Bridgetown, a significantly understaffed branch, had even higher caseloads of TANF cases and were among those most likely to describe their jobs as extremely stressful. As Todd Eitzen, a white case manager told us, "[Bridgetown] used to have a reputation as a hell hole and it really wasn't. Now it really is. We have all of this stuff and we are under stress. Management won't hire the people [we need]. When you are under stress you want to get out."

No doubt some case managers were able to effectively manage *some* cases, but as one case manager put it, high caseloads mean you can only "go through the motions" of case management with many others—marshalling clients through the bureaucratic steps of assessment, employment development plans, and the JOBS program, but, by and large, unable to take the time necessary to effectively plan or manage their steps to self-sufficiency.

The fragility of branch-level worker discretion and empowerment was further revealed by the crisis over the Food Stamp error rate that we discussed in the prologue. Although Oregon's TANF program allowed for deviation from federal rules because of the waiver the state received, rules for the federally financed Food Stamp program were *not* similarly relaxed. When the U.S. Department of Agriculture threatened to smack the state with a $16 million penalty if Oregon's Food Stamp error rate (13.5 percent in 1998) was not brought down close to the national average (10.7 percent in 1998), agency leaders and managers took swift action. Unfortunately, those actions further undermined case management, from the perspective of case managers, leaving workers feeling re-regulated by managers, rules, and new practices of surveillance.

Reducing Food Stamp errors quickly became a top agency goal, and district and branch managers devised mechanisms to quickly respond, with little attention to the newer modes of participatory decision-making the agency had instituted and lauded. One measure required workers to recertify the eligibility of most Food Stamp recipients every three months rather than every six to twelve months, as had been recent practice. The other measure required review of *every* Food Stamp case to ensure that each eligibility item was thoroughly documented, every name correctly spelled, and every address consistently and correctly entered.[7] These measures affected both case managers and family resource workers because case managers determined eligibility for all assistance for TANF clients, almost all of whom received Food Stamps. Both measures intensified pressure in already high-pressure jobs.

These pressures, however, varied among branches, as did the methods of reviewing cases for errors, reflecting the varying organizational climates. In Bridgetown, mangers decided that every case was to be reviewed by a reviewer with a background in eligibility work. Workers whose cases had an error rate of 10 percent or more were to receive a "letter of counseling," which recommended specific training(s) and was to be put into their personnel files. The practice was intended, according to one operations manager, not "to be punitive, it is meant to get their attention, it is meant to redirect them, it is meant to identify training needs and what they need to do." Some case managers observed that it was "meant to redirect them" away from case management and back toward a focus on eligibility. Workers in Bridgetown signed a petition against the policy (this was never actually delivered to the district manager), and the union called a meeting to air workers' grievances. In a meeting with union leadership, district management agreed to some, not all, of the workers' requests.

In Woodside, worker concern was less acute though still present. The ops managers established a buddy system through which workers informally reviewed each other's cases. More formally, the branch also instituted another practice that had been adopted in Bridgetown; staff members, often reassigned from the ranks of family resource managers (technically below case managers in the hierarchy), reviewed all Food Stamp applications on a full-time basis. Workers in both Bridgetown and Woodside, especially case managers, resented the surveillance over their work and felt that they were being pitted against each other. Marc Mendez, a Latino case manager, summed up his frustration with the process:

> If you asked almost any worker, they had to deal with [the Food Stamp application reviewer] at one time or another, and we get tired of it. It's frustrating because it's like something you do that you work over and

over and over and you feel like a kid going to ask mom for five bucks when she's already said no the first time.

Coastal was much more relaxed about the problem because district and branch managers were convinced that the error rate determination was deeply flawed. They reported to the researchers that the auditors' procedure entailed drawing a sample of cases to examine and calculating an error rate from that sample. We were told that, for Coastal, the sample was two cases. They found errors in both cases; thus, the error rate for the branch was 100 percent. Ops managers and workers objected to both the sampling procedure and the definition of an error, which, in addition to miscalculations of benefits, could be any issue in the verification and narration (documentation) of the case. Although Coastal complied with the instructions to review cases, the atmosphere of tension around "the crisis" that existed in the other two branches was lower.

The Food Stamp error rate crisis touched a nerve among staff in the Woodside and Bridgetown branches. Many workers voiced distress over how the crisis had shifted their workloads; for example, Graciela Gonzales, a Latina family resource manager with seven years experience with the agency, said:

> It is putting a lot of stress on us; we are not able to meet the deadlines anymore. We understand the clients. But the clients don't understand that. They don't understand the change…Here these clients are used to walking up to the desk and getting what their needs are. If they don't get what they came here for, they rant and rave until they are seen by a supervisor and they get their way. That is putting a lot of strain on us because of all the paperwork on us.

Not only did workers need to complete more paperwork in the attempt to lower the error rate (more case reviews, more recertifications), but, according to this worker, they were also under increased fire from clients who did not understand why their benefits were delayed. As Food Stamp applications went through the review process, they were often backlogged for two to three extra weeks. With their attention turned to recertifying food stamp cases more frequently, workers now had less time to do case management, as Ann Sage, a mixed-race case manager with just under five years experience at AFS, explains,

> Yes, it has taken me so much longer to do recertifications than it used to. I have cut down my office time with clients. I used to try to see two, four, five a day in addition to my assessments…I am down to three clients a day and that is really pushing. Because if I have a stack of recertifications on my desk like tomorrow, I just can't schedule any appointments…

Distress was not reduced when AFS lead administrator Sandie Hoback framed the agency's renewed emphasis on Food Stamp accuracy as a challenge that workers could address by better "time management" and "reduced expectations of what they could do for clients," as we saw her do at the December 1998 workshop described in the prologue. The Food Stamp "crisis" marked a return, for at least a period of time, to a stricter enforcement approach, affecting both workers and clients. Like high caseloads, the responses to the error rate curtailed case managers' capacities to spend constructive time with clients to determine how best to help them.

This situation was exacerbated as caseload reduction began to plateau (largely, managers believed, because a higher portion of the caseload was now what they called the "hard to serve") and budget reductions occurred, related to the state's ongoing fiscal crisis. This combination forced managers to reduce and more intensively monitor the financial resources case managers could use managing cases (i.e., "assessment" and JOBS payments). As Christy Kahoe, an ops manager put it, withdrawing the resources that had helped case managers be successful with clients caused a lot of "confusion" for workers:

> Recently, with our caseloads, a lot of our case managers have come in really confused as to what we are trying to accomplish. We are asking them to reduce their caseload; however we are asking them to reduce their expenditures and so a lot of them are really confused as to what we are doing.

She continued, suggesting that staff morale had been affected by the recent changes:

> When welfare reform first came about, I think, the people that could got jobs almost immediately. Now you're sort of dealing with people who have lots of barriers and just working through those barriers with clients and keeping staff motivated so they can motivate clients, I think that is one of the hardest parts, especially when you are dealing with a lot of 1:90 [caseload] issues and [reduced] expenditures.

Unquestionably the resources that case managers had available either for "assessment" payments or JOBS payments were among their most important and valued tools in doing effective case management. The money for these payments came from "savings" resulting from reduced caseloads (less money being paid as cash assistance). This pool of money more than doubled between 1993 ($40 million spent) and the end of the decade ($90 million), although it fell dramatically in later years, beginning a sharp decline in July 2001 (Leachman, Merten, and Sheketoff 2005). We discuss this further in the conclusion. Nevertheless, even before the sharp decline, the die was cast. We saw agency leaders and ops managers already beginning to rein in and more carefully monitor case managers' spending toward the end of our fieldwork. Workers were beginning to express concern about this in their interviews with us. In Coastal, where staff teams designed program details, the decision was made to issue "checkbooks" to workers with a monthly deposit for these payments; workers were supposed to think about how to spend their own limited funds rather than dipping into the larger pool of money allocated to the branch. In practice, workers traded funds and could ask managers for additional money at the end of the month if they ran over their allocation. In some offices monthly spending total per case manager was posted on bulletin boards (e.g., along with performance measure data), in full view of others and managers. The reining in of spending was not a whim of agency leaders; it was a response to real pressures on the agency's budget and to decisions made about how to prioritize funds that grew scarcer over time. Nevertheless, it meant that workers had less and less to work with to meet the never-dwindling needs of their caseloads.

Being empowered to decide how best to help clients facilitated case manager buy-in to the enforcement of work expectations. Discursively, empowerment cohered with deeply held values of choice, self-determination, and individualism. Yet, in practice, the agency's power structures and practices of management and bureaucratic regulation, as well as growing pressure on its budget, truncated case managers' power. Empowerment did not fade as an ideological *promise* to workers, but it became a more diluted promise, as case managers' jobs were more fully circumscribed, a reality many workers recognized and struggled with.

Managing the Work of Welfare from the Perspective of the Workers

Doing the work of welfare in Oregon's restructured public assistance system plunged agency workers into a mass of contradictions among the publicly proclaimed goals; the actual practices and policies instituted to achieve those goals; and the realities their clients faced, both as low-wage workers and poor, or near poor, breadwinners. Contradictions persisted between imagined ends—self-sufficiency and the end of reliance on the public safety net—and available means—working for low wages at insecure jobs. Agency workers also grappled with contradictions between the constructed claim that clients have choices and the effective absence of choice. Though, in theory, agency workers were empowered to make decisions about how to help clients, in reality, they were restricted by confining rules about how to do so, the workload demands of their jobs, and changes in the resources they had to work with. The agency's new mission was positively framed and its organizational restructuring was real, but the realities of gender, race, and class inequities within a capitalist society affected different welfare workers both *as workers* and as the implementers and enforcers of the restructuring of welfare. That restructuring, grounded in neoliberal ideas and deeply marked by gender subordination and racism, had mixed, and sometimes harsh, consequences for clients.

At the same time, though, stark differences existed among the branches we studied. The same policies were administered in more punitive or more supportive ways, with much of the difference resulting from local socioeconomic, political, and racial conditions as well as local leadership. In Bridgetown, the racial composition of the staff and the racial structuring of authority, with whites placed in higher status positions, contributed to racial tensions, racial inequities, and negative attitudes toward clients. Depressed local economies also affected the actions of staff in various ways; at the Coastal office, where workers were well aware of structural labor market conditions, this awareness contributed to a less punitive evaluation of clients' problems than we saw in Bridgetown.

Each of the contradictions facing workers "on the ground" reveals significant ideological work that held, sometimes precariously, the neoliberal objectives of welfare restructuring in place. Most workers accepted the widely promoted idea that "work is better than welfare," but they often had to close their eyes to the full significance of the hardships these policies caused. Like the agency leaders who so insistently encouraged their workers to frame what they were doing in positive terms, workers often focused quite explicitly on the successes they had with some clients, even when those successes might be temporary, rather than dwell on families "falling between the cracks" or those struggling with sanctions, ticking clocks, or troubles that workers could not help resolve. Workers emphasized the positive values they associated with self-sufficiency and saw themselves as able to provide more valuable services and more resources than when cash assistance was an entitlement. This was an important dimension of how they constructed themselves more as "helpers" than as "enforcers," a distinction Evelyn Brodkin (1997) uses in her analysis of frontline welfare workers.

This portrait of welfare restructuring draws on research conducted during some of the best years of this process, at least as measured by a continuing decrease in the number of clients on the TANF rolls, clients' ability to secure jobs in a relatively strong economy, and agency resources. These all helped to fuel workers' relatively positive perspectives on welfare restructuring. Especially for case managers, the work of welfare provision became more challenging, but also more fulfilling. Agency leaders and managers worked hard to keep workers' eyes on the goals of caseload reduction and work promotion, rather than focusing on how little they were accomplishing to meaningfully address poverty or promote economic security.

What was most visible was what conformed to the agency's changing mission, what was measured, and what was ideologically and institutionally reinforced. What was less visible, or what workers preferred to keep in the shadows, was what they could no longer do for or provide to families struggling with economic and other crises—the coercive effects of a diminished social safety net; of public assistance benefits contingent on conformity with agency policies; of time limits, sanctions, and penalties; and of decreased choices for poor mothers about either whether or how to combine paid and unpaid work or whether to pursue education to bolster their chances for better jobs.

Workers clearly did not see their jobs as enforcing neoliberal values, nor did they see that they were helping to perpetuate the low-wage labor force or the production of poverty. But their own struggles to manage the work of welfare under varying conditions did create some fissures in the narrative of policy success. Some saw a side of welfare "reform" that they could not ignore completely, not when needy, sometimes desperate, clients sat across from them or left messages on their telephones. In the next two chapters we pivot our vision to the other side of the desk, examining how the women (and some men) who were the primary targets of welfare restructuring interpreted and experienced these new policies very differently from either agency administrators or workers.

THE OTHER SIDE OF THE DESK

Client Experiences and Perspectives
on Welfare Restructuring

Betty Wooten, an African American fifty-year-old mother, is employed full-time as a certified nursing assistant (CNA) at a residential home for the elderly. Her minimum wage job barely allows her to make ends meet, even with the small check she receives from Social Security, because her ex-husband's illness prevents him from working. Over the past twenty years, she has worked mainly as a CNA, turning to public assistance when she did not have a job or after the births of her children. She has endured years of economic hardship, and her troubles continued unabated over the two years of this study. Wooten sees little resemblance between her lived experience and the rhetoric and policies espoused by policy makers who "don't know what it's like" but have the authority to make the rules.

> Being there firsthand on the receiving end of all these things, I think that more people that have been in the positions that I have need to have some input...you know. Instead of the people that have never had to receive this assistance. They're out there making the rules and they don't know what it's like, you know they don't.

The experiences of many of the families we studied diverge sharply from the way they are portrayed both by the media and by the policy professionals that shaped and promoted the recent changes to the welfare system. Although the hundreds of women and men we studied do not speak in one voice about work, family, or public assistance, many share Wooten's beliefs that the realities of their lives and their perspectives have been virtually ignored in public discussions of welfare "reform." Up to this point we have examined welfare restructuring from the vantage point of agency administrators and workers, but on the other side of the desk sit agency clients, the objects of agency policy and essential participants in welfare bureaucracies. Client experiences with welfare restructuring provide a very different angle of vision on how the paradigmatic change in U.S. social welfare policy and ideology became concrete in peoples' daily lives.

The clients whose perspectives we examine in this chapter are much more likely than the administrators and workers we studied to question the "success" of welfare reform.[1] Many were astute in their assessment of the large gap between what they needed and what they received from the agency, although some felt that their needs had been fully met. Many also had different, and more complicated, understandings of the agency motto "work is *always* better than welfare." Clients, as a group, have a very different stake in welfare reform than agency staff. While Adult and Family Services (AFS) administrators and workers labor under the mandate to reduce welfare caseloads and promote nonstate forms of provisioning (wages, help from partners or extended families, or assistance from other agencies, especially private organizations), clients come to AFS precisely to secure public assistance, often, as more than one client put it, as "a last resort." They need help with housing, food, health care, vehicle repairs, and past due utility bills. They seek assistance in digging out of deep financial holes and sustaining their families.

Here we explore the most recurrent themes that emerged from client descriptions of their experiences as AFS clients. Based on these data, we describe a powerful culture of compliance and work enforcement that confronts those who apply for or receive aid from AFS, especially the female heads of household on Temporary Assistance for Needy Families (TANF). Welfare restructuring involves an explicit ideological policing that is embodied in mundane, everyday welfare-to-work practices; the more intense surveillance and the system of rewards and punishments are meted out by welfare workers; and less targeted but powerful ideological messages about welfare, work, and family circulate in the wider culture (Roberts 2002; Davis 2006). But none of these processes are deterministic.

While poor women do share, to varying degrees, key assumptions embedded in the new welfare policies, many also hold alternative ideas about personal responsibility, motherhood, education and mobility, poverty and inequality, and "deservingness"—ideas that sometimes coexist with and sometimes contest the dominant cultural understandings. We explore these alternative perspectives later in the chapter. Their actions and degrees of what the agency calls "compliance" vary. Despite the powerful hold the agency exerts on them, especially while they sit across the desk from workers, many struggle to negotiate the powerful culture of compliance in ways that allow them, albeit in highly constrained ways, to exert some agency over their lives. From their positions "in the system" they have developed their own ideas about how agency services and programs could be changed to far better address their multiple responsibilities and needs, which we take up at the end of the chapter.

The analyses in this chapter are based on four sources of data described in the introduction: (1) fieldwork in three Oregon welfare offices in 1998; (2) responses from current or former AFS clients to two telephone surveys at two different points over two years (1998–2000); (3) two additional in-person, in-depth interviews with seventy-five women and three men chosen from the larger sample, conducted in between the two telephone surveys and again six months afterward; and (4) additional in-depth, in-person interviews conducted with thirty women from the original study three and a half to four years after leaving welfare (in 2001 to 2002). The sample of the original study consisted of 47 percent chosen randomly from a group the agency categorized as *Food Stamp "leavers"* (those who left Food Stamps in the first quarter of 1998), 31 percent from *TANF "leavers"* (those who left TANF in the first quarter of 1998), and 22 percent as *"diverted" from TANF* (those who applied for but never received TANF in the first quarter of 1998 because they found a job, became frustrated with the process, et cetera, before the thirty to forty-five day "assessment" period ended). However these distinctions are less meaningful than they might appear. Many categorized as Food Stamp leavers had been on TANF at some point in recent years, and more than half of the "diverted" ended up receiving TANF during the period of our research (Gonzales, Hudson, and Acker 2007).

Who Are the "Clients"?

These women and men mirrored the demographics of public assistance use in Oregon in the mid- to late 1990s. The respondents for both the telephone survey and the in-depth interviews were mostly women: 93 percent of TANF leavers, 86 percent of Food Stamp leavers, and 79 percent of TANF diverted in the telephone surveys; and 96 percent (72 of the 75) of the in-depth interviews. More than 80 percent of the TANF leavers and over 60 percent of the other two groups were the heads of single-parent households. Like Oregon's population as a whole, and its public assistance caseload, the sample was overwhelmingly white: Over 80 percent of each of the groups identified as white. Because we thought it was important to ascertain how race mattered for those affected by welfare restructuring in Oregon, we oversampled women of color among those we interviewed in-person. Of the 78 individuals we spoke with in the first round of in-depth interviews, sixty-six percent (51) identified as white, 14 percent (11) as African American, 8 percent (6) as Latino, 6 percent (5) as mixed race, 4 percent (3) as Native American, and 1 percent (1) as Asian American.

Compared to national samples of welfare leavers, this subsample was a slightly more educationally advantaged group; 38 percent of the sample had either a high school diploma or a GED. Although 35 percent had taken at least one college course, fewer than 10 percent held either associates or bachelor's degrees. Fifty-eight percent of those whom we followed most intensively were employed either full- or part time over most of the two years of the study (i.e., at either three or four contact points). Five percent were employed at only one point of contact, and 14 percent were not in the paid labor force at all during this period.[2] As a group, they faced considerable economic hardship and insecurity. Almost half of the families had incomes below the poverty line eighteen to twenty-one months after exiting or being diverted from public assistance in 1998. Only a handful of families had household incomes above "twice the poverty rate"—a more accurate reflection of actual poverty in the United States according to many policy makers and scholars (Bernstein, Brocht, and Spade-Aguilar 2000). Their limited means explains the continuing reliance of the vast majority of these families on one or more forms of public assistance at some point or continuously during the two years after their exit or diversion from public assistance in early 1998.

Labels such as welfare "client," TANF "leaver," or Food Stamp "recipient"—categories that make administrative or academic sense—obscure much about these women and men.[3] It is highly unlikely that any of them would choose these categories as salient identities. She might well think of herself as poor, as a struggling single mother who needs "a little boost," turning to the welfare agency to seek "help" out of a financial hole or because she has no viable alternatives means of support for herself and her baby. But she doesn't generally identify with the stigmatized category "welfare recipient" or even welfare "leaver," and the fact of being a "client" of AFS, while accurate, is low on the list of salient identities for most of the women we interviewed.

As we have maintained, it is important to examine the intersections of gender, race, and class in studying the lives of welfare clients. Most of the women we interviewed are embedded in gendered, raced, and classed webs of relationships and responsibilities that they bring with them, sometimes physically, to the welfare office. These relationships and responsibilities constitute a major reason for their need and eligibility for assistance. One of the most remarkable, but least remarked on, facets of welfare restructuring is that most of the people affected by or involved in the everyday work of welfare are women. This fact often lurks just beneath the surface of most research or policy discussion of welfare restructuring, but we suggest it is problematic to leave it subterranean.

Individual recipients experience welfare restructuring differently. Two different sources of the variations we analyze are those *between* agency workers and clients and those *among* clients. Some agency personnel have firsthand experiences with poverty, racism, and gender subordination; some do not. Additionally, the circumstances that create dire financial need among clients vary, encompassing some who have never known economic security and others facing "dire straits" only recently. Issues relating to gender, race, and class often have a role in shaping these relationships. A second source of difference, especially among clients, has to do with the relationships they have with their workers: Some clients get resources, and others do not as a result of these relationships. Differences also result from how welfare reform is organized and implemented within branches and among workers. We turn now to an exploration of clients' perspectives on their interactions with agency workers.

"It All Depends on Your Worker"

Cheryl Lions, a single mother in her twenties, has worked full-time at a factory doing assembly work for nearly three years. She has received TANF, Food Stamps, and Oregon Health Plan (OHP) benefits sporadically since the birth of her first child, in between jobs, and immediately after each of her subsequent two children's births. Lions characterized the relationship between clients and welfare workers:

> It depends on who you are, who's your caseworker, what they suspect of you. It all determines what, if they are going to help you, if they are really going to give you a lot of help or not help....I figured it should go, as everyone equal... [but] it's not, it just depends on how your caseworker wants to do your case and how much they want to give you and how much you have to do.

Clients believe that much depends on who they are, to what worker they are assigned, and what that worker "suspects of you." Lions' interesting turn of phrase melds together the combined brunt of worker expectations and the climate of suspicion that greets many clients. The "chemistry" between individual workers and clients has long been a factor in human service relationships, and there is a considerable literature that analyzes the various reasons why relationships between welfare workers and clients are often strained, and sometimes even adversarial (e.g., Kingfisher 1996; Seccombe 2007).

But, as we saw in chapter 4, welfare workers now wield more discretion because the entitlement of income-eligible families to cash assistance has been replaced with a system of contingent assistance. The consequences of what workers call "flexibility" or "empowerment" and what clients often experience as caprice are considerable: what kind of assistance is offered or withheld, how long a client has to wait for services or benefits, the nature of the requirements listed on the employment development plan (EDP), the slack offered or consequences imposed for noncompliance, and how the worker makes the client feel across the desk. Because so much is embodied in any interaction between agency workers and clients, it can be difficult to say with certainty which characteristics of workers, clients, or their relationship determine the quality of the service provided or the nature and quantity of the help given or not given. However, our research unearthed some patterns that suggest strongly that gender, race, and class inequalities are very much in play during agency interactions.

For example, two women who left TANF in early 1998 had very different experiences with AFS despite considerable similarities in their needs and circumstances. Connie Rounds is a white woman in her early forties, a divorced mother of two teenagers. Teresa Pena is a Latina in her late thirties with a baby, a ten-year-old son, and a fiancé who has a chronic and serious health problem. Both work as certified nursing assistants (CNAs). Rounds was on TANF for five years, beginning after she left an abusive husband. She suffers from a number of health conditions, including fibromyalgia. Over the past decade, Pena has worked a series of low-wage service-sector jobs, including the CNA job she had in 1999 at a local nursing home when we interviewed her. In between jobs and after the births of both children, she was on cash assistance. At the time of our first interview with Pena in 1999, she had just returned to work, three weeks after a C-section, because the family was desperate for money. She worked nights so she could care for her family and attend classes to complete a medical tech training program. She was not receiving help from AFS for that training.

Rounds was very grateful for the help she had received from AFS. She described the agency as "very supportive…emotionally as well as financially." Rounds worked part-time during much of the time of our study, a decision her case manager supported because of her chronic health problems and so she would have the time needed to complete a course to recertify her licensed vocational nurse (LVN) credential. The agency also helped pay for that training. In addition, Rounds reported that the agency "helped pay for my car insurance, and they've just helped pick up the pieces when I couldn't carry everything myself." She did experience problems with changing eligibility for OHP benefits, causing problems that we discuss later in the chapter. But, in general, Rounds's experience led her to believe that "public assistance helps maintain people so they can feel protected and feel that their needs are going to be met. So then their mind is free to move on to higher things."

Pena's experience was very different. She described her experience of seeking help as "rough," feeling that "they don't want to help you." She understands that "they don't want to give you a free ride…they want to give you a push in the right direction, get self-sufficient, but they make it real hard when you're starting off with nothing. It's like you have no home, no food, no nothing." Pena received almost no help for the one and a half months while she was in assessment (the diversion period): "[D]uring those weeks I was sweating it, you know. I thought that was a little harsh. They gave you bus fare to find work, but that was it." She asked her case manager for help with the required deposit for an apartment the family found. But despite being told at the group assessment meeting that this kind of help was possible, her case manager said no.

Pena was working full-time, but she could not afford the health insurance premium on the employer-provided health insurance, and the family's income put them just over the limit to qualify for OHP. Thus, there was a significant mismatch between Pena's needs and the help she got from AFS:

> The main reason you usually go to [AFS] is because you're destitute at that moment. You have no money, no house, no food. You know, it's like, give me a little hand so I can get on my feet. I need a roof over my kids' heads and food in their bellies so I can go out and get a job and support our family. But they just said, "Well, here's information."…What really sticks out in my mind is that point where they say they'll do this and this and this, but then they didn't, you know, especially when you need it most. It's false advertising or something.

Like Rounds, Pena also struggled with fluctuating income and, therefore, benefits that went up and down. She described as "painful" the fact that "they start taking it [health and child care subsidies and Food Stamps] away at such a fast rate it does not balance" your income. We pick up this point about fluctuating benefits later in the chapter.

The differences between Rounds' and Pena's experiences are typical of the variations of support we saw in our observations and learned about in the interviews with clients. Though we have limited information about these women's case managers, the outcomes the clients experienced suggest that each worker interpreted each woman's circumstances differently. It may be that Rounds, who is white, divorced, and has chronic health problems, is seen as more deserving than is Pena, a woman of color who is partnered, but is not married to the unemployed father of her youngest child. Not surprisingly, personal histories and individual attributes, including race and family forms, seemed to play a role in how workers responded to individual clients—that is, what the "chemistry" is between them and how workers use their discretion based on their impressions.

In particular, each of us observed cases in the branch offices that supported what a number of the women of color we interviewed stated explicitly or implied: that race colored relationships and may have been a key factor in how they were treated by agency staff. For example, after turning down a black pregnant client's request for help with moving costs, one white worker at Bridgetown told us that when she sees "multiple kids by multiple men," it "bugs" her and that this particular client represented a "sore spot" with her, reminding her of another "demanding" young black mother with whom she had wrangled. In chapters 3 and 4 we described how workers in Bridgetown, the branch in a predominantly black neighborhood, tended to see clients through the racialized lens of stereotypical "welfare recipient," while Coastal workers, serving a predominantly white clientele, extended more empathy in their assessments of clients and tended to acknowledge the ways labor market conditions curbed job opportunities. This is consistent with a significant body of evidence that documents women of color being more negatively affected by key provisions of welfare reform nationally and more vulnerable to harsh and coercive practices.[4]

Some especially difficult situations were reported by the "diverted" clients. Some received more generous "assessment payments" (to help pay the costs of housing, utilities, expenses related to seeking a job, etc.) than others with apparently similar needs. Ann Clay, a white married mother caring for her grandchild, recounted how the case manager questioned her after explaining the diversion program: "I guess I had a dumbfounded look or something because she said, 'Do you understand?'" Ann shared what she told her: "Yeah, I understand. You ain't giving me no money, no help. I totally understand. I think it's stupid, but I understand." On the other hand, Darcy Williams, a divorced white woman in her early twenties, felt she got what she needed during the work search process, "[they gave me] close to $400 [for] the vehicle just to keep me out on the road...I never thought I could find something that could help me so much."

Case managers of course, do not have limitless funds to work with. In addition to the choices they make based on their individual discretion, they work within agency-imposed limits, as we discussed in chapter 3. Our analysis of AFS administrative data shows that the mean assessment cost per participant per month rose from $278 in 1998 to $340 in 1999 and declined to $260 in 2000. These averages are below the meager maximum TANF cash grant for a family of three, which was frozen at $460 from July 1991 through April 2006 (Leachman and Merten 2007). The experiences of the clients we interviewed took place during a period when funds were more generous than they later became, as funds for the assessment program continued to decline after 2000. These variations in what clients secured during the assessment period depended on their workers' decisions, branch policies and practices, and fluctuating agency budgets and spending priorities. There were similar kinds of differences in JOBS payments, another pot of money workers had available to assist clients who had gone through assessment and were now on TANF. Here, too, worker discretion and attitude toward clients played a role in shaping clients' experiences.

Client Experiences of the Agency

Client assessments of the agency were sharply affected by the way they were treated by agency staff. More than half of those we interviewed in person expressed a negative assessment of agency personnel, particularly of the frontline staff at reception and some of the multiple case managers clients were assigned. Clients often felt that agency staff did not see or treat them as "people," as individuals with problems. We heard over and over that their case managers did not "care about them." They resented the very common experience of being "judged" by case managers and of having their stories treated as "lies" or as attempts to "milk the system." Many described the treatment they received as "unfair" or "rude," sometimes as "discriminatory," and repeatedly as "demeaning" or "humiliating." They observed that many case managers did not listen well, were stingy with assistance, failed to follow through with paperwork or requests, took "forever" to return telephone calls, and/or were "intimidating" or "threatening."

For example, Kim Smith, a white single mother, believed that many workers were "just clueless," suggesting an awareness of the ways her resource deficits and struggles were overlooked by the agency. Here the gap between those agency staff who enjoy class, and sometimes race and gender, privilege, and the majority of clients who do not, is extensive. Smith, a student and a cocktail waitress, felt judged and dehumanized, "lumped" into a stigmatized category; she explains:

> They treat you awful, like you are stupid....You are not a person, you are a number to them. And you know, if you *are* a person it's because you are a *bad* person because you are not well off, or you know, because you've had issues in your life that have brought you to where you are.

Jean Glass, a white mother of a young son who has worked as a hairdresser for years, "dreaded" going into the welfare office because

> When you go in, they, like, belittle you. I mean they were rude....They would treat you like you were a nobody, like you were a lowlife...I think they treat everybody that goes in there like they are taking advantage of the system. And for those who are working and trying to provide a life for their child and their selves, I mean, and just want a little bit of help just to kind of help pull them up in life, you know, and get on the right track and stuff. It is like they weren't there for you.

Clients reported that the problems begin the minute a client enters the welfare agency into what is often a crowded waiting area staffed by workers who hand out lengthy and complicated forms that have to be filled in, inform clients about the (often onerous) procedures that separate them from the benefits they probably need (and won't get) right away, and enforce long waits, as we detailed in chapter 3. Applicants for assistance, especially if this is a new process for them, are often on guard when they enter. They may be battling discomfort, shame, or fear, and some of them feel desperate because their disinclination to apply for help held them back until their situation had reached crisis proportions. Unlike case managers, about whom there was a mix of positive and negative comments in the interviews, the only specific comments about frontline staff we heard in the interviews were negative ones, references to those staff as "unfriendly" or "unhelpful."

The most significant interactions with staff were with case managers. As we discussed in chapter 4, the "assessment" meeting is the first contact with the case manager. Depending on how this interview is handled, a client can feel she has been treated with sensitivity or that she has endured a grilling. We saw and heard descriptions that fell across this spectrum, but the feeling of being intensively "cross-examined" is surely justifiable. Clients expect to have to answer questions. What they object to more are the underlying negative judgments they hear in the kinds of questions asked and the failure of case managers to be as curious about larger circumstances that many of these women feel are at the root of the struggles they and their families confront, what Tara Sanders called the "real issues" that the agency basically ignores.

Sanders, a married African American mother of a four-year-old, applied for assistance because her minimum-wage job as a child care worker did not cover her family's basic needs. She was dismayed that someone like herself, from "a working class family...[who has] worked as much as you possibly can" would be subjected to what essentially felt "like they were being interrogated, because of why they need assistance." It was enough to deter her from seeking further help.

> It's bad enough going in there and asking for help....And then to be—have all the questions and all the suspicions and everything entailed with it....That's why I haven't done it anymore.

While women of all racial and ethnic backgrounds reported that they found the questioning uncomfortable, a higher proportion of women of color used language that indicated they felt suspect, and sometimes they used words such as "interrogation" to describe their meetings with case managers. Lydia Mendez, a forty-four-year-old Mexican immigrant mother of two children who was separated from her husband and has a long history of doing agricultural work, felt humiliated by persistent questioning, especially about her sexual and reproductive history, and unsolicited advice that she should seek family planning. Given her age and that she has two children, she experienced the insinuations about her fertility as offensive, leading her to conclude that "there's people [at AFS] who discriminate."

While women have to divulge intimate details of their lives to workers, to become, as one client put it, "an open book," they found their workers to be the opposite: inaccessible and not always forthcoming with the information clients needed. Erin White, a white single mother of one school-aged child who lives in rural eastern Oregon, complained that her worker was stingy with information, leaving her to feel like "you're…a mushroom, kept in the dark and fed a lot of bull." Quite a few clients explained that they learned about certain benefits or resources from other clients, not from their workers, leading them to indict workers who act like the "money is coming from their own pockets." Many clients complained that case managers didn't return their calls in a timely manner, or at all, prompting Sally Reid to suggest that it takes "an act of Congress to talk to a real human being."

Another double standard, and a source of significant problems for some clients, had to do with the consequences of errors. If a client made an error in filling out forms or providing documentation or was not timely with that information, her benefits suffered. When you are living on the financial edge, this can be serious. On the other hand, when case managers made mistakes, and this was not rare, penalties accrued to clients instead of the agency or the worker being held accountable. Several clients described situations where worker errors resulted in overpayments, for example, in Food Stamps, that were later picked up in audits. When the error was detected, the client was responsible for repaying the amount overpaid, even though it was not her fault. In an agency where the rhetoric of personal responsibility and accountability was ubiquitous, this did not feel fair to clients.

What is striking about so many of these stories in which relationships with agency workers are described as humiliating, unfair, and unhelpful is how far these experiences are from the belief of many workers that with welfare "reform" they are better able to "really help" their clients (i.e., to become independent, productive, good role models, solid citizens). And there were instances where this promise was fulfilled. When clients did describe positive relationships with case managers, they used words such as "helpful," "supportive," and "caring or described them as "allies," "advocates," or "mentors"; they praised workers for treating them with "respect" and seeing them as "individuals."

Diane Wheeler, a separated white mother in her forties with two teenaged children who lives in a small, economically depressed rural community in eastern

Oregon, is one such example. Jobs in her community are scarce, but she has had a long string of low-wage jobs, and had a part-time clerical position in a nonprofit agency at the time of our research. She is classified as a Food Stamp leaver, but also got OHP, although she received Aid to Families with Dependent Children (AFDC) years ago after the birth of her oldest child. Wheeler felt supported by her case manager, and even though she, like so many others, struggled because her wages and public assistance benefits together did not add up to making ends meet, she thought the agency treated her well:

> They know people as individuals....You aren't, in a small community, made to feel like you're just a sheep....So I guess it's more of a comfort thing than an actual dollars-and-cents thing. They helped me keep my sanity as far as how I was going to keep my child fed while I was looking for work.

Similarly, Pam Stewart, a white single mother of two, said, "I've had a couple of really good ones [workers] ...I couldn't say enough good stuff about them....But initially, you know, to walk in there, it's not very friendly." But even some who praised the treatment they (sometimes) got recognized that their treatment was unusual, that they were on the winning side of the much critiqued "favoritism" that wider discretion can foster. Some clients empathized with their workers, seeing the pressures they were under and that the agency staff was overworked. Diane Wheeler recognized how tough the jobs of case managers are, and that they functioned in a morass of rules and financial limitations, so she understood how they could become inured to their clients' needs:

> Once you have so many people go through your office in a day wanting a certain kind of help, that you would have to have a certain buffer to be able to stay in that position...and probably have to turn people away at times due to not meeting criteria or whatever it might be. There have been times that I have felt lumped into a category maybe, of why aren't you responsible, why aren't you working a job like I am working?...I think it's sometimes hard for people [the workers] to understand, you know, or empathize...I think they probably do the best they can with what they have.

Others understood that overworked case managers have trouble juggling the large caseloads, the extensive documentation required, and the plain hard work involved in doing what the agency mission requires. Some clients thought the agency workers were also intensively monitored, undermining the ability of case managers to use the discretion they were given to truly help their clients. Lilly Cantwell, a white single mother who had been a Food Stamp recipient while also working as a cashier at a convenience store, echoed the sentiments of others that she had experienced a range of workers from good to bad. She had perceived a recent worsening of relationships between case managers and clients that she thought came from pressure on workers "from above" to save money.

Other clients suggested astutely that workers were under pressure to "make the agency look good," so that it was more important to get "the numbers right" than to actually meet client needs. In chapters 3 and 4 we examined these pressures, analyzing the larger policy and organizational constraints under which agency leaders and staff worked. The organizational culture that developed in response to both these constraints and the allegiance of agency leadership to the welfare-to-work ideal shaped a culture of compliance and work enforcement that characterized AFS in the mid- to late 1990s.

The Culture of Compliance and Work Enforcement

Janis Woods is a married white woman in her early twenties who went on TANF soon after the birth of her now (in 2001) three-year-old son. For several years the family received various combinations and amounts of TANF, Food Stamps, OHP, and Employment Related Day Care (ERDC). Woods was now employed full-time in a clerical position, her best job to date. She attributed her success in getting the job to the community college degree that her worker allowed her to complete while on TANF. Woods reports using TANF "as an aid because I didn't have any other support there for me." She was among a handful of mostly white women in the study who were permitted to use postsecondary education as partial fulfillment of TANF work requirements. Nevertheless, she still found the JOBS program a poor match for her needs:

> If they didn't have so many rules and regulations now, and you could just sit down with a caseworker and tell her what your needs are and resolve issues personally....But I had so many issues going on that I didn't fit their—if I didn't walk their line, there was no other line to walk. You know what I mean? There was just one path from here to there. You are going to jump through all these hoops on your way and they would threaten you, whatever is going to happen to you by eliminating that check. And that is probably the worst thing that they can do.

Despite having a comparatively flexible and supportive case manager, welfare-to-work for Woods consisted of "hoops" and "threats" that restricted most women to walking the "one" path AFS offered: rapid labor force attachment. The culture of compliance and the culture of work enforcement—the singular path, the hoops, the enforcement mechanisms—we discuss in this section are mutually supporting sets of discourses, originating in and depending on stigmatized conceptions of welfare recipients. These discourses inform and are embodied in a series of routine practices that constitute welfare as we now know it. That welfare functions as a form of social control, a means of "regulating the poor" (Piven and Cloward [1971] 1993) has been well established in the literature on U.S. welfare both pre- and post "reform." In 1971, Piven and Cloward published the classic formulation of this argument, analyzing how welfare aimed to discipline the poor, to simultaneously reinforce the work ethic (and supply workers for the lowest wage jobs), and to provide minimal support to the poor to reinforce the legitimacy of capitalist states. However, the new welfare regime has shifted the balance between these functions of welfare, emphasizing more and differently than previously a culture of work enforcement (Piven 2001, 2002). While the exhortation to work is not recent, agency workers have new, and more powerful, tools to firmly require recipients of public assistance to seek and accept jobs. These tools range from work requirements to time limits, penalties, and sanctions that have made the new welfare regime both more forceful and more punitive. These are the "sticks" that accompany the positive incentives to work, the much valued "carrots" of work supports that help "make work pay."

Although Oregon's welfare policy has been judged "kinder and gentler" than many other states, many clients experienced Oregon's welfare policies as coercive. For example, Ellen Durant, a white woman with two children who struggled with a series of serious health problems and homelessness for years while she was on and off public assistance, described the agency as having her on a "choke chain." Tamara Ryan, an African American mother of four who lives with her partner, says Oregon has used "scare tactics" to achieve Oregon's goal of "keeping Oregon number one for welfare reform." Mary Torres, a non-English-speaking Latina in her late twenties, whose husband was deported, leaving her with five dollars and a brand new baby and a toddler, felt "confronted" by her case manager; her experience was that the agency was "going to give you the help but in a bad way." Agency rhetoric cloaked the coercion in a vocabulary that emphasized self-improvement, self-sufficiency, choice, responsibility, accountability, empowerment, and conciliation. But the experiences of surveillance, regulation, and punishment were anything but empowering for the majority.

Frances Fox Piven (2001, 2002) has suggested that a more intensive culture of work enforcement emerged from a combination of the growing influence of neoliberal ideologies and the global and national economic restructuring that has resulted in the loss of family-wage and production of many more low-wage jobs. With as many as 39 percent of female workers paid low wages at the start of our study in 1998 (Kim 2000) and approximately one-quarter of U.S. workers earning low-wage wages in 2007 (defined as ten dollars an hour or less) (Acs 2008), some individuals who are unable to secure higher paying jobs because of education, skills, family obligations, or occupational segregation and discrimination based on gender and race have to be prodded (economic and political elites believe) into taking "bad" jobs. The culture of work enforcement provides the prod, one felt forcefully by many clients. Taken together, miserly, short-term welfare benefits, cultural disparagement of welfare recipients, valorization of paid work, and a welfare bureaucracy that is onerous and stigmatizing to navigate combine to construct any type of employment as a more attractive option for many women, no matter how poorly paying or unresponsive to the needs of mothers with children. Low-wage work is, thus, enforced.

Beyond the ideologies that promote paid work are the actual policies and practices of welfare agencies that constitute the heart of work enforcement, as we discussed in chapter 3. In Oregon these included freezing the amount of the cash grant in 1991 so its value shrank markedly each year, strong diversion tactics to achieve caseload reduction by keeping people off welfare, strict and intensive work requirements for almost all TANF applicants and TANF recipients, and a system of disqualifications (sanctions) to promote compliance and punish noncompliance. The heart of welfare-to-work in practice is the obligation to seek employment, which takes the form of a signed contract, allegedly negotiated between worker and client—the employment development plan (EDP). But in our observations of TANF intake meetings, there was little to no "negotiation"; workers interviewed clients, developed an EDP, and told clients that any further aid was contingent on signing and complying with the EDP. In none of our interviews did clients describe being actively involved in coming up with these plans; indeed, they were painfully aware of how little power accrued to their side of the desk.

Clients were similarly disenchanted with their job readiness classes. It was a rare client, either from the telephone survey sample or among the seventy-eight whom we followed most closely, who spoke highly of these classes. Although over half of TANF clients in the survey said that AFS helped them look for jobs, very few of those we interviewed face-to-face agreed that AFS actually helped them (as opposed to exhorted them) to find a job. The main exceptions were those who were placed in "Work Experience" (subsidized) temporary jobs. Client after client described the mandated classes as "unhelpful" or as "stupid," "a joke," or a "waste of time." One client said the classes were like "elementary school"; this not only offended her but stood in contrast to the postsecondary education she would have much preferred. Adding insult to injury for some clients was the relatively long distances they had to drive to get to mandated classes, posing both a time and financial drain. Clients frequently described the intensive monitoring as "strict" and "inflexible" and a clear message that the agency lacked faith that they could determine for themselves the parameters of their job search.

In chapters 3 and 4 we heard case managers applaud the flexibility the EDP process gave them to individualize a self-sufficiency plan for a client. And there were a few clients whose positive experiences are attributable to case managers who used that flexibility to allow, for example, clients to count community college classes or training programs toward the work requirements. Clients who were immediate survivors of domestic violence were usually released from the stringent work requirements for a time and able to get on TANF right away. In cases where case managers suspected or had evidence of drug or alcohol addiction or serious mental health problems, the EDP often included mandated treatment. But our observations of TANF assessment intake interviews in the three branches found that much more often than not the standard template, or something very close to it, ruled.

One serious objection some clients had about the way the work search program worked was the practice of case managers in some branches of threatening them with loss of benefits if they turned down *any* job offers, or warning clients that if they had not found a job after two weeks that the agency would "place" them in a job. Lela Barnes, a white married woman with two young children, who lacked only twenty-five credits toward a degree in psychology and who had extensive job experience mainly in low-wage service-sector jobs, was "horrified" by that warning:

> The JOBS program here, if you don't get a job within two weeks of going to these little morning sessions, they put you in a job. Telemarketing. Burger King, McDonalds, Dairy Queen…I was shocked. I mean I have three years of college education. To go to work at Burger King is horrifying to me. AFS told us in the JOBS program, if you turn anything down…your case will be automatically closed for six months. It is very clear. It is very harsh.

Barnes understood that "the state has a limited amount of funds," but she saw forcing people to take such menial, minimum-wage jobs as coercive and counter to the larger agency goal of keeping people off welfare. "It seems to me," she said, "you would see a lot less people going back on the system if the system would help them get a decent job."

Due to the discretion that case managers have, situations such as Barnes describes are not ubiquitous. Nevertheless, we heard the same complaint from many others: They were told they would have to take whatever jobs they could find or face their case manager's ire, job placements over which they had no choice, or being out of compliance and then vulnerable to sanctioning. This was true even in Portland, the site of a highly lauded welfare-to-work demonstration project, described in chapter 2, praised nationally for encouraging clients to "hold out" for better jobs as part of the Portland JOBS Program. As we showed in chapter 2, changes in this program implemented during the period of our study, but *after* the original study that found it so successful, were in the direction of faster labor force attachment.

For some clients the rules, or the way they were implemented, created a palpable climate of fear. Vicki Jones, a white divorced mother in her early twenties who reported feeling extreme stress from her dealings with the agency, was "overwhelmed" by the requirements she had to comply with. But she did not feel she was in a position to really be honest with her case manager about how overburdened she felt. She admitted to feeling "scared, it's like I feel I can't tell her how I'm feeling or what I can do, you know to be involved with this without her saying, 'Your benefits are going to stop.'"

Although one infraction rarely resulted in having a sanction imposed, multiple infractions, even minor ones, could and did trigger sanctions. Sanctions were progressive and involved financial penalties. These sanctions could have significant repercussions for families living well below the poverty line and on the edge of economic crisis. In Oregon the final sanction in a series of six penalties was loss of the entire cash grant. While this was rarely imposed, because the agency had to prove that the "full family sanction" would not harm the children on the grant, even the threat of this sanction constituted a powerful regulative mechanism.

Since case managers had considerable discretion in deciding what level of noncompliance to tolerate before initiating a sanction, they wielded a great deal of power over clients. In previous chapters, we discuss how workers defined the disqualification process as a means of "engaging" clients, a distinction important to some case managers that differentiated this process from punishment. But we never heard a single client talk in positive terms about the "re-engagement" consequences of sanctions. Rather, sanctions were the force behind the "choke chain" of the work requirements.

AFS data from 1998–2000 indicate that statewide the percentage of the TANF caseload disqualified per month in Oregon was in the range of about 3.5 to 5.0 percent (table 1). There were differences in these rates by branch and by year. Table 1 shows the range each year in the percentage of disqualifications for the state and in the three branches we studied over the three years of the study. Over the course of a year the numbers added up to thousands of clients statewide who were disqualified at some level of severity.

Table 1 Disqualification Rates (combining six levels of sanctions) for TANF
Clients in Oregon and Three Branch Offices, 1998–2000

YEAR	STATE (%)	BRIDGETOWN (%)	WOODSIDE (%)	COASTAL (%)
1998	3.3–4.9	2.4–6.4	4.1–7.8	2.3–6.7
1999	3.4–3.7	2.6–5.7	2.9–4.8	3.0–7.4
2000	3.5–4	3.3–4.9	2.0–5.2	3.1–8

Source: AFS administrative data, 1998–2000. Calculated from administrative data available at the Oregon
Department of Human Services website, http://www.oregon.gov/DHS/assistance/data/archive.shtml#2001.
Disqualification rates back to 2001 are available in the monthly reports titled Branch and Service Delivery
Area Data.

The negative impact of sanctions was intensified when clients either did not understand why they were sanctioned, when the sanction resulted from (the common) errors or delays in reporting by JOBS subcontractors, or when the sanction represented an unfair denial of the client's perceived extenuating circumstances. Although (as discussed in chapter 3), sanctions could be lifted when clients participated in "conciliation"—a meeting with their worker that involved her acquiescence to fulfill the work requirements—any future sanction would trigger the next of the six levels of possible disqualifications.

Sanctions are part of a much broader atmosphere of coercion that weighed heavily on clients. Many clearly felt that agency rules strongly constrained their choices to determine what was in each client and her/his family's best interest. The pressures brought to bear on clients were infantilizing, at best; at worst they connoted the surveillance and punishment usually associated with the criminal justice system. Clients sometimes explicitly invoked the latter through the language and metaphors they used to describe their experience with the agency. A higher proportion of those using this kind of language were women of color.

For example, Elana Heiser, a mixed-raced single mother who was experiencing dire financial problems and facing benefit losses tried to fend off her case manager's pressure to take a minimum wage job rather than hold out for a better paying job. Her situation, as she admitted, was "complicated." But her frustration was palpable, and she likened the agency to a prison. "They got you. I mean, that's what, the system doesn't care anymore. They just, it's like they want to *incarcerate* you." Tamara Ryan, a black partnered mother of four children, said, "[O]nce you sign the papers [the EDP] you are '*in the system*'…once I signed those papers they were all over me. 'You have to do this and we want you here.'" And earlier we quoted a young African American woman, Tara Sanders, who likened her AFS interview to "being *interrogated*." Practices and experiences reminiscent of criminalization are widespread in this "reform" regime. A 2008 study found a strong correlation between highly punitive state-level penal policies and punitive TANF policies (Soss, Fording, and Schram 2008; see also Haney 2004).

Some clients responded with indignation or anger to these forceful institutional practices. But most learned, sometimes the hard way, to mute their feelings in the presence of authorities. In both the in-depth interviews and the telephone survey, however, complaints about perceived mistreatment or indignities were common. Adele Fenstermaker, a married white woman with a toddler, speaks for many in expressing anger about the treatment she experienced:

> They look at me as if I don't deserve it. As if I'm just trying to get something for free. And that makes me angry. I mean I could see if I wasn't trying to get anywhere, but I am....And it just really makes me mad.

Expressing anger or indignation or contesting policies or practices, however, can get a client branded as a "troublemaker" by workers who have the power to retaliate in many ways. Elana Heiser, a mixed-race woman in her early thirties, recounted how she learned to mute her anger in front of her worker. During one appointment, she expressed considerable anger toward her ex-husband, who was suing for custody, and at particular agency rules. Her worker warned that her behavior, that is, acting angry, could hurt her case. Heiser confronted her case manager, asking for empathy:

> And I flat-out asked them, Are my reactions—don't I have a right to be angry? "Well, yes. If I were in your situation I would be angry too." I said, then why don't you just take that into consideration? "Well, it's the way that you react. You get angry and start yelling"...I had every right to be mad. I had every right to be angry.

Heiser conveys her sense of injustice in the face of painful circumstances and disempowering negotiations with a powerful regulating institution. But her "right" to be angry was heavily constrained within an organization in which she has no power or authority, where others make the rules.

Lisa Dodson and Leah Schmalzbauer have argued that poor women, used to being suspect, employ "acts of strategic self protection," silencing their real beliefs and feelings and/or "telling [workers] what they want to hear" (2005:951). Ironically, the culture of compliance that helps to shield case managers from unpleasant interactions with their clients also inhibits the candid discussion or critique of policies by clients that could otherwise prompt some case managers to question the policies and practices they enact. But just because clients may learn to not *express* their opinions or feelings does not mean that they are not defiant. Their frustration and anger signal their discontent, their refusal to completely relinquish their own authority, and the staying power of their own perspectives in the face of the powerful culture of compliance.

When expressions of dissent are muted as a form of self-protection, it may be difficult to discern the potential counterhegemonic values and beliefs that often survive just below the surface of the culture of compliance. But these fissures exist. Under a relatively shallow veneer of consent, we found not only righteous anger but explicit critique of the new welfare regime. This brings us back to the beginning of this chapter—to the introductory statement by the client whose perspectives on welfare restructuring constitute alternative perspectives rarely taken seriously in the public dialogue about social policy. In the following section we discuss the counterhegemonic frameworks and alternative policy prescriptions offered, mainly by women, who yearn for economic security but are forced to bear the brunt of agency policies and practices from institutionally relatively powerless gendered and racialized class positions.

Counter Perspectives on Welfare Restructuring

Sally Reid is only one of the many women we interviewed whose perspectives on welfare restructuring differ substantially from the policy makers who mandate, the administrators who manage, and the workers who implement welfare "reform." She is a thirty-eight-year-old white single mother of three teenagers, who provides in-home care for her elderly grandmother. She has worked most of her adult life as a low-wage caregiver and received cash assistance for seven years when her children were much younger. At the time of the second interview in 1999, she was employed by private agencies doing mostly hospice work for which she earned seven to eight dollars an hour. Her hours were variable and she had no benefits. Her children were covered by OHP, but her own coverage was affected by her fluctuating income that sometimes put her just over the income cutoff for OHP. In this interview, she mused about her "daydreams" of economic stability:

> [T]hings that I daydream about is having a job. It seems like out of this world that I would ever have enough money to put down on a house. But that's what I daydream about. I daydream about…going to school…just hav[ing]…a good job, and to be able to just provide for my kids. Just, I guess, the American dream, the apple pie thing, the little white picket fence…I don't want a Mercedes. I don't want a speedboat…I've got a little…TV back here. That's fine. I've got cable. So I daydream about a house and being on the Internet and reliable transportation and medical.

Just being able to provide, and be happy and healthy and maybe you don't have to live large but to be able to enjoy things once in a while.

Reid's version of the "American Dream" is not striking it rich or owning luxuries. For her it is a better job, an education, health insurance, reliable transportation, and maybe home ownership. This is her image of escaping poverty, perhaps achieving economic security. But Reid perceives these goals as "daydreams," not as things she is positioned to get. Interestingly, Reid also used the vocabulary of daydreaming months later, during the second in-depth interview. This time she described as a "daydream" the belief by policy makers that welfare "reform" is producing self-sufficiency:

> You have all these seedlings and some of the seedlings are a little bit bigger and stronger. They still all need water and fertilizer. I feel like poverty just, it's a vicious cycle. I mean if you get your head above that water, then they're going to drop you.... You know they are going to let the air out of your lifejacket and you go back down to the bottom rung again.... You know we all are just kind of treading along. And maybe if that support [public assistance] is ongoing and continuous, that somebody is strong enough, truly strong enough to support themselves the way that they daydream that you are when they cut you off.

There is a lot packed into Reid's articulation of the difference between her experience and what policy makers imagine happens when they "cut [clients] off." Her choice of words and images constitute a very different image of welfare recipients and welfare, including her astute substitution of poverty (for welfare dependency) as the definition of the crux of the "vicious cycle" that social policies should be aiming to ameliorate. From her particular gendered and racialized class position—a white unpaid caregiver at home, a low-paid caregiver at a job that offers no health coverage, a female head of household with so many responsibilities further education is not viable and better jobs inaccessible, a client in an agency with policies designed to "cut off" clients before their economic circumstances promise any degree of economic security—she sees poverty, the employment practices she confronts, and a safety net full of holes as the real threats to her family's security.

Sally Reid is only one of the many women we interviewed whose perspectives on welfare restructuring differ substantially from the policy makers who mandate, the administrators who manage, and the workers who implement welfare "reform." They do not always articulate full-blown counterhegemonic arguments. Many accept some of the basic, as well as some of the most pernicious race- and gender-inflected assumptions of the dominant discourse. But anyone concerned with developing meaningful antipoverty polices, or with getting a fuller, more accurate picture of what welfare restructuring has meant for low-income families, has much to learn from these women whose lived experiences call into question, implicitly if not explicitly, the triumphant narrative of successful welfare "reform." For the remainder of the chapter, we explore how the clients we interviewed contest the hegemony of underlying ideological assumptions and the practical realities surrounding personal and social responsibility, education and mobility, motherhood and carework, poverty and inequality, and claims of "deservingness."

Personal and Social Responsibility

Welfare "reform" enshrines the doctrine of "personal responsibility." Almost to a person, the clients agreed with the value of personal responsibility. They expressed both their obligation and, usually, their desire to provide for their own families. They diverge from policy makers on two key points that concern responsibility: First, having been low-wage workers they know that many jobs do not pay wages sufficient to achieve self-sufficiency and usually lack key benefits that are essential to self-sufficiency (e.g., health insurance). Given this, they argue that the government has an obligation to help. They see themselves, and sometimes the other women who also depend on public assistance, as deserving of assistance because the circumstances they face are either beyond their control or because, whatever else, their children are needy and as mothers they are trying as hard as they can.

Sally Arnold, a single white mother who battled cancer (and ultimately died) while being subject to work-first mandates clung dearly to the goal of being self-sufficient. Arnold had an extensive job history in clerical work and accounting, but after her divorce and, especially, once she had a cancer diagnosis, her life spiraled out of control. She was earning $7.25 per hour but could not afford the health insurance premiums associated with her job, and as her chemotherapy progressed, she had to reduce her work hours. She was grateful for the help she got from AFS with Food Stamps, OHP, and child care, but her family's economic security was severely strained. She recognized that self-sufficiency was beyond her reach and her control:

> I don't like to ask for help. It embarrasses and upsets me…it makes me feel I'm not doing a good job of being self-sufficient or taking care of my family. Even though it's out of my control. I can't put food on the table for them. Or keep a roof over their heads.

Rhonda Long, a forty-five-year-old white, partnered mother, identifies an irony: policy makers can compel poor women to take "menial jobs," but they can't or *don't* require employers to pay living wages. She does not comprehend how forcing people to take dead-end, low-wage jobs will improve their lives:

> [T]he welfare department can't create jobs. I don't know how they're going to do that…force someone to pay more money for wages or—a lot of those jobs, they were just menial jobs where you wouldn't want to stay there. There was no future in those places. And there's no…insurance. I don't know why they thought that was some sort of improvement.

Tom Nelson, a white married male in his early forties, explicitly contrasted his definition of self-sufficiency with AFS's definition; he also resented that AFS forces two-parent families to rely on two low-wage jobs instead of one family-wage job:

> [T]he government's interpretation of self-sufficiency and my interpretation of self-sufficiency are…different.…What I understand as self-sufficiency is being able to provide for my family and have a certain standard of living. For me, that means if my wife chooses to stay home and be a mom, that is her choice.…What I perceive the government thinks is self-sufficiency is that she go get a job at $6 and hour and I go get a job at $6 an hour, and together we are making $12 an hour. And for them that's self-sufficiency. And for me it's not.

Nelson speaks from a (former) position of some privilege as a white man with a college degree and a long, varied work history. But he suffered a work injury that has left him with chronic back pain, and his family lives in a rural area with very limited job opportunities. Now, like most of the female heads of household we interviewed, he recognizes that the lack of family-wage jobs stands between his family and self- sufficiency. He was not the only one who lives in a community with a limited supply of decent jobs. And as another male recipient put it, "We can't all live in Portland!"

Education and Mobility

One of the most vehement criticisms of current Oregon welfare policy expressed by the women and men we interviewed was the illogic and unfairness of policies that denied poor clients access to postsecondary education or job training. Because Oregon's welfare rules did not allow most women to count these activities as fulfilling the stringent work requirements, they could not see how they would ever get ahead. Maya Bronson, a white single mother in her twenties with one daughter, worked at a convenience store earning about $1,000 a month. She wanted to go to college and become a pharmacist, and started along that path by taking some community college courses a couple of years before the study. But the stress of school, work, and single motherhood took a toll, and she had to leave school. When her daughter was a little older she told her case manager she was ready to try school again but was told "you get nothing if you go to school...We will have to take away all of your benefits." Bronson's reaction was anger and amazement:

> That made me so angry. I had a few things to say about that when I left there....You would think they would want you to go out there so you were able to eventually to get a job that would support you, take care of you...I expected some reward for going to school, you know, that is an accomplishment. That's an important step. And they say "no."

Bronson was one of the many women and men we interviewed who were frustrated by AFS's decision not to count education toward the work requirement for TANF and by the agency policy to not provide Food Stamps to full-time students. Yet 84 percent of the larger sample desired more education or training. Even some who were trying to complete high school faced problems. Lorraine Tenney, a nineteen-year-old Native American mother of a toddler, thought she had everything arranged to go back to school. Her employer at the gas station helped her fix her schedule so she could take a class, and Tenney thought she had gotten the go-ahead from her case manager to phase in cash assistance once she proved she could manage part-time work and the high school classes. But a month later her Food Stamps had been cut, and when she finally was able to reach her worker she found out that the worker had misunderstood and thought she had quit her job, and that she "felt that was irresponsible of you so we cut you off." Tenney explained to her worker that she *was* still working and that she had tried to follow her instructions, including making an effort to get an appointment:

> I am still working. I've got my pay stubs....You told me to go down to part-time and get everything going the way I need to and to try setting up a meeting with you. And I've been trying for a month now and you never returned my calls. And she said, "Well I have been busy." And I said, "Well look now where I am." And that's when everything went downhill for me.

There is little doubt in the larger culture, or among policy makers, about the value of postsecondary education for the general population. Thus, between the neoliberal welfare-to-work policies and the dramatically rising costs of higher education, low-income women face dim prospects for securing a college degree.[5]

And the assumption that low-income women are somehow different, that they can succeed in an increasingly tight labor market without educational credentials, simply on the basis of their hard work, is untenable (Jones-DeWeever and Gault 2006). Many recognized this and wanted to be able to pursue postsecondary education or vocational training as part of, not in addition to, their work requirements.

Motherhood and Care Work

Ideologically, welfare "reform," as it was designed by social conservatives, used the language of family values, especially the valorization of marriage, nuclear families, and marital childbearing, as a justification for contracting the rights of poor single mothers to prioritize and provide care for their children (Mink 1998). Those mothers who strayed beyond the traditional bonds of marriage and nuclear family formation were redefined by "work first" policies as breadwinners first. The logic policy makers used was to portray nonemployed single mothers as poor "role models" for their children, putting them "at risk" (as the discourse defines it) for poverty and welfare dependency because of a failure to embody the value of "work" (Oliker 1990, cited in Cancian and Oliker 2000). The unpaid labor in the home for which feminists so recently won some degree of social recognition has, with welfare reform, become discursively invisible, except among the worthy mothers who married well-paid male breadwinners.

The mothers we interviewed clearly felt caught between their multiple responsibilities, which we investigate in chapter 6, and various ideologies and values about motherhood. But many of them also adopted the agency rhetoric about the importance of modeling a strong work ethic for their children, consistent with the culture of work enforcement. Most echoed the sentiments of Janis Foster, a hairdresser and single white mother of two, who said:

> I think your children learn what they live…if they see things that are being, you know, done right, they'll know that's the way things are. That they need to grow up and do the same things. Work, and, that's what normal people do. Right? [laughs]

Foster, like others we discuss in greater depth in chapter 6, struggled mightily to try to balance her paid work and the unpaid care work her family needed. But, as other mothers said, this difficult combination of responsibilities often resulted in feeling that they did not have the time and energy to be the kinds of mothers they believed their children needed and deserved. When asked about balancing work and family, they tended to blame themselves for not being "good mothers," rather than looking to the limitations imposed on them by the labor market and agency practices. For example, Pam Reiss, a Native American mother of two, felt she did not always "manage it [this balancing act] well."

> It makes me feel like I am a bad mom sometimes because I don't get to spend the time with my kids, and the good quality time—I try to make the time that we have together the best I possibly can. But with me not being there sometimes I can feel them kind of like drifting further and further away, not having the respect for me to listen or mind or anything…and I come home so exhausted, and I try really hard not to bring home the problems of the day, but sometimes you can't help it.

Like Reiss, many felt beholden to a mothering discourse that assigned them full responsibility for producing well-adjusted children, regardless of their circumstances. Though seemingly conflicting, the expectations of good mothering worked hand in glove with the expectations that they should also serve as employed role models for their children. Women escaped stigma and signified as socially appropriate individuals with a healthy work ethic by aligning their actions with the culture of work enforcement, while the mothering discourse helped them to read their difficulties as their *own* inabilities to cope with balancing work and family. Thus, the two discourses worked in concert to individualize the struggles mothers encountered in the low-wage labor market, deflecting women's attention from the conditions under which they care for children and back on to how they, as mothers, are fulfilling narrowly defined ideological obligations as "good workers" and "good mothers."

Their commitment to motherhood pulses through the interviews. These parents, in many instances, refused to accept hegemonic understandings of their lives, conditions, and identities, developing counternarratives to commonsensical perceptions of those who live in poverty as neglectful mothers. They did this by insisting on the primacy of their roles as mothers in word, and, when possible, in deed.

Some also explicitly rejected the wisdom of Oregon's demand that a new mother is mandated to search for work and accept a paid job as soon as her infant is three months old. Connie Rounds believes mothers need more choice about when to return to work and whether to work full-time, adamant that "a [welfare] worker needs to be sensitive to that bond between the parent and child." Amy Manasoto, a thirty-five-year-old Asian American mother of four, including recently born twins, agreed. She has a college degree and had been an elementary school teacher and a housecleaner, but was at home with her children during the last interview, though she was struggling financially. She critiqued AFS policies as they affect the choices that mothers have to make:

> See, that's crazy…to suddenly be faced with, "Oh I HAVE to go to work. In order to get by, I have to leave my baby" probably to make not very much money.…[T]hree-month-old babies need to be with their moms. They need to be breast-feeding and, with, and bonding with their families.…I would think if you've got kids under five or six years old, you should be exempt from that…because before that—I mean, maybe she can't find good child care, or you don't know what kind of child care you're dropping your kid off to.…It's crazy. So, if you're working full-time, you come home and you're tired…you're not going to be the best parent that you could be. And you don't have very much time with them…I think in the long run, you're going to have less crime, more stable citizens, if those kids get to be raised by parents that are not freaking out because they don't have enough money and have to work ten hours a day.

Child care problems are particularly onerous for these families. Many of these women have strong reservations about the child care arrangements they often had to settle for. As we commented above, as much as they valued the Employment Related Day Care (ERDC) program that subsidized child care costs, quite a few mothers criticized the low reimbursement rates the state paid and the growing copayments they owed, both of which constricted their options for child care. They also wanted to see improvements to the many "hassles" involved with applying and reapplying for ERDC and getting payments to providers in a timely manner, things that position them to lose their child care.

While these mothers ultimately patch together resources and arrangements to the best of their abilities, as we will discuss in the next chapter, some of them think beyond their individual situations to make a claim on the state to play a much larger role in solving this problem. Rhonda Long, a forty-five-year-old white woman, advocated "government backed and funded" child care that could better guarantee children's safety:

> I think there ought to be somewhere in this state, in this whole United States, child care that is government backed and funded…a place that's safe where you could take your child, a big, safe center with a lot of people in it and monitoring and all that.

Long's suggestion is evidence that some women resist the goal of fully privatized social support that is a key element of neoliberal social policy. Moreover, as long as most low-income mothers have no paid maternity leave, TANF becomes the only viable economic alternative when they have babies. In the absence of universal family leave policies, poor women, and especially single parents, want and need public support.

Poverty and Inequality

Against the powerful discourses so widely integrated into the programs' design and implementation—which blame individual's "poor choices" or nonnuclear families for their poverty and economic insecurity—some women adopted an alternative framework, analyzing their circumstances in terms of structural constraint and the larger processes of social inequality. For example, Michelle Moran, a white single mother and former TANF recipient who works a full-time warehouse job to support herself and her nine-year-old daughter, suggests that her abusive ex-partner, the government, and the proclivity of employers to pay low wages to enrich themselves shape the economic hardship she faces, *not* her "poor choices":

> I didn't choose to be, I left an abusive relationship. Maybe the person I chose was wrong. But I didn't choose to be in the situation I'm in now.... It's very difficult.... You know the right people and can get into the right job to be, you know, not in poverty.... It's the, I don't know who they are, the government or the President or whatever that keeps the wages the way they are.... They don't pay people enough for their job.... Everything else goes up but the wage.... Because if they brought up the wage instead of giving themselves raises and making, you know, $100,000 a year.... Have them live like the average person lives. And they'd change their tune.

As a survivor of domestic violence, Moran makes clear she did not explicitly choose single parenthood; what she *chose* was safety for herself and her child. Poverty makes it difficult for low-income women to leave abusive situations, despite the fact that they experience higher rates of intimate partner violence than do middle-class women.[6] Women of color, who have higher rates of intimate partner violence than whites (Davis 2006), share this tough choice with white women, but their difficulties may be exacerbated by racism when they report it to authorities, including the police and welfare workers. The experience of having their stories be suspect or their reluctance to feed racist cultural stereotypes about "dangerous" men of color create more precarious and stressful circumstances to navigate when compared to the circumstances of white women.

Moran was not unusual in contesting individualistic explanations for dire economic circumstance, but she was more explicit than many others we interviewed in articulating a structural analysis of poverty and inequality. She understands that poor women lack the connections that others have to land better jobs and blames employers who enrich themselves at the expense of those whose wages they keep low. She is not sure exactly where to point the finger within government, but she realizes that policy makers help to "keep…wages the way they are."

Viola Prince, an African American child care worker we discussed earlier, articulated a class-based analysis about the differential rewards of "hard work" in this society.

> I am like, you see, any hard-working person at a law firm or at a corporate office…I am up early in the morning, and last night I didn't get to bed until one o'clock in the morning because I was up getting things prepared for the next day. So I am just like any hard-working person out there. I pay taxes like everyone else does.

Prince knows her perspective differs from many policy makers in pointing to the social forces that keep many people who are "trying their best" in poverty. That is why she supports government spending priorities that help poor families.

> There's a lot of people out there that are on welfare that are trying their best to get off welfare, but they can't.…And it's like society is keeping them in poverty.…Let's look at the things we're putting our money toward that we don't really need. And put it to work in something that we do need. I mean we've got people on the street that are hungry.…My thinking is not the ways the society thinks. You know what I am saying, the government?

Connie Rounds implicitly sees the negative effects of class polarization, leading her to make what she sees as a radical policy suggestion. She believes that universal health care is warranted not only because of the desperate need for unaffordable medications but also because wealth is accruing at the expense of those who are "struggling":

> I mean I know it sounds like socialized medicine, but it just seems like everyone should have access to medical care and medications.…Medications are incredibly expensive. I think that's an outrage…they probably don't need to be that high. I mean, maybe I'm misinformed, but I just feel like there's probably people getting rich off of medications while there's people struggling to live because they have to have them.

Rounds is not "misinformed." But her caveat ("I know it sounds like socialized medicine") speaks volumes about the lack of an accessible alternative to the neoliberal and conservative ideologies that permeate the media and policy discussions. The absence of significant counterperspectives that analyze gender, race, and class dynamics as foundational to the U.S. economic and social order deprives everyone of alternative explanations for the inequalities disadvantaging more and more Americans.

But lacking a full-blown analysis of structural inequality or suggestions for systematic change in workplaces and economic and social policy did not keep the women we interviewed from recognizing major fallacies with current welfare policies and practices, many of which we have discussed above. Rarely did respondents feel they had a full grasp of welfare policy, writ large; their concerns tended to be concrete and the result of the problems they faced in practice. While as a group they were articulate about the conditions they faced, they were clearer about what was *wrong* than about how to fix it. In the absence of structural solutions to the nation's degrading supply of good jobs (a problem few of the rest of us know how to solve either), they had three main kinds of concerns: (1) removing barriers to education and training so they could get better jobs; (2) changing welfare-to-work policies that channel and threaten people into having to accept "bad" jobs; and (3) expanding Food Stamp and OHP eligibility and child care and housing subsidies so that those in these jobs have and retain access to public assistance to help make up the gap between wage income and household need.

The need to fix the glaring holes in the social safety net was one of the most common concerns and solutions offered by this group. The criticism that welfare policies themselves constitute a significant barrier for low-income families working themselves out of poverty by reducing (or ending) benefits such as Food Stamps, OHP, and housing and Employment Related Day Care subsidies before family's incomes replaced the value of these benefits in higher wages. This is what Sally Reid (above) referred to as the agency letting "air out of [her] life jacket." More than 200 of the 756 respondents in the telephone survey and almost all of those we interviewed in-depth raised this as a key problem with social welfare policy. Getting a raise often triggers benefit losses that far outweigh the wage gains, as Sally Arnold, describes:

> Every time I get a raise in pay or a bonus they make me pay more child care and cut my Food Stamps. Instead of letting me get ahead. And it ends up costing me more.

Pamela Stewart, a white single mother of two children who works in retail, suggests that "It's important when you are moving up not to take things way from you so fast. It makes people feel like they are being punished for doing better." They also advocate a more realistic income cutoff for Food Stamps and OHP, higher child care and housing subsidies, and a schedule of benefit reductions with growing incomes that are more gradual. Along the same lines, they advocate lower copayments for OHP and ERDC to make these programs more affordable, and, therefore, valuable.

Claiming Deservingness

Perhaps the most insistent challenge clients have to the prevailing discourse is their self-identity as deserving of public assistance; they contest the presumption that they are bad mothers or morally wanting, that they are lazy or out to cheat the system. In addition to the concrete changes they recommend in particular policies, they constitute a strong chorus of voices maintaining the importance of treating clients with respect and dignity. In response, to the negative treatment these women experience from workers, clients define themselves as deserving, referencing their own work histories or the circumstances that landed them in "hard times," explaining how they are trying to get off public assistance, and claiming as legitimate their "real" need for help.[7]

Susan Wells, a white single mother, only challenged her internalized cultural stereotypes about welfare when her own dire circumstances sent her to the welfare office in need of help. Becoming a client made her reconsider the false cultural stereotypes and led, ultimately, to her seeking a job at AFS:

> I think it wasn't until I was a client and I needed it and I realized that not everybody there is just trying to get a dollar they don't deserve, is when I decided I wanted to work there. Because I wanted to help people like myself who had gotten into a situation and didn't have any place to turn.

Tamara Ryan, an African American woman, also mentioned the almost requisite concern about clients who might be "working the system." But she believes this is not true of "most" TANF recipients, who, as researchers have documented (Spalter-Roth et al. 1995), cycle on and off welfare because of getting, then losing jobs:

> I'm pretty sure there are a lot of people like myself who'd be working and then end up having to go back on welfare to get cash assistance to get whatever. It's like a little circle, you do good but then you fall, or you get fired, or you get laid off or whatever.

Despite their strong sense of deservingness, many did not extend the presumption of deservingness to all, or most, TANF recipients. Of the seventy-five women and three men in the sample we interviewed in person, more than one-third made a negative reference to other welfare recipients. White respondents were more likely than women of color to deploy negative images of other recipients of public assistance in order to compare themselves favorably and justify their own deservingness, and some, a minority, but a significant minority, actively perpetuated the racist dominant discourse. Recipients seen as undeserving—"takers," as one respondent called them—were seen as unwilling to work and "milking the system." Commonly those who allegedly stayed on welfare beyond when they "really needed it" were blamed for making it hard for those who *are* really trying or really needy because they are responsible for widespread social perceptions that welfare recipients abuse the system. Sally Arnold, who is white, contrasts her legitimate need against those who allegedly abuse the system:

> A lot of them just don't want to work. They want to be on the system.... They milk the system. I'm not one of those people, but I take the brunt of it for the people that do milk the system.

She continued by drawing on and reproducing the pervasive racialized discourse that defines immigrants, in particular, as unfairly drawing on welfare:

> I wish there was a way to weed out the people that get it that shouldn't... I hate to say it, but most of them are migrant people. I have nothing against Hispanics, different nationalities, as long as they come here to work. But when they come here and abuse our system and take it away, then when people that have lived here all their lives can't get it, that's not fair.

Sally's perpetuation of the undeserving racialized welfare "Other" legitimizes the intense surveillance practices (a "way to weed out") that welfare recipients are often subjected to.

Erin White, a nineteen-year-old single mother who lives in an agricultural community in eastern Oregon, received TANF because her wages from a fast-food job were so poor, also believes that "the people that need that welfare can't get it because of the people that abuse it." To prove her point she complained of long waits for services made worse by her perception that immigrant clients were put ahead of her in line to see a worker:

> Well, a family of like ninety, hundred Hispanics came in and they all went before me. And I was the first one there, and it's supposed to be first come, first served, and I was mad. So I stood up and I said, "What, you have to be Mexican in this town just to get anything done?"

While most of the references to illegitimate recipients of public assistance named Latino immigrants, respondents in other areas explicitly referred to "Russian," "Asian," or (Vietnamese) "boat people."

A second set of negative images of undeserving recipients came in the form of gendered, often racially coded, references to promiscuous and/or fecund women, echoing the racist dominant discourse that focuses on African American women. These kinds of statements were articulated, for example, by two white women who repeated the kinds of judgments opponents of welfare often lob at African Americans: "babies having babies and where's the family unit gone?" and "people that just keep having kids just to keep on it…eight, nine kids, it's ridiculous." Delores Johnson, a white single mother, expressed her anger at being unable to get Food Stamps because she wanted to go to school by railing against the fact that welfare was willing to support "drug addicts and the whores and the prostitutes that are out there, you know, and the wife beaters and the women who abuse their children," but not her or others who were trying "to get ahead."

In the absence of a welfare rights movement that has the potential to demonstrate both that judgmental treatment is a shared negative experience for all women *and* that racial disparities do differentiate agency treatment of clients—for example, the higher rates of sanctioning of African American clients and that they are less likely to be referred for education and training (Kalil, Seefeldt, and Wang 2002; Gooden 2003)—low-income women and men have limited access to research or information gained through working together that would dispel the false stereotypes and buttress a collective claim to deservingness. Counter-hegemonic ideologies may well be generated by the disjuncture between received ideas and lived experience, but these alternative frameworks are most robust when they are embedded in a systematic understanding of the extent and dynamics of social inequality. Given that the deeply entrenched legacies of race and gender discrimination in the labor force continue to help shape rates of employment, jobs, and differential wages and opportunities for upward mobility, welfare policies that channel the poor into a labor force laced with unequal opportunity help guarantee that women of color will have the hardest time finding family-sustaining jobs. In turn, their continuing higher rates (and extremity) of poverty will further racialize the demographics of the TANF caseload, a pattern that has, nationally, worsened markedly since 1996 (Schram 2006).

Even without benefit of this kind of analysis, clients clamor for better treatment, based simply on their sense of fairness and human dignity. They want agency staff to extend to them more support and trust, better communication and more information, and less—far less—coercive treatment. Welfare restructuring exposes them to less protection from market forces that dramatically curtail their economic opportunities and consign them to a daily grind that offers little hope of escaping poverty. This is not a story of welfare policy success. We now turn to experiences in the labor market as we conclude our examination of how poor women's lived experiences caution against facile evaluations of welfare reform success.

LIFE AFTER WELFARE
The Costs of Low-Wage Employment

Delores James, a white single mother in her early twenties, was raising her school-aged child in an urban community. Like most other women and men we interviewed, her relationship to welfare, employment, and family was fluid, changing as she tried to make ends meet while being what she considered to be a "good mother," coping with the trying conditions of poverty. For six years she received varying combinations of TANF, Food Stamps, Oregon Health Plan (Medicaid), and child care assistance either while she was working or between jobs. At the time of our final interview with her, she was unemployed and had moved in with her own mother, with whom she had a conflicted relationship. She explained her family's transition to paid work in the following way:

> Delores James [DJ]: Before you went to work, and you were being a welfare tramp—that's the best way to put it—you were miserable, you were totally embarrassed with yourself, you hated your life, and you took it out on your kid.
>
> JW (interviewer): So this is you? Are you talking about yourself here?
>
> DJ: This is me…I got a job. I felt much better about myself…I was able to afford to take my daughter skating…movies,…I'm not paying the bills still…I live with somebody still. I'm still a dependent.…But I'm independent enough to go out and buy my daughter, you know, a new pair of tights, every day of the week if she needs them…
>
> JW: So…you're feeling good about yourself?
>
> DJ: I was feeling good about myself.

JW: And how does that play out in your relationship with [your daughter]?

DJ: Financially, she liked it. Emotionally, she hated it.... I'm back to not having a job, but I'm not on welfare. I will not go back. I'm still a dependent, with ... what? Roughly 500 a month, if that.... My daughter is much happier emotionally that I am at home, and she's starting to learn the concept of money now.

James's story begins to reveal the more complex realities facing low-income families that we examine in this chapter. Whether the many hardships, constrained choices, and sacrifices they experience are intended or unintended consequences of "reform," they are important aspects of the story of welfare restructuring and the dismantling of important strands of the U.S. social safety net. In this chapter we trace the many costs of welfare restructuring for the families we studied, looking at both the material consequences of "reform" and how these policies have helped to reshape family relations and dynamics, the social relations of distribution in society, and a redefinition of women as individuals and citizens.

Life in the Low-Wage Labor Market

The jobs former and current public assistance recipients secured offered them numerous benefits. For some, employment gave them increased self-esteem, new feelings of competence, time off from trying teenagers, increased adult interaction, less stress surrounding making ends meet (but more around arranging work and family), and the reduction of stigma, consistent with other studies which have linked these gains to more positive parenting.[1] However, their lives were complicated in ways that often undermined their families' long- and short-term well-being.

Mainstream discourses about welfare restructuring rarely raise concerns about the shortage of living wage or "good" jobs. Instead, the focus is on the improvements in income that result from even low-wage jobs accompanied by other income such as the Earned Income Tax Credit. Because welfare benefits have been pegged at very low levels in states such as Oregon, as we have previously discussed, almost any job results in higher income than welfare benefits. In Oregon, and nationally, the available jobs have low wages in an economy generating relatively few well-paying jobs but an abundance of low-paying ones. The Northwest Job Gap study documented that approximately 76 percent of all jobs and 77 percent of all job openings in Oregon paid less than the living wage for a single adult with two children (Northwest Policy Center 2001). Nationally, the low-wage service sector is the fastest growing sector of the labor market today

(Mishel, Bernstein, and Boushey 2003). At issue is the structure of the job market and the quality of jobs.

Nationally between half and more than three-quarters (depending on the state) of the people who left TANF during the period of dramatic welfare caseload decline in the mid- to late 1990s were employed when they left.[2] Oregon mirrored other states in that about two of every three welfare leavers had jobs (Acker et al. 2001; Loprest 2001), mostly low-paying jobs in the gender-segregated service sector with highly limited opportunities for vertical movement (Boushey et al. 2001; Cancian et al. 2002). At the time of our second survey, the most common jobs were medical or health care aide, general office clerk, child care worker, general laborer, food service worker, and retail worker. Women more often reported employment in health or personal care work, general office work, child care, retail, and food service; men were more likely to be employed in general labor, janitorial services, agricultural work, automobile repair, and heavy equipment operation.

Being employed in such jobs, even full-time, meant that these workers earned wages so low that almost half—48 percent—of those we surveyed had family incomes below the official federal poverty line two years after they left TANF or Food Stamps. In real numbers, the average monthly take-home pay for respondents at the time of our first telephone interview was $995.60, rising slightly six months later to $1,016.32. Using a measure that calculates what a true "living wage" would be in Oregon ($2,835 per month for a single parent with two children), 98 percent of the families we surveyed made at or less than this wage (Northwest Policy Center 2001). Gender and race affected wages. Women, on average, earned less than men: $939 versus $1,325 twelve to eighteen months after leaving assistance, and $966 versus $1,348 twenty-one to twenty-four months after leaving assistance. Latino families had the lowest average wages of all racial groups and were more likely to be in poverty than any other racial group.

This echoes other research that has found gender and race inequities among U.S. workers throughout the labor force. For example, Sarah Burd-Sharps, Kristen Lewis, and Eduardo Borges Martins (2008) show continuing gender and race wage differentials that constitute the hard realities the families we studied confront (table 2).

Jobs, of course, provide more than wages. They either do or do not offer benefits and family friendly or flexible work environments. Using data about the jobs held by the women and men in our study, we constructed a measure of "good" jobs and "bad jobs."[3] Using conservative criteria we defined a "good job" as one that was at least thirty-five hours per week, had monthly take-home pay over $1,200 (this is just above the poverty level for a three-person family), had

Table 2   Median 2005 Earnings for Full-Time U.S. Workers by Race and Gender

WORKER GROUP	MEDIAN EARNINGS ($)
White men	37,269
Asian men	37,035
Asian women	26,138
African American men	26,086
American Indian men	24,315
White women	23,388
Latino men	22,471
African American women	20,915
American Indian women	17,589
Latino women	16,147

Source: Data from Burd-Sharps, Lewis, and Martins (2008), 162.

predictable shifts, and offered sick leave, paid vacation, and health insurance. The majority of jobs held by the women we interviewed were "bad" jobs using this measure. Nearly 87 percent of the jobs held by interviewees almost two years after leaving welfare lacked one or more of the characteristics of a "good job."

The jobs held by the women and the few men we interviewed after they left public assistance in early 1998 were fundamentally similar to the kinds of jobs most held before their recent exit or diversion from public assistance. All but a tiny percentage of them had previously worked for wages and most had held a number of jobs, including some who had lengthy job tenure in a particular job. The architects of welfare "reform" portray welfare-to-work as transforming welfare-dependent women into disciplined, productive, self-sufficient breadwinners. But in reality most welfare and Food Stamp leavers in Oregon already had work histories, albeit mostly in the low-wage labor force they were back in.[4]

The Promise of Self-Sufficiency versus the Reality of Economic Insecurity and Hardship

The promise of self-sufficiency was heralded as the crowning achievement of welfare reform nationally and in Oregon. Get a job, policy makers declared, and you will fulfill the moral requisite of personal responsibility and your family will be on its way toward self-sufficiency. The problem is that the rhetoric does not translate to reality. Low-wage jobs do not lead to self-sufficiency, nor do they allow most single mothers to "make ends meet" in a sustainable manner (Edin and Lein 1997). This was the case before welfare "reform" and it remains true today.[5] Having to depend on low-wage work leaves millions of families facing a combination of job insecurity, inadequate household income, long hours of work, unsatisfactory child care arrangements, and lack of health insurance, sick leave, or retirement benefits.

Thus, over and over we found families struggling mightily to make ends meet. Commonly they scrambled to pay their bills. Three-quarters of families we surveyed reported that they had difficulty paying their bills at our first point of contact, twelve to fifteen months after their exit or diversion from TANF or Food Stamps. Six to nine months later, even more of them, 82 percent, reported that they had difficulty paying their basic bills. Thirty-eight percent of the sample was trying to dodge calls from collection agencies. Tight budgets meant more than anxiety; they forced difficult choices. Between a quarter and a half of the sample at the first survey either put off needed medical care, had their telephone disconnected, skipped meals to stretch their food budgets, or turned to a soup kitchen or got a food box to help feed their families, while smaller proportions dealt with utility disconnects, repossession of their cars, or evictions (table 3). While the numbers who faced such difficulties decreased somewhat by the second survey (see table 3), economic hardship and its consequences remained all too real for many families. Moreover, these tough choices were at a time when Oregon's economy was relatively strong, before the deep recession and jobless recovery of the early twenty-first century.

Table 3 Economic Hardship as Measured by Coping Strategies for TANF and Food Stamp Leavers and Diverted in Oregon 1998–2000

STRATEGY	RESPONDENTS REPORTING IN 1ST SURVEY (%)	RESPONDENTS REPORTING IN 2ND SURVEY (%)
Ate at a soup kitchen or got a food box	42	25
Didn't go to doctor or purchase needed medical supplies	27	23
Telephone disconnected	25	10
Skipped meals	24	17
Utilities turned off	12	6
Vehicle repossessed	7	3
Evicted or did not pay rent	5	3
Kept children home from school until clothes or supplies could be purchased	3	3

Source: Acker et al. 2001, 60–63.

Hardships like these were still common even three and a half to four years after our initial contacts. Interviews conducted with a subsample of thirty women in 2001 and 2002 found just over half still experiencing such significant hardship that they were forced to forgo medical care, to visit a food bank, to deal with their utilities being turned off, or to go without food. For example, Jenny Nall, a white mother of one who worked in retail and was attending college, told us in the last in-depth interview that medical care was "the worst stress in [her] life right now" and that her elementary school–aged son was "not getting to the doctor as many times as he should." Others told us that they "have to be dying" to go to the doctor or that they were fortunate enough to avoid getting sick.

In an effort to make ends meet, many continued to rely on benefits from Adult and Family Services. AFS data indicate that at some point during the two years of the main study, fully 90 percent of our telephone sample used Food Stamps, 87 percent relied on the Oregon Health Plan (OHP), and 42 percent used Employment Related Day Care (ERDC). Fifty-four percent of those who had been categorized as TANF diverted in our study experienced enough financial difficulty that they received cash assistance again in the eighteen months following their 1998 diversion. Of those who began the study as TANF leavers, 24 percent returned to TANF during the two years of the study. Many respondents who tried to get back on TANF reported many of the same reasons that lead most poor families to apply (table 4).

Under these conditions, self-sufficiency was elusive for many families. Former clients did not turn a corner to financial security once they relied primarily on wages instead of (or in combination with) welfare because basic living expenses far outstripped what they were able to earn in the low-wage labor force. As we

Table 4 Reasons Given for Reapplying for TANF during Study Period

REASONS[a]	REPORTED BY REAPPLICANTS ORIGINALLY CLASSIFIED AS TANF DIVERTED (%)	REPORTED BY REAPPLICANTS ORIGINALLY CLASSIFIED AS TANF LEAVERS (%)
Income too low to support a family	59	72
Lost job	39	29
Medical problem for self or family member	22	37
Pregnant or just had a baby	12	14
Recently separated or divorced	12	20
Attempting to escape from domestic violence	8	9

[a] Respondents were able to choose more than one reason.

mentioned, of the thirty women with whom we sustained research contact over three and a half to four years, 40 percent reported that they still struggled to make ends meet. Over half reported hardship in recent months, and 40 percent were still or recently reliant on Food Stamps, ERDC, OHP, and/or housing subsidies. Four others told us they were planning to reapply for Food Stamps in an effort to help feed their families.

Though making ends meet was precarious for the majority of families, it was especially difficult for families with acute or chronic health problems that often landed them in very difficult financial straits. Former recipient Connie Rounds' experience brings together three of these destabilizing conditions as just one of many troubling stories we heard—changes in public assistance benefits, health issues, and debt. Rounds, whom we discussed in chapter 5, left TANF when she secured a half-time position as a certified nursing assistant in a residential facility for the elderly. Because she worked part-time, she did not qualify for health benefits through her employer and, instead, relied on the Oregon Health Plan. When she was not working, Rounds worked toward reclaiming her certification as a licensed practical nurse, which she had lost during a long chronic illness.

At one point in our first study, in order to cover an employee shortage, Rounds' boss instituted mandatory overtime. She complied to keep her job, but soon found that she had been cut off OHP because she earned $10 over the eligibility limit in the previous month. Shortly thereafter, Rounds' medical exam uncovered a suspicious breast lump. Assuming that she would requalify for OHP when her income dropped, Rounds grappled with putting off a surgical biopsy and lived with the fear. She eventually decided to have the biopsy, which, to her great relief, came up negative but put her back $3,000. In the midst of the cancer scare, she struggled to pay for medications (normally covered by OHP) to control the pain brought on by a chronic illness. Monthly, she decided between buying medication that helped with the pain and allowed her to work or paying basic expenses such as food, the electric bill, and car insurance. During this period she sought and received help from AFS with her electric bill and car insurance. She considered increasing her hours or finding a new job, but feared that she would not finish her licensed practical nursing recertification course, which she saw as her ticket to a higher paying job.

Rounds' experiences illustrate common barriers to the ability of families to make ends meet. A change in earnings affects one's eligibility for public programs, which many low-wage workers rely on to supplement their pay. A small raise—even one as small as twenty-five cents an hour—can result in the loss of a critical housing subsidy, child care assistance, Medicaid, or Food Stamps, unexpectedly setting women back hundreds of dollars each month. Kim Smith, a white single mother of two children who worked as a cocktail waitress, explains further this irony:

> Even though you get a dollar raise an hour…it knocks your copay for your day care up, your copay for your medical up, and your Food Stamps down…and your rent up…that dollar an hour cost you three bucks an hour…the more you make, the more they skyrocket everything and take everything away…so, you end up having less. When I got my raise I told (my boss) I didn't really need one. Because it wasn't going to make a difference anyway.

Like Smith, it is not uncommon for low-wage workers still reliant on public assistance to forgo raises or working more hours in order to retain safety net benefits that were worth more than slightly higher incomes.

Connie Rounds was only one of a significant number of people we interviewed who became mired in debt when they were cut off from public assistance. Debt breeds more debt as utilities are shut off and require additional payment for reconnection, late payments accumulate, and people turn to high-interest lenders such as payday loan companies to make ends meet. Financially strapped families are forced to choose between, for example, purchasing food or the pain medication that allows them to work, rent or transportation to work, or medical care for children or the water bill. Health problems are frequently the catalyst for spiraling debt. For others, going without health insurance either because an employer does not provide it or because premiums are unaffordable, coincides with illness, an accident, or the worsening of a chronic health problem and worsening debt.

Some individuals in this study might have been able to secure disability benefits through Supplemental Security Income (SSI) before eligibility for this program was also tightened in recent years. Now some of the poor have much reduced means of basic support even when they are quite ill. Irene Miller, a white mother of three adult children in her early forties, lost eligibility for TANF when her youngest child turned eighteen. Although she had worked for years as a cafeteria aide, often while on cash assistance, a chronic pulmonary condition and other health problems had left her too weak to work when she ended up in this study. She was (barely) surviving on about $300 a month from Senior and Disabled Services, a Food Stamps allotment of $125 a month, and OHP. But this combination of resources confines her to a tiny, moldy trailer; she is always behind on her bills; and she now suffers from depression. For over four years she and her physician have been trying to get her qualified for SSI. In an era when public assistance is shrinking and welfare agencies focus on promoting employment, women like Irene Miller are stark reminders that neoliberal dictates about privatization, reliance on the market, and self-sufficiency fail to account for people who cannot work and who live without any degree of dignity or security under the new conditions of public assistance.

(The Myth of) Job Mobility

Policy makers marketed welfare reform on the promise of job mobility, presuming that employment would ultimately allow women to achieve job mobility so that they would, at some point, be able to support their families without public assistance. Meaningful job mobility, however, was relatively rare among the women (and the few men) we studied. Few avenues upward existed; when they did exist, they offered increased responsibilities but marginal wage gains. Additionally, though nearly half of the employed reported that they saw opportunities for mobility in their jobs, many also reported that family obligations would or had thwarted their efforts to take advantage of these ladders.

Participants in the study were fairly split in their perceptions of the mobility available to them, but perceptions differed from realities. Donna Murphy, a single white mother of one who worked in group homes and special vocation programs, saw little room for upward mobility:

> It was frightening because I had a full-time job and knew how much I was making. It was the same every day, and I hated it. I didn't know where my income was going to come from but I couldn't do this anymore. There was no room for advancement. It was terrible.

Murphy was part of the 55 percent of our in-depth sample who felt stymied by the lack of opportunities in their current jobs. However, 45 percent of the survey sample reported that they did perceive opportunities for advancement in their jobs; 38 percent reported that they were satisfied with the potential for a raise or promotion that their jobs offered, while 34 percent were not satisfied with the potential for a raise or promotion (27 percent did not comment on this aspect because they were not employed). Those who felt more positive about their opportunities for advancement tended to work in public-sector jobs, growing private-sector firms, or unionized workplaces. Among those who felt they had limited opportunities were agricultural and food service workers, health aides, retail cashiers, service station attendants, and, often, workers in rural areas. Union members were considerably more likely to describe themselves as more satisfied with the potential for wage or position mobility than nonunion members.

Though nearly half of the in-depth sample reported that they could imagine advancing with their current employer and over a third of the survey sample described themselves as satisfied with their opportunities for wage increases or promotion, our data suggest that such mobility was relatively exceptional. The interviews with the subsample of thirty women revealed that three and a half to four years later, only three individuals (10 percent) had experienced any job mobility.

Potential for mobility was hindered for some because the job search requirements of AFS' JOBS program left clients believing they had no other choice but to take jobs with limited or no opportunities for advancement. Some took the first jobs that they were offered because they were told they would be denied benefits if they turned a job offer down. What mobility we observed generally looked like the conditions in which Ellen Durant and Darcy Williams worked. Durant and Williams, both white mothers of two, had worked their way up to assistant managers at a convenience store and a gas station store, respectively. They earned $7.00 and $8.50 an hour, respectively. Both worked a great deal of overtime, sometimes racking up as many as sixty hours per week. Williams was on-call twenty-four hours a day to troubleshoot issues at the store. Durant worked erratic shifts due to staffing shortages; in any given week, she would be required to work day, swing, and/or graveyard shifts, sometimes back-to-back, exhausting her and exacerbating her health problems. Both lamented that they had little time for their families and were experiencing difficulties with their children, aggravated by long hours at work. Williams had been told that she would be able to reduce her hours and hire additional workers when the store began making more money. Similarly, Durant's employer tied the promise of a raise to greater sales:

> Right now, I'm making seven an hour, you know, until the store starts making more money...the store has to make more money before I can get a raise....So, and I'm influencing quite a bit of the customers into coming back a lot. Our sales are up.

Job mobility in low-wage jobs tended to be more beneficial to employers, often offering employees opportunities for more responsibility but not necessarily pay commensurate with that responsibility. Some "promotions" were merely additional duties without an accompanying raise. Such was the case with Lily Cantwell, a white mother of three, who was promoted from desk person to lead desk person at a large retail outlet, a position that required her to supervise fellow employees, but did not offer her higher pay.

Many mothers reported that they could not realistically accommodate the demands of the job ladders that they thought were available. They believed they would be unable to fulfill the time obligations required given their family responsibilities and the resources available to them. For example, Amber Alexander, a white mother of a preschooler, worked as a cook during the first study and in the deli of a grocery outlet in the second. When asked if she could move up with her current employer, she replied,

> I don't want to do that job. They call you—somebody calls in sick, if you can't find somebody to come in you have to go in no matter what's going on in your life. I don't want that, they're calling me all the time, questions and I don't know, it's just a lot of responsibility that maybe if I was single—if I was single it would be a good job. But being that I'm a single mom it's not a good job for me.

Education represented another arena in which women were compelled to curb their long-term security for their short-term well-being. With a few rare exceptions, those who were pursuing an education, or had pursued an education in the past, put off occupational tracks that offered wages that would have been more likely to allow them to escape poverty. Hence, women in our study opted for short-term training programs that prepared them to become, for example, hairdressers, phlebotomists, or certified nursing assistants, rather than pursuing two- or four-year degrees. This strategy enabled them to move quickly back into the workforce full-time to support their families, but it also kept them in the low-wage sector of the labor market.

Kim Smith, the cocktail waitress and mother of two introduced earlier, exemplifies this trend. She began college with the intention of pursuing a four-year nursing degree and eventually becoming a doctor. As she began to more fully understand the time commitment, financial sacrifice, and toll this was having on her family, she downsized her plans to a two-year degree as an emergency medical technician (EMT). She would be able to begin supporting her family sooner but with considerably less income than she could earn as a nurse.

> I was going to go through the nursing program....But...it's too far off to where I can work. And I'm sick of—now that my scholarship's up at school, I have no money that I'm so far behind in bills and stuff, you know. So I'm going through the EMT program, so that I can work and go to school both, and have actually some money....My goal is eventually to get into medical school—eventually.

By the third interview, she was beginning to see this goal as unrealistic. Her mother fell acutely ill, leaving her in the middle of the semester without the free child care she relied on. She dropped out of school temporarily and then had to repay $1,800 in educational grants. She considered herself nearly too old (she was twenty-four) and hesitated to put her children through the strain that attending school and working would wreak on their family: "It's too much school and it's too long for them to be, for us to be tight on money and me to be stressed out going to school." When we last spoke with her three and a half years after leaving welfare, Smith remained out of school, working full-time as a cocktail waitress with the hope that she would be able to save enough to pay off her educational debt and resume the EMT program.

Low-income mothers like the women described above had few institutional supports to assist them in pursuing their educational objectives and securing more financially viable futures. In many cases, women were forced, by necessity, to relinquish the educational and occupational opportunities available to them. Parenting responsibilities and a lack of resources kept them entrenched in low-paying jobs, even when they could see, and had the motivation to pursue, paths out of their predicaments. Our data suggest that the potential for mobility, which served as a key component of welfare reform's foundational argument, is faulty. Not only do few opportunities for mobility exist, as our data and national data attest, but when they do exist, women are often too constrained by their circumstances to fully take advantage of them.

Unemployment and Nonemployment after Welfare

Consistent with national data, a sizeable proportion of our sample was not working at some point during our studies: 34 percent and 28 percent at the first and second telephone survey, respectively.[6] Between 1998 and 2000 Oregon ranked within the top ten states for its relatively high unemployment rate,[7] with an economy rebounding after the bottom fell out of the fishing, timber, and agricultural sectors. The unemployed were individuals with varied experiences, which nonetheless intersect in a common set of socioeconomic conditions: a lack of "good" jobs, restricted safety nets, and an ideological terrain that valorizes work and serves to "disappear" the experiences of the nonemployed.

A closer look at those who were unemployed in our sample refutes assumptions about the work ethic and histories of the once welfare reliant. Two-thirds of those not employed told us that they wanted to work (the other third reported that they were home because they were keeping house). Nearly all with whom we spoke had employment histories; only *3 percent* of the unemployed respondents had never worked. At the second telephone survey, nearly one-third of the unemployed had worked within the last six months.

Very few participants in our study became chronically unemployed after leaving welfare. Those who did remain unemployed can be categorized as people desperately in need of a safety net, individuals with intractable mental health issues, learning disabilities and/or physical issues, and/or exceedingly complicated life circumstances, people falling through the cracks of the safety net. They included people such as Vicki Jones, a white divorced mother in her early twenties with mental health issues and a learning disability. When we met Jones she reported that she was suicidal and having anxiety attacks. She had worked in the past but had difficulty meeting employers' expectations, not infrequently resulting in her being let go. She told us, "I want to work but I'm so scared people are going to put me down. Because I want to tell them I learn a little slower and I'm afraid they won't hire me." Dealing with her mental health issues and learning disability without adequate support had left her with diminished self-esteem: "I'm always feeling like a failure, and I'm no good and I'm not smart enough."

Those who were unemployed were not a homogeneous group. Respondents reported sundry reasons for being out of the labor force (table 5). Their stories were as divergent as those of Freda Perez, a disabled Latina in her fifties with grown children, and Lily Cantwell, a white mother in her thirties with three young children. During the course of our study, Perez suffered from a debilitating health condition that left her unable to work in jobs for which she had experience—agricultural and cannery work—though she was eager to work. She and her husband subsisted on Food Stamps and help from relatives. She cared for her four-year-old grandson full-time. Cantwell, fortunate enough to rely on the wages of her partner, was unemployed because she took seven months off to be home with her newborn child during the nearly four years we had contact with her. Though financially comfortable, she returned to work to supplement her family's income and to "escape" the kids.

As Cantwell's example suggests, unemployment was not a static condition; in fact, the term *unemployment* is a misnomer for describing those studied, one implying a fixed state *in opposition to* employment. The "unemployed" we studied could more accurately be described as experiencing periods of both planned

Table 5 Reasons Given by Unemployed Respondents for Being out of the Labor Force

REASON	AT 1ST SURVEY (%)	AT 2ND SURVEY (%)
Keeping house	36	33
Looking for work	23	20
Unable to work due to disability	15	19
Going to school	12	11
Unable to work for some reason other than disability[a]	5	4
Temporarily laid off	4	1
Retired/not looking for employment/volunteering	4	11

[a] For example, caring for a sick or disabled family member, lack of access to reliable transportation, child care problems.

and unexpected *non*employment, intermingled with employment. With a few exceptions, people tended to move in and out of work as their life circumstances dictated. Mostly, the unemployed were experiencing situations similar to those described to us by Margaret Lowery, a white single mother of a preschooler. Lacking paid maternity leave, Lowery quit her job at a discount retail store just before giving birth to her daughter and went on TANF. As Lowery was searching for work when her child was three months old, her mother fell seriously ill. Caring for her mother derailed Lowery's employment plans for another six months, time she used to volunteer in an AFS-sponsored Work Experience position. She then worked in a human service agency, subsidized under JOBS Plus. When the placement ended and the agency was not able to hire her because of budgetary constraints, she began looking for work again. Again, her mother fell ill and Lowery went back on TANF for a few weeks before securing a job in retail.

Though varied, the experiences of those we interviewed frequently met at the crossroads of "bad" jobs and inadequate safety nets. Like Perez, Cantwell, and Lowery, many of those who were unemployed might well be working if their jobs or public assistance policies provided them with the benefits or flexibilities needed to combine employment and their family obligations. Examining people's reasons for leaving their last jobs buttresses the argument that spells of unemployment could have been minimized, or circumvented altogether, with better jobs and better safety nets (table 6).

More than a third at each survey quit for reasons they identified as directly related to job deficiencies—for example, hours that did not mesh with family obligations, demand for contingent labor, and unsafe labor conditions—conditions identified as frequently coexisting with low-wage labor (Shulman 2003). Furthermore, an additional significant proportion reported that they quit their jobs for personal/family/pregnancy-related reasons; reasons that could, in theory, be mitigated by access to paid family and/or maternity leaves. Though some readers

Table 6 Reasons Given by Unemployed Respondents for Leaving Last Job

REASON	AT 1ST SURVEY (%)	AT 2ND SURVEY (%)
Job related[a]	35	37
Personal/family/pregnancy	25	19
Fired	12	23
Attending school/training	3	3
Other reasons	7	7

[a] Including temporary/seasonal job, slack work, quit because of bad hours, quit because of bad tasks/personnel/equipment.

Table 7   Reported Barriers to Getting and Keeping Jobs

BARRIER	EMPLOYED RESPONDENTS REPORTING (%)	UNEMPLOYED RESPONDENTS REPORTING (%)
Job and/or labor market-related characteristics[a]	27	15
Health issues[b]	9	35
Child care issues[c]	19	14
Transportation	11	11
Lack of skills and training	8	11

[a] Including jobs with low pay, irregular hours, or lack of benefits or a lack of jobs, in general.
[b] Including one's own health, permanent disability, and pregnancy.
[c] Including cost, trouble with arrangements, and access to quality arrangements.

would surely point to the fact that 23 percent left their jobs in the last six months because they were fired as evidence of the poor work ethics of former welfare recipients, data from our qualitative interviews suggest that family obligations and the lack of leeway to deal with them contributed greatly to this rate.

Survey respondents identified barriers to getting and/or keeping jobs that reveal similar patterns regarding the potential for "bad" jobs, lack of family supports, and poor health to disrupt employment (table 7). When compared to the employed, the responses of the unemployed respondents expose barriers slightly less job-centered and more focused on health

Though the unemployed consisted of both those who chose not to work and those whose bouts of unemployment were unexpected, unemployment nevertheless took a toll on families' resources and welfare. Compared to those who were employed, unemployed respondents in the first survey reported lower rates of family well-being; only 3 percent of the unemployed reported that their family's well-being was "excellent" (vs. 10 percent of those employed). Twenty-three percent reported their family well-being was "good" (vs. 45 percent), 53 percent reported "fair" (vs. 39 percent), and 21 percent reported "poor" (vs. 6 percent). Unemployment, not surprisingly, increased the probability of subsisting below the poverty threshold. At the second telephone survey, 42 percent of those employed had incomes below the poverty line, while 63 percent of the unemployed were in poverty.

Family Supportive Policies and Arrangements

Welfare restructuring has reframed and complicated the obligations of women, transforming them into neoliberal individuals whose main commitment is to paid work and "independence." This ideal neoliberal individual is presumed to be unencumbered by daily family maintenance responsibilities; these tasks are carried out by someone else, a wife in most cases (Acker 1990). In reality, women's obligations to children and family care cannot be erased, even if they are obscured by policy dictates. The Personal Responsibility and Work Opportunity Reconciliation Act (PRWORA) enforces these gendered double demands by eliminating the entitlement of single mothers and their children to income support from the state. The result is that single parents are often the sole supporters of their children, and if they are poor, forced to cope with very little help from the state unless they can comply with the rules for time-limited TANF eligibility.

Similarly, most jobs are structured around the implicit assumption that the worker can give themselves totally to the demands of the employer while at work. Randy Albelda (2002) has expressed this dilemma in another way, turning the welfare-to-work phrase "job-ready" on its head and arguing that most of the jobs available to mothers leaving welfare are not "mother-ready"; the employment options available to these mothers fail to offer conditions that would enable them to care for their children without compromise and hardship. Mother-ready jobs would have living wages, ladders for advancement, adequate flexibility, paid leave, assistance with child care, and health insurance. In reality, low-wage jobs in the United States are less likely than higher paying jobs to offer employees key supports that facilitate combining family obligations and employment. Employers of low-wage workers are less likely to allow employees to adjust their schedules to accommodate family needs, to provide employees paid holidays, sick leave, or vacation, and to offer health insurance (Shulman 2003). Welfare leavers, in particular, find themselves in jobs with limited flexibility or stability (Boushey et al. 2001; Cancian et al. 2002). Access to quality, affordable child care is similarly problematic (Chaudry 2004). Data from our studies reveal a similar dearth of family-supportive policies. We have described the struggles of many mothers with employment situations that weakened their abilities to create solid and lasting financial foundations. Next we look briefly at the family supports provided through employment and policy and some key strategies that women use to accommodate this lack of support.

About half of the respondents to the surveys reported that they received paid vacation and a third received paid sick leave. However, employees often could access these benefits only after working for a period of time, often, among this group, after a year. Still, having a benefit and being able to actually use it are not always the same. Paid time-off, for example, generally required advance notice to one's employer, making it hard to use in the case of children's' illnesses or family emergencies.

In both surveys, 40 percent of respondents had access to employer-provided health insurance. Unfortunately, for many the cost to employees was prohibitive, significantly reducing the number who could take advantage of this benefit. As Janis Foster, a white hairdresser who declined her employer-provided health insurance, said, "I just try not to get sick...I just remember looking at it and going 'there's no way I can take that out of my paycheck.'...It was quite a bit...like a hundred and something, a month."

Respondents to the telephone survey also reported that they had a degree of flexibility in their jobs. Eighty-one percent of those employed in the second survey reported that they were satisfied with the flexibility their jobs offered to allow them to meet their families' needs. Ninety percent of the employed in the first survey reported that they could leave work if a family member became sick or was injured; eighty-nine percent said they could adjust their schedule to take a family member to the doctor at the beginning or end of a workday; and eighty-two percent said they could take a leave without pay and get their job back if a family member needed help for an extended period of time. However, face to face we heard a very different story, as women described highly constrained arrangements such as trading pay and other benefits for access to meager flexibility, and then only using that flexibility in rare instances. The flexibility they used was infrequently formalized through policy; thus, women relied on relationships with employers. The contradiction between what was reported in the telephone survey and what we learned when we interviewed women in greater depth was that their overall expectations for flexibility are low. We explore these issues below.

Strategies for Accommodating Family Obligations

The women we interviewed took great pains to secure and maintain the flexibility they were able to access. Consistent with a "compensating amenities" argument (Estes and Glass 1996), in which mothers forgo higher wages to obtain other benefits such as flexible workplaces, the mothers in our study often accepted and stayed in lower wage jobs with few opportunities for advancement because the working conditions were more conducive to meeting children's needs. For example, these jobs were close to home or child care, the hours suited the needs of school-aged kids, or the boss was perceived to be relatively flexible about allowing time off. Consider the following two quotes:

> I couldn't ask for anybody better as far as [flexibility to meet family needs], I mean, that's why I'm still there. I have no medical benefits, I have no paid vacations, I have no sick days or anything like that. But

there's not too many jobs out there that are so lenient either....[H]e's done the kid thing you know, and he's older. I mean, he understands. He's really good. (Kim Smith, white mother of two, cocktail waitress)

Don't get benefits, don't get paid the same amount as other people out there doing the same kind of work. But to me having the boss that I have kind of makes up for that. Other bosses wouldn't have been so understanding when you have kids that are sick or when you need to attend something at their school...but he's real good about that. (Pam Reiss, Native American mother of two, factory worker)

Like many others in our study, both of these women sacrificed critical resources—benefits, prevailing wages, and paid leave—for employment arrangements that allowed them some flexibility in caring for their children.

These compromises, however, were precarious. Like Smith and Reiss, many relied on individual relationships with supervisors that needed to be cultivated and maintained. In short, holding onto flexibility required work and sacrifice on the part of employees. Because this flexibility is not institutionalized, there is no guarantee that these mothers will have ongoing access to these arrangements should the conditions of their jobs or their relationships with their supervisors change. When women found these relationships, they felt fortunate; employers who cooperate with employees' familial responsibilities were perceived as a scarcity. The assessment that good bosses were hard to come by contributed to some women's hesitation to use the very flexibility for which they bargained away pay, benefits, and mobility. Thus, women were under the impression that they can use their flexibility only sparingly.

Often when women needed flexibility in their schedules to attend school events, doctors' appointments, or be at home with sick children, they used unpaid time off, most often by calling in sick—the arrangement they could most quickly and reliably access. Though half of those employed at the time of the telephone surveys had paid vacation leave, using this benefit was complicated, as discussed. Most of these women used their flexibility only rarely because there was no room in their budgets for unpaid days off or to pay for additional child care if their employer allows them to make up missed time. Mothers frequently stated that employers worked with their families' needs because, in the words of Margaret Lowery, they were "not big ones that called in all the time." Mothers reported that they were able to maintain their relationships with their supervisors and employers, in part, because most were careful not to ask for too much. Thus, it was not uncommon for mothers to take children to day care when they were sick, even when their day care did not permit sick children, or for mothers to miss significant school events such as conferences or performances.

Women who have been in the low-wage labor force for most of their lives expect little of their jobs, even though they need much more than they either expect or get. What flexibility they do have has to be measured against what they give up to hold on to jobs that they can manage to make work, albeit not well, for their children. Even those benefits they have are often hard to use because they cannot afford to take time off, they cannot afford to pay for insurance, and they cannot afford to alienate bosses who hold the key to the limited flexibility they have.

Child Care

Child care is another vital element in an overall family-supportive work environment. As a number of studies of low-wage families have found, mothers faced many structural constraints in finding and maintaining child care.[8] Mothers in our study navigated issues such as irregular or unpredictable work schedules that often conflicted with child care availability, incomes too low to afford safe and reliable care, the necessity of working long hours to make ends meet, inadequate child care subsidies and the inability to meet copay obligations, limited transportation options, a lack of other resources such as kin networks.

A report released by the Oregon Commission for Child Care during our fieldwork found that child care accessibility and affordability were particularly problematic in Oregon. The report identified a "persistent need for specific areas of care that include infant/toddler care, special needs care, extended hour/odd hour care, sick child care and school age care" (1998:11). In 1997, the year before our study began and just as welfare reform went into effect, Oregon experienced a *decrease* in child care slots. The report showed that only 41 percent of low-income families had "affordable" child care, defined as no more than 10 percent of a family's income (Oregon Commission for Child Care 1998). Janis Woods, a white mother of two in our study, summed up the constraints she faced: "There's just not very many options when they're zero to three. So, I felt that money was kind of an issue, and location was another issue, that I just was—you know, I didn't really have a lot of choices."

One of the positive effects of welfare policy changes was an increase in the availability of child care subsidies for employed parents. However, Oregon's child care subsidy program, called Employment Related Day Care (ERDC), was far from a panacea for the many child care problems families faced. Perhaps most problematic, in Oregon and nationally, was that the need for subsidies surpassed what was available due to funding constraints (Mezey et al. 2002). But this was not the only problem. For example, the subsidies reimbursed child care providers at relatively low rates. Second, eligibility for ERDC capped out at relatively low incomes in Oregon ($25,060 for a family of three), compared with what federal guidelines allowed ($33,000). Furthermore, ERDC copayments were relatively high because they were based on a higher proportion of one's income than was the case in almost every other state (Oregon Commission for Child Care 1998).

These conditions aggravated accessibility, affordability, and quality of child care for women reliant on subsidies. As we discussed previously, as women's incomes rose, their subsidies dropped at a faster rate, leaving them without the resources they needed to make up the difference. Providers who charged more than the ERDC rate either refused to accept ERDC or charged parents the difference between the reimbursement and their regular rates, leaving women to pay *both* their copays and the extra charges out of pocket. This was another reason that women in our study often struggled with meeting their copay obligations. Viola Prince, an African American mother interviewed for this study, provided child care for low-income women. She asserted that because ERDC reimbursement rates were so substandard, providers who accepted them compensated by taking more clients, which sometimes lowered the quality of care they could provide.

These realities were reflected in the lives of those we interviewed. At both telephone surveys in our study, over one-third of the employed respondents reported that they had one or more problems with child care. The most common of these problems included cost (25% in the first survey, 22% in the second survey), transportation (8%, 13%), locating high-quality care (25%, 25%), and other troubles with child care (15%, 18%). Problems were particularly hard for families with children under six years old; half of them reported problems with child care in the second telephone survey.

It was in the in-depth interviews, however, that we learned the most about the nature and severity of the child care problems many families faced. When we explored the child care arrangements these families had, most described arrangements that were complicated, occasionally unreliable, and required considerable coordination. Mothers characterized these arrangements as workable because, on most days, they did work but not without exacting emotional, physical, and material tolls on children, mothers, and kin.

Vicki Lenz was one such mother who considered her arrangements "workable," though to us, they seemed very complicated. To accommodate a shortage of income, care options, and access to subsidies, Lenz "patched together" care from a variety of sources (Scott, London, and Hurst 2005) and tried to uphold basic standards of quality while choosing some providers because they were affordable (or free), some because they offered flexible care or pay schedules, and some because they were conveniently located. Lenz, a white partnered woman who lived in a small city in southern Oregon, relied on an in-home day care provider for two days of the week, a friend on Saturdays, her fiancé on Sundays, and, two days a week, on two neighbor girls, aged ten and twelve, who watched one child for free while Lenz brought her infant to work for a coworker to keep an eye on. Though Lenz reported that she was satisfied with this arrangement, she admitted this was stressful on days that she used her in-home provider because it required an hour of transportation time each day. She also reported that she was not technically allowed to bring her baby to work and so relied on her coworker to help keep the child's presence a secret, at risk of both of them losing their jobs. Though the cost of child care was a chronic concern for her, she did not qualify for ERDC, the child care subsidies offered through the state, because her partner's income was too high.

As is evident from this examination of policies and supports, most of our respondents did not benefit from "mother ready" work environments (Albelda 2002). Indeed, the expectation that workers will be unencumbered by care responsibilities helps to render these gendered obligations invisible. Inability to fully rely on state or employer supports to manage work and family lives means that low-wage mothers absorb extra gender- and class-based labor, stress, and hardship into their lives, conditions that—combined with low wages—also shaped their family relations.

Restructuring Family

The material conditions under which parents (mostly mothers) in the low-wage labor market operate also affect family life. Without question welfare restructuring helps to contour family life. Women's familial experiences serve as portals through which to explore a number of theoretical issues involving welfare restructuring: the privatization of social reproduction, the shifts in relations of income distribution, the erosion of women's autonomy, and the slow unraveling of women's citizenship.

According to previous research, post-welfare employment has both positive and negative effects on families (see, e.g., Brady-Smith et al. 2001; London et al. 2004; Zaslow, McGroder, and Moore 2000). Mothers who enter the workforce after receiving welfare have been found to experience increased self-esteem, increased feelings of independence, perceptions of positive role modeling for children, and/or increased income, all of which have been observed to have a positive impact on parenting (Chase-Lansdale and Pittman 2002 Monroe and Tiller 2001; Scott et al. 2004). On the negative side, the logistics of combining low-wage work and family have been detailed and described as "wreak(ing) havoc" on families (Garey 1999, 95). As Beth Shulman (2003), in her book on the low-wage labor market, writes: "Most Americans juggle work and family life. But for low-wage workers it is more than an issue of juggling. In many cases, it requires sacrificing the needs of one's family to have a job" (34). The conditions of low-wage work can reduce time available for children, increase physical exhaustion and stress (Butler and Nevin 1997; London et al. 2004), intensify health issues (Kurz 2002), increase parental absence contributing to behavioral or school problems in children (London et al. 2004), and/or increase reliance on mothers' abusive ex-partners for financial and logistical help (Brush 2001; Scott et al. 2002a). Researchers agree that families leaving welfare for employment fare better when their material circumstances are boosted through work supports, higher incomes, and/or better jobs (see, e.g., Chase-Lansdale and Pittman 2002; Scott et al. 2004).

We echo some of these findings here, but we also focus on the commonly expressed theme that mothers felt unable to care for children in ways they saw fit. Our data suggest that some mothers do experience some of the positive paybacks of working; parenting in difficult circumstances can be made easier when parents and children experience less stigma associated with being degraded welfare recipients and have more disposable income, as former client Delores James suggests at the beginning of this chapter. The few who described their situations as "manageable" tended to have greater access to resources that allowed them some choice in how to care for their children. Mothers' concerns about how they cared for their children centered around three overlapping issues: (1) being physically, emotionally, and mentally available for day-to-day needs, (2) maintaining the parent-child bond, and (3) providing adequate supervision and safety. Pamela Stewart, a white single mother of two who worked at a nonprofit organization, believes her job prevented her from being available to her children to the degree she thought best:

> If I had the opportunity, I'd be home more with my kids than I am now. I would be more involved in their life. I would certainly like to have the choice. I think that's very important...My job takes away too much from me. There's not enough left for me and my kids when I get home. I'm flat too tired.

Similarly, Amber Alexander, a white single mother of a preschooler, was concerned that she could not be more available to meet her child's emotional needs:

> [S]he tells me all the time that she misses me. And she's really clingy, usually. And, I think, that if I didn't leave her so much she wouldn't be like that. I think she'd be more secure. I think that she's a little insecure because she's left so much. Because now it's not just with my mom. Now it's with Rosita [a friend], it's with day care, it's with Aunt Jan,...she has to spend nights there...when it's time for bed, she wants to be home.

Her fluctuating work schedule meant that she depended on a number of child care providers and that her daughter sometimes spent nights away from home (fairly common in our sample). Alexander and Stewart speak for many of the other mothers we interviewed who worry that they are not able to be as emotionally and physically available to their children as they thought their children needed. Mothers commonly told of being too tired, too preoccupied, or unavailable—as a direct result of the demands of their jobs, the stress of making ends meet, and their constrained choices—to care for their children in ways they felt were appropriate.

When mothers spoke of being unavailable or lacking adequate time with children, they often revealed fears about damaging the bonds they shared with their children. Some spoke of the importance of maintaining strong connections with children in order to guide them through the terrain of growing up under tough circumstances. Janis Foster acknowledged in an interview that she felt her children were more susceptible to drug abuse, crime, and teen-aged pregnancy because she was a single mother:

> Well, I think it always, is in the back of my head that, you know, that could [pause], that's why you just never let them go, all the way. I think if you let them go too far, then those things can happen. But as long as you have a relationship that's with them, and it's…just kind of a connection that you have. And if you keep it, then I think you're okay…

Amber Alexander, who above described her daughter as insecure, explains how her connection with the preschooler improved when she was unemployed and job searching, compared to when she was working full-time:

> But when I was off for that month, we really got close and [pause], she changed a lot towards me. Because she was like Grandma's girl and…she loved me but she didn't really want to be with me…I could just see a big difference and, it's like she loved me a lot more. It's like…maybe she was mad at me before or…something.

Many of the women we interviewed reported that employment interfered with their ability to supervise older children. Not only were they physically unavailable, but they also felt their connections to their children were attenuated, undermining their parental control. Pam Reiss, quoted above, reported that her work schedule prevented her from maintaining crucial parental oversight. She offered a recent example of arriving home early to find her eleven-year-old daughter riding her bike on a busy road with a neighbor's twenty-one-year-old male cousin, instead of playing at the neighbor's home as arranged. The incident "was against all my rules," Reiss relayed. She expressed the concerns of a number of mothers as she spoke about her daughter "getting into things that are totally against my thoughts, my wishes, my beliefs":

> I think if I was there more often I would know where these things were coming from and figure out exactly how to kind of get away from that. I don't know if it's coming from the neighbor's household…from people at school, I don't know. I'm feeling like I'm knowing less and less about what goes on in my eleven-year-old's life. And she's coming up to junior high next year and that's where a lot of bad things are possible of happening. I don't think that she would do drugs. We have a lot of talks about that. And having sex at an early age—we are open and have a lot of talks about that too…I really feel she's hanging out with some of the wrong people. And without being around her I don't know which ones they are.

Ellen Durant, a white mother of two, offered another example. Her position as an assistant manager at a convenience store required her to work on average of fifty to sixty hours per week. Her hours were unpredictable; in any given week, she would work multiple day, swing, or graveyard shifts, sometimes back-to-back, exacerbating her health problems. In addition to unpredictable work hours, she worried that "What time I do have, I'm either asleep or running errands." She described multiple incidents of her children, aged 12 and 14, sneaking other children into the apartment, against her wishes, when she and her partner were both working graveyard; one such incident resulted in injury to one of the children and subsequent police involvement. She reported that she was at her wits' end with her eldest because of his anger issues, problems in school, and increasing disobedience.

Although employment gave these mothers more cash income than welfare, what they lost was the opportunity to provide more direct care for and supervision of their children. Stacey Oliker has argued that welfare reform subjugates children's needs to workplace needs and strikes a harsh blow to mothers' discretion, which she characterizes as "a moral grounding and a constitutive ingredient of care" (2000, 176). Diminished discretion deprives mothers of their most basic rights in parenting—their ability to choose the path they find most appropriate; moreover, their ability to achieve that path may be further impeded by the consequences of low wages, inflexible workplaces, limited opportunities, long hours, and/or a lack of other resources.

Shifting Relations of Distribution

As Acker has argued (1988), class (and gender and race) can be conceived of as patterns of interaction that constitute relations of production, reproduction, and distribution (both personal and state-related). Thus, class is best understood not as a rigid position in a social hierarchy but as a set of relationships to the labor market, care obligations, and other individuals and institutions that can provide access to income (e.g., partners, kin, welfare). In the United States, poor women have a long history of cobbling together different income sources to support their families, including wage work in the formal labor market, under-the-table jobs, income from partners and other kin, and, when available, public assistance. Welfare restructuring drastically reduced access to cash assistance from the state to support care work, altering the relations of distribution and, thus, class/gender/race relations themselves. Given the inadequate wages so many women earned, as well as the instability of employment, welfare reform further privatized family support by making poor women ever more reliant on kin and male partners to supplement or substitute their own low wages. Though the distribution of wages has always been a process embedded in the socioemotional relations of the family, the new welfare regime explicitly promotes self-support in ways that affect parenting and complicates kin relations and heterosexual partnering. Examining these relationships reveals the dynamics and significance of the resulting changes on the relations of distribution and on women's lives.

Reliance on Men

The preamble to the TANF legislation states explicitly the law's aim to encourage marriage as a means of mitigating poverty and overcoming welfare dependency—in effect, welfare restructuring aims to transfer women's reliance from one mode of distribution to another (PRWORA 1996, Pub.L. 104-193, 110 Stat. 2105). In support of this objective, the Deficit Reduction Act of 2005 (Pub.L 109-171, 120 Stat. 4), which reauthorized welfare reform, allocated $1.8 billion over six years to marriage education and other programs designed to promote marriage (Legal Momentum n.d.). The soundness of encouraging marriage has been questioned by social scientists because there are compelling socioeconomic reasons people do not get or remain married.[9] As wages stagnate for men without college educations, it becomes increasingly difficult for working-class men to support or contribute to the support of families. The effects of economic hardship on men and the fallout on families are well documented (e.g., Rubin 1994).

Others criticize this objective of welfare reform on the grounds that it feeds gender inequity. Gwendolyn Mink argues that welfare reform "disable[s] women's citizenship" (1998, 6), in part, by removing state supports that previously enabled them to move more freely in and out of relationships with less concern for economic constraint. Policy that locks women into dependence on men overlooks, or perhaps conveniently ignores, the reality that the family is a particularly gendered site of inequality (Mink 1998, 18). Though welfare has traditionally been patriarchal in form and function, it at least provided women with some choice about how to combine employment, partnership, and care work in ways that allowed them to be "a little less vulnerable and a little more independent in the face of male power" (Thomas 1995, 122, quoting Block et al. 1987, 98) and in a better position to fight for rights collectively rather than "having to plead behind closed doors" (Thomas 1995, 122, drawing on Pateman 1988). In addition, welfare pre-reform, though comparatively limited, represented a potentially more reliable source of income for poor women than marriage or employment, given high divorce rates across the class spectrum, a strong correlation between poverty and divorce, and the instability of jobs in the low-wage labor market.

The undermining of income distribution brought about by welfare restructuring is particularly detrimental for poor African American women, who are disadvantaged in both the marriage and labor markets (Thomas 1995). Racism plays a significant part in creating this disadvantage. In comparison to white men, African American men have higher unemployment rates, lower wages, and higher rates of incarceration, illness, and homicide, reducing the pool of potential marital candidates for black women (Brown et al. 2003; Roschelle 1997). What are the consequences of a policy for African American women that assumes women will opt for partnership to gain access to wages they themselves may not be able to earn in the labor market? Structurally, they are granted even less autonomy than their white counterparts and will be more forcefully regulated into low-wage work, maintaining and perpetuating the raced, classed, and gendered nature of the labor market. The capacity of welfare policy to encourage marriage is, to date, not empirically documented; a relationship exists, but it is not a simple one (Christopher 2004). While we do not argue that welfare reform increased partnerships, it was clear that women in our study were partnering with men, even as some expressed ambivalence or stated explicitly that partnering was a bad idea.[10] For example, interviewee Mary Harman, a partnered white mother of four, explained her observation that tough economic times compelled women to rely on family and men who were not necessarily good for them:

> Well, I think what I'm seeing happening, because it happens all around me all the time...in the building I work in...is single moms [pause] relying on friends and family and, clinging onto boyfriends a little bit tighter. And, lots of times being stuck on stupid, you know, and not moving forward...

According to administrative data from the state, at case closure, 13.4 percent of the households from the first survey reported a male head of household.

Twelve to fifteen months later, when we did our first survey interviews, 31 percent reported that they lived in a two-parent household. Eighteen to twenty-one months after case closure, 33 percent of the sample was cohabiting or married. In the third set of in-depth interviews, 70 percent of the sample was partnered or married. One-third of those partnered or married in this last interview had been single at the first telephone survey.[11] Our data suggest that finances clearly play into some women's decisions regarding partnership—whether to enter into and when and how to exit relationships, which is consistent with other data (Scott et al. 2001). Our data do not allow us to fully tease out people's motivations for partnering; these decisions are a complicated calculus of the practical and the romantic, a fact of life for women across the class spectrum. But choice has become far more constrained for poor women with the replacement of AFDC with TANF, and the consequences of reduced choice bears down hardest on families with the most limited means.

The women we interviewed cited multiple benefits of partnering, often in instrumental terms; relationships help women to make ends meet, accomplish everyday logistics, balance work and family, and give children, especially boys, male role models. The most common benefit women mentioned was that partnership had ameliorated their financial picture. For example, as she discussed how her new partnership had shaped the last several months of her life, Jane Andersen, a white mother of one, said, "financially it's better...and I guess worrying about how I'm going to feed us is better." Linda Agnaci, similarly reported that, though her partner had added a great deal of "burden" to her life, she felt somewhat "de-stressed" by having access to more money. When asked if her life would be different without her partner, Vicki Lenz, a white mother of two, said, "I would probably be a mental case. Because he does take a lot of my stress off my shoulders....Like I don't worry about bills. I don't worry about...having food in our house...because I know that he's, he can do it."

While it is not a new finding that heterosexual relationships hold the potential to be oppressive for women, it is important nevertheless to document how this plays out in a context of limited choices. Partnership had its benefits, but women's domestic labor, their care work, the strife in their lives, their compromises, and their stress levels frequently increased when they entered into partnerships. Mundane, everyday complications accompany partnership and sometimes strain women's emotional and financial resources and prospects in ways that can potentially be destabilizing to their families over the long run.

One of the most common complications we observed was the sapping of the time and energy that women had and could be investing elsewhere—in employment, in education, or with their children. Ironically, men *increased* the time women spent on household labor, rarely pulling their weight on the home front, according to their partners. When asked whether her husband helped with the housework, Linda Agnaci replied:

> I don't know what he does. He feeds his…cat. He helps haul the kids around, now and then. Take [sic] care of his girls, sometimes on his day off. He's been helping, you know…he cleaned off the deck one day when I was at work, and he had the day off. I was like, wow. I didn't have to actually give him instructions. Because it's been kind of like, having another kid around.…But, he just makes the money and [pause] I don't know. We haven't really been together long enough in our marriage to actually…figure out who's in charge of what yet.

Though they had not yet "figure(ed) out who's in charge of what," Agnaci and her husband had quickly established a fairly traditional division of labor. She had already reduced her work hours, shifting her time and labor investment from her own employment and wages to her husband's. Many other women reported that they had reduced their work hours or privileged their partners' employment over their own, a strategy that holds the potential to both reduce their power within the relationship and undermine their future stability if these relationships deteriorated. When asked if she could work nights, for instance, Vicki Lenz stated, "[her partner] has all different kinds of hours that he has to wake up. And he's our breadmaker, so I couldn't ask him to do that [take care of the children at night]."

Jane Andersen reported that her new boyfriend and his teenage son had brought so much additional work to her household that she was on the verge of dropping out of college in her third year, "to hold the family together." She described how, in addition to taking on the additional housework required for her partner and his fifteen-year-old, she frequently had to step in to deal with the son's behavioral problems at school because his father tended to have a hands-off approach to parenting. She was overwhelmed by her unpaid workload in the home and by combining it with her education, her job, her new relationship, and her parenting. She told us, "So, school, our relationship was falling apart, I wasn't able to handle all the, you know, responsibilities at home."

Janet Phillips was a white mother of two, who married between the second and third interviews. Phillips worked full-time as a welder while her new husband worked only sporadically, contributing little to the household finances. Though she had a painful degenerative muscle condition and no health insurance, her husband did not share in the household tasks or the child care in any systematic way, much to her aggravation. "[W]hen I have the battles with Jeff," she said, "there are times that I need him to cook so I can go to bed at five o'clock. There are days when I just am hurting and tired [from her medical condition]."

Moreover, he did not get along with her children ("my children are not fond of him"), causing great stress in the household. Echoing Linda Agnaci's sentiments, she said, "I'm to a point with my frustration with him that I need him to be the adult. I need him to pull his weight...there are too many times that I feel like I have three children. And it blows me away."

Some of the women we interviewed also reported considerable strife in their relationships, which affected both their parenting and their work. Delores James, quoted at the beginning of the chapter, was in and out of the labor force and in and out of cohabitation with her partner during our study. At the end of the study, in the midst of a bad financial year for both of them, she said, "[I]t's gotten so bad with our—we're really angry, really angry people right now. And we really show it and we're not having a lot of success right now with our relationship...[her child] is feeling the effect of it too." She reported that they fought over childrearing (he had three children from previous relationships), his "controlling" behavior, and their shared guilt about living together before marriage.

A number of those who were partnered also said that their partners interfered with their parenting. Some mothers were concerned that these situations affected their relationships with their children and carried additional material or emotional costs for children. In some cases, male partners practiced different parenting styles that contradicted the mothers' styles. Others reported that partners fought with their children or robbed mothers of time with their children. Despite such difficulties, ending a partnership did not appear to be an easy solution. Not only do women (and their children) suffer emotionally from the demise of relationships (a much more frequent occurrence for poor women), but they also had to cope with the very stressful financial consequences when relationships end without the safety net of welfare.

We identified many potential consequences of the shift in the relations of distribution. Our data show that partnering can interfere with women's health, their economic independence, their investment in work, their pursuit of education, and the safety and well-being of their children. Though only a few of the women interviewed for our studies reported domestic violence since leaving welfare, other studies have documented a link between domestic violence and welfare reform (Scott, London, and Myers 2002a and 2000b; Brush 2006; Riger and Staggs 2004).

These difficulties, of course, are not limited to poor women. More affluent women may face similar problems. However, the thin financial cushion available to low-income women exacerbates these problems. Moreover, we do not suggest that partnership is *always* detrimental for poor women, but neither is it, as the framers of TANF implied, always good for families. Reality is more complicated. Even as some saw themselves as benefiting emotionally, financially, and logistically

from partnering, their partnerships—often accompanied by the stress and uncer-
tainty of low incomes—frequently interfered with their efforts to build stable and
secure lives for themselves and their children. Many women in the United States
face or have historically faced this tradeoff. But what is noteworthy here is how the
unraveling of the safety net combines with the precariousness of women's lives,
destabilizing their families over the long run. Welfare restructuring shifts the relations of distribution so that poor women have fewer options, placing them in a
heightened position of trading male financial support (or the promise of financial
support) for their emotional, domestic, and sexual labor, embedding them more
completely in the web of disadvantageous gender, class, and race systems.

Reliance on Kin

The assumption that poor women have strong kin networks to fall back on was
implicit in welfare restructuring (McDonald and Armstrong 2001; Roschelle
1997; Seccombe 1999), despite research that suggests that kin reliance, especially
among those minority families who are economically most vulnerable, is becoming a less reliable strategy (Menjivar 2000; Roschelle 1997). Anne Roschelle con-
tends that this assumption of strong family networks reflects misconceptions
that welfare recipients have mostly been people of color, as families of color have
historically relied on extended kin networks to protect and bolster their families
in the face of racism and labor market inequities (1997). This faulty class- and
race-based expectation, which, to some degree, guided the change in policy, begs
the question of why these racial stereotypes are woven into welfare restructuring
and also suggests willingness on the part of policy makers to burden extended
families of color.

Many of the low-income mothers we interviewed did rely on kin. Approximately 85 percent of them received some form of help from family three and a
half to four years after leaving or being diverted from public assistance, though
the levels varied greatly. Help ranged from transportation, child care, and logistical assistance such as dropping off and picking kids up at child care and school,
to food, money, clothes, housing, and long-term custody of kids. Without such
assistance, work would not have been an option for some. However, knowing that
many do rely on kin in order to care for children, eat, keep a roof over their heads,
and maintain employment, belies the complexity of tapping into this resource.
Not all women have kin to fall back on, nor can it be assumed that such an
arrangement represents a straightforward shift from one set of resources (the
state) to another (one's relations).

Three loose patterns of kin reliance emerged from our data, two of which
reveal the problems inherent in private extended families compensating for the

difficult conditions of the low-wage labor market: (1) relatively conflict-free kin support, (2) a lack of kin support, and (3) conflicted kin support. First, kin reliance was a feasible arrangement for some women, though they still struggled with the complications and hardship brought on by inadequate wages and supports. The kin assistance they received caused few conflicts within their family networks. In most cases, those with more help from family were experiencing less hardship and more stability. Second, a number of our respondents were disadvantaged because kin support was not forthcoming. Not surprisingly, those who lack regular kin support, because of geographical distance, relationship issues, or material lack on the part of their kin, were often among the most desperate we encountered. Third, some who relied on kin to make ends meet dealt with complicated familial dynamics that both highlighted the degree to which they lacked control over their lives and undermined their attempts to create stability for their families.

Sharon Janey provided an example of how ideal kin reliance might operate. A divorced, African American mother of a preteen son, she benefited from fairly regular financial infusions—a car, a computer, community college tuition, and occasionally, cash—from her parents. Her sister provided free child care during school vacations, and other relatives provided general parenting support and extra care when she needed it. Because she was able to take computer courses at the local community college (financed by her father), she made the transition from day care provider to office assistant, a job she hoped would provide more occupational ladders. She reported no difficulties in relying on her kin.

Janey was fortunate. Few other former clients could count on such obliging relatives with plentiful resources. Roughly 15 percent could not or did not rely on any family members. For example, Jean Glass, a white hairdresser who had one preschool child, said "I guess I'm the kind of person that really doesn't depend on anybody, because I've been so…turned down in my life, I guess. It's just, don't want to deal with the drama." Her family actually had the capacity to help, for they possessed both the time and money. But their strained relationship made it impossible for her to ask. Glass worked long, irregular, constantly shifting hours and struggled logistically and financially to cover child care with the resources she had available. Though her employer offered health insurance, she could not afford the premium and, consequently, suffered with a diagnosed but untreated, or sometimes poorly treated, mental health condition. Overwhelmed with working, making ends meet, and parenting, she revealed in one interview that she had seriously considered giving up her three-year-old for adoption shortly before the interview. Though clearly one cannot read a direct causal relationship between Glass's circumstances and her lack of familial support, her inability to rely on kin certainly aggravated her hardship and played a critical role in perpetuating it.

Others relied on their kin but not without costs. Vicki Jones, a white mother of one who was homeless for part of the study, described jumping between friends' and relatives' households. She sporadically stayed with her mother and was inevitably kicked out each time. After one such incident, she had her mother arrested for assault. Jones, who suffers from mental health issues and learning disabilities, often had trouble finding and keeping employment. She depended on her mother to care for her son for several months during the study, further straining the relationship. Jones's mother provided key strands of Jones's very frayed safety net, though this relationship was fraught with tension and insecurity. At times, Jones had no recourse but to rely on her mother despite the fact that doing so kept her enmeshed in dynamics that perpetuated her mental health issues and precarious subsistence.

In other cases, relying on kin did not constitute such an undermining force in women's lives, though examining these arrangements reveals the degree to which they lack the structural capacity to be self-determining. Many of the women who relied on kin reported making serious compromises in the ways they wanted to raise their children or arrange their lives. For example, many women who relied on relatives for child care were not satisfied with the quality of care relatives provided; however, they could not find or afford other care and had no choice but to accept this help.

As other studies have documented, women in poverty turn primarily to female relations to mitigate the conditions of the low-wage labor market (Seccombe 1999; Stack 1974). Assistance from children's grandmothers, aunts, and older sisters was sought when mothers lacked financial resources, when they needed extra logistical help with difficult and shifting schedules, or when they were unsatisfied with the quality or safety of care on the market. Our data are rife with examples of mostly female relatives sharing, sometimes willingly and sometimes not, precious resources with former clients who worked for minimal pay at jobs that did not provide much material and logistical space for care work. This assistance was reciprocated when resources were available, but, frequently, they were not, so these mostly female kin sacrificed their own time and resources.

Welfare is not, nor has it ever been, an easy way to access income support. Welfare has historically been a time-consuming, hassle-filled, stigmatized mode of distribution. Welfare benefits have historically been paltry, such that—even before "reform"—recipients commonly relied on the help of kin or partners to make ends meet (Seccombe 2007). Yet, entitlement to welfare offered women some capacity to structure their own lives by granting them one additional route to income than they currently had (Block et al. 1987; Mink 1998; Pateman 1988; Thomas 1995). Looking beyond claims of reform success exposes the costs borne by families when women have fewer options—the resentment, the expectations of reciprocity, conflict, stress, lost opportunities, and instability that can emerge out of forced associations with kin and partners. It also overlooks the practical and emotional hardships of not being able to parent in ways that one finds acceptable. While this reality exists for many families in the United States, not only those on welfare, the complicating attendant stresses and deficits of poverty are particularly onerous when it comes to caring for families. Looking beyond individual-level hardship, however, we can observe the ways these shifts change the nature of women's citizenship, as Mink (1998) claimed they would: by removing entitlements that remunerate care work, restricting women's autonomy to enter or leave partnerships and dependencies on kin, and restricting "vocational liberty" by obliging "single mothers either by law or by economic circumstances to chose wages over children" (Mink, 9). Indeed, Julia O'Connor, Ann Orloff, and Sheila Shaver (1999) argue that the right to make decisions about household formation, unencumbered by financial constraint, is an important indicator of the gender equity of a society.

Taken together, it is clear that the people who left the welfare rolls faced many difficulties in making ends meet and caring for their families. Measuring the success of the program by the number of people who were no longer on assistance is a gross oversimplification, producing inaccurate claims to success. The narratives of these individuals suggest that, contrary to the official credo of welfare reform in Oregon, work is not *always* better than welfare. While women reported some positives to working and some women were faring better than others, low-wage work clearly holds the potential for financial, familial, and logistical hardship that can undermine long-term security. The complications these families experienced demonstrate how starkly neoliberal trends—the unraveling of the safety net that moves them into the labor market, the preponderance of "bad jobs" that keeps them in or near poverty and the lack of "mother-ready" employment conditions, the ideological classification of poor women primarily as unencumbered workers rather than mothers with care obligations, and the valorization of work, regardless of its outcomes—shape their lives.

Laying bare the conditions under which families labor reveals the class, race, and gender assumptions and outcomes of welfare restructuring. It is women who bear the consequences of these policy changes in their lives, whether through accommodating to jobs that overlook their care obligations, laboring to compensate for poor child care options, struggling to meet their care obligations and feeling that they are failing, relying on men or kin who potentially complicate and destabilize their lives, or being more forcefully regulated into low-wage work because institutional racism constrains their options. Women's experiences in dealing with life after welfare expose the many ways in which welfare restructuring has solidified the privatization of social reproduction to individual women and their families and rigidified race, class, and gender inequities. From the client perspectives, welfare reform is hardly the picture of resounding success yet it is instructive, nonetheless. How could we construct a "successful" and equitable safety net? What kinds of policies would support *all* families in the low-wage labor market to raise children without the struggles women told us about? In the concluding chapter we consider some of those possibilities.

REFORMING WELFARE "REFORM"

Welfare reform failed to give the majority of mother-headed families receiving public assistance in Oregon meaningful self-sufficiency; that is, secure employment with earnings sufficient to meet family needs. Most of their family budgets were stretched thin as they tried to get along on wages below or close to the federal poverty line. By further shredding the country's already tattered safety net, Temporary Assistance for Needy Families (TANF) promoted greater economic insecurity, reduced women's social citizenship rights, and undermined, for many, their ability to care for their families in ways consistent with what they believed was good for their children. This is not to say that there were no positive effects of welfare reform for some clients, in some circumstances, and in the context of a strong economy.

This conclusion echoes a significant body of research.[1] The reasons that welfare "reform" failed to fulfill its promise are complex, rooted in misdiagnosis of the reasons that millions of families are poor and dependence on a set of neoliberal policy solutions that intensified economic insecurity and reproduced inequalities more than they fostered poverty reduction or economic opportunity. Real reform would recognize and target the overriding economic, social and political conditions that shape the extent, severity and demographics of poverty instead of defining poverty primarily as a consequence of poor individual choices or intergenerational dependency on social welfare programs.

These conditions are: first, the current form of capitalist markets which make profits for owners and shareholders an overriding goal, neglecting the wage and benefit needs of workers. This leaves millions of breadwinners without adequate resources, *despite* hard work and has resulted in a profoundly inequitable distribution of the prosperity that workers, managers and owners generate together. The second condition is the continuing reality of race, gender, and class inequalities that, despite some change, structure disadvantages for women, people of color and low-wage workers. Low-income communities of color and women raising children on their own have borne the harshest effects of the market fundamentalism of the last 25 years. Moreover, across all strata of society the absence of sufficient social and public resources for addressing families' needs means that unpaid care work, provided mostly by women, constrains the kind and extent of paid work that many women do. Rather than addressing these complex social realities, welfare reform focused on cutting welfare caseloads and mandating employment, demanding that individuals take "personal responsibility" for widespread social and economic problems, most well beyond their control.

We have spent many pages detailing the consequences of an approach to welfare that forces millions of breadwinners to wage an often losing battle to attain real self-sufficiency or provide for the many needs of their families. Our conclusion that welfare reform needs reform emerges not only from assessing its most severe consequences for the families who have suffered the most, but also from looking at the everyday struggles and needs of the families deemed welfare reform successes, who try to make ends meet or to get ahead, but who find that real self-sufficiency eludes them. Thus, we argue, to assess welfare reform as less successful than its adherents claim does not require findings that show absolute destitution among most families affected by the elimination of the entitlement to cash assistance. Furthermore, examining the work of implementing welfare reform puts in stark relief the difficulties facing welfare staff who are also stretched thin as they somehow work with diverse clients' needs, constraining agency rules and mandates, and the realities of local labor markets and available public services.

Most research on welfare reform, including ours, took place before the economic woes of the last eight years: a recession early in the new century, a long "jobless" recovery, and, recently, the worse economic crisis the country has faced since the Great Depression. TANF no longer serves, as did Aid to Families with Dependent Children (AFDC), as a viable safety net of last resort for the most vulnerable families during severe recessions (DeParle 2009). Despite serious economic problems, welfare rolls have risen only slightly in comparison to recessions in the pre-PRWORA years. TANF caseloads continued to decline nationally in 2007 and 2008, down to about 1.6 million cases in both years from 1.9 million in 2005. While Oregon witnessed a slight rise in cases in 2008 (to 20,000 cases, up from about 19,000 in 2005), the 2008 caseload remained less than half the numbers reached in the last recession before welfare-to-work was implemented.

In 1994, 42,000 Oregon families facing a bleak economy received AFDC. (U.S. Department of Health and Human Services, 2008).

Although TANF caseloads did not rise sharply, other programs sensitive to the economy have seen big caseload increases. Unemployment Insurance applications rose steeply, Food Stamp caseloads soared, and local food banks are struggling unsuccessfully to meet the spiraling need. Work-first welfare in an economy hemorrhaging jobs will mean far more widespread and severe hardship as millions of families find a social safety net all but destroyed by successful "reform."

Poverty alleviation, particularly in periods, regions or communities facing extensive jobs losses and limited economic opportunity is not easy. Moreover, one policy will not address the different needs of the families we studied, the ability of welfare workers to provide services as their agencies' budgets are slashed, or the conflicting pressures on welfare administrators who face growing demand for services and budget cuts. One size does not fit all when it comes to either the reasons individual families are poor, the pathways out of poverty for families facing different combinations of issues, or the ways in which structural conditions shape insecurity and poverty at particular times in particular places. Policy to address economic hardship and insecurity will require solutions far beyond "fixing" welfare reform. When millions of even middle income families are facing home foreclosures, outsized debt, job loss, wages or salaries that have not kept pace with rising costs, declining health insurance coverage, and unaffordable college tuitions, new solutions to growing economic insecurity are needed.

We argue that it is vital *not* to lose sight of the particularly harsh realities facing the poor in the current economic crisis. Although media coverage and policy maker concern about the current crisis has been intense, the most visible targets of attention have been the millions who have lost jobs, homeowners facing foreclosure, owners of stock whose portfolio values have plummeted, and banks, other financial institutions and corporations that have seen their profits disappear and face deep debt. Savvy politicians have signaled alarm about what is happening to the middle class, even as the bailouts focus on corporations, with hardly a nod to the mostly low-income families forced to weather the crisis with no financial cushions and almost no defenders.

Listening to the women and men who participated in this study and thinking about what we learned about individual, social, economic and political realities, contributes to thinking about different policy strategies and concrete recommendations that can ensure greater economic security and more equitable opportunity, as well as rebuilding the tattered social safety net. The evidence leads us to conclude that those who declare welfare restructuring successful are not simply mistaken. The facade of policy success is an obstacle to even having the hard policy discussions we need to develop real solutions to the problems of poverty, inequality, and insecurity in this country. We hope that this book will contribute to a renewed and energetic debate on these issues.

The Myth of Successful Reform

As we have shown, national and state politicians, along with top administrators of state TANF programs, applauded the restructuring of welfare as a successful innovation in public policy. But they relied on selective readings of results, often from the early years of reform, during a period of economic expansion, when much of the available research on welfare was conducted. After the applause ended, public scrutiny of the new law mostly evaporated. Welfare and poverty were once again consigned to the footnotes of political agendas. There was a brief reprisal of some debates about welfare reform during the various phases of TANF reauthorization in Congress from 2002 to 2006. But serious reconsideration of welfare-to-work as a strategy and market fundamentalism as a policy direction did not occur. As the current economic crisis worsens, market fundamentalism is facing critical scrutiny.

Among researchers there is no consensus on future directions for welfare policy despite a wealth of data showing its promises have fallen short. Some—concluding that welfare reform has caused great harm to our nation's most economically vulnerable residents, reproduced inequality, and undermined social citizenship—call for fundamental changes in policy.[2] Others argue for reforms consistent with the current direction of welfare policy.[3] A heated debate remains between those who credit the declining poverty rates and growing rates of employment of single mothers in the mid- to late 1990s to welfare reform per se and those who attribute these results mainly to the "boom" economy and the resultant growth in wages, jobs, and economic opportunity.

Our research shows that "success" on the ground is very much in the eyes of the beholder, and that beholders define success in ways much influenced by their locations within and outside "the system." In Oregon, assessments of success varied significantly across differences in participants' relationships to the agency, relationships that are deeply etched by gender, race, and class. Welfare administrators had the least nuanced, most positive assessments of the three groups we studied. They defined success as declining caseloads and clients leaving the TANF roles for employment, even when low-wage jobs kept these families poor enough to continue to need and rely on other safety net benefits. But as other chapters in the book document, statistical measures showing steep caseload decline and strong employment for at least a significant number of clients obscure the realities associated with low-wage and dead-end jobs, lack of affordable and high-quality day care, high housing costs, difficulties in paying for medical care, and relentless (and often losing) struggles to make ends meet. Oregon's welfare administrators chose not to judge their program in terms of its success in reducing poverty. Instead they chose measurable outcomes that could make the agency look successful in an era of outcome-based public policy. In so doing, they lost touch with the real outcomes of the policies.

One crucial case in point is the overriding importance attached to TANF caseload decline. When declining caseload statistics are taken out of the context of poverty reduction, they become an inaccurate proxy for poverty reduction. For example, if TANF caseloads decline when poverty rates climb (as was true in most of the post-2000 period), caseload decline counts as a positive outcome, even when it means fewer needy people are getting help. A similar logic pertains to what happens when caseload decline occurs, as it did for years in Oregon, in large part because of the decision to freeze the gross monthly income limits to qualify for aid or to freeze the amount of the cash grant, making it decreasingly worthwhile to receive TANF. These bureaucratic decisions reduce the pool of families eligible for or who try to get assistance without reference to the actual needs of desperate families. To be fair, and as we argued in chapter 2, despite being positioned at the more powerful top of the agency hierarchy, AFS administrators too were highly constrained by both fiscal and political realities, including legislatively mandated cuts in welfare caseloads, conflicting policy demands, and inadequate budgets.

Frontline workers, especially case managers and family resource managers, held more measured views of success than their bosses. Many judged the program to be working well if individual clients made modest progress toward (though never reached) self-sufficiency. They appreciated the new monies they now had to provide subsidies for child care, health care, housing, and help with employment-related expenses. Sitting across the desk from individuals with widely varying circumstances, resources, and needs, workers navigated the complicated realities of clients' lives, agency mandates, and their own highly constrained time and resources. Most were enthusiastic about the new mission of the agency and, particularly among case managers, about their new job responsibilities, but a significant number harbored concerns or outright critique of facets of agency policy.

Some workers, for example, admitted the contradiction between the agency's rhetorical respect of clients' choice and the fact that clients had only a very limited range of choices available to escape sanctions. Feeling successful, for agency workers, was highly dependent on resources of money and time. Over time they had less of both. Their already outsized caseloads of ninety clients in the late 1990s climbed even higher in the 2000s as TANF caseloads climbed and agency budgets were effectively contracted. The pot from which assessment and JOBS payments came shrank (Leachman, Merten, and Sheketoff 2005). The ghost of the Food Stamp error rate, with its attendant federal penalties, continued well into the 2000s, reinforcing the old benefit eligibility model and taking valuable time away from effective case management. Workers were able to do less for clients even as their own jobs became more difficult, pressure-filled, and insecure. With fewer dollars for JOBS and assessment payments, workers lost much of the most valuable tool they had to help clients. Therefore, despite a palpable enthusiasm and commitment to the idea of welfare reform, those women and men who actually implemented welfare restructuring had a more realistic, and, over time, a less affirmative appraisal of welfare reform as successful.

Clients had the most diverse, and, certainly, the most critical perspectives about welfare "reform." Some believed the agency or, usually, a particular worker or program came to their aid at a critical moment, helping them in ways they saw as positive for their family. Others expressed serious reservations about or explicit criticisms of welfare restructuring. Moreover, our examination of the lived experiences and consequences of welfare "reform" on the diverse group of individuals and families subject to its provisions provides a direct challenge to the distant, but more visible, claims of success by policy makers.

Some of the core rhetorical promises of welfare reform—self-sufficiency, the dignity of work, being good role models for their children—had strong resonance for clients. When they perceived the agency as helping them to get decent jobs, get through an emergency situation, make ends meet, and/or provide a more secure environment for their child(ren), they expressed gratitude. But they consistently argued that they needed more, not fewer, resources; that both eligibility for and the value of TANF, Food Stamps, the Oregon Health Plan, housing subsidies, child care assistance (through Employment Related Day Care [ERDC]), and Emergency Assistance should be expanded. They welcomed advice, assistance, and support from those case managers whom they saw as "friends," "mentors," or "advocates." Most wanted to have jobs and believed parents should provide for their children. They also desperately wanted to escape poverty.

But the resonance of the rhetoric of welfare reform faded for many when they experienced the agency as being insensitive to the needs of their families, unresponsive or stingy with resources, or creating hoops and unrealistic barriers to the help they needed. In contrast to the optimistic self-appraisal of many workers that they were able to "really help" clients, many clients talked about a punitive culture of compliance they faced, describing AFS as "scary," "intimidating," "disrespectful," "humiliating," "suspicious," or "unhelpful." The frequency of these comments raises considerable doubt that the agency had successfully changed its practices in ways that empowered clients, respected their dignity, or helped them chart a positive course for their lives.

At the heart of many critiques of welfare reform by clients was the belief that agency policies were out of touch with the realities of their lives. Clients, often with long histories as low-wage workers, knew that "rapid labor force attachment" to "bad" jobs would not lead to self-sufficiency or improvements in their children's lives. Most struggled with low incomes and jobs that gave them little flexibility, forcing mothers to make painful tradeoffs in income or benefits, limiting occupational mobility, and producing significant hardship. This encroachment into families' lives was far-reaching, recontouring mothering, partnering, and kin relationships. Thus, some clients questioned the logic of policies that overlooked their family obligations.

Although the agency shied away from the goal of poverty reduction, escaping poverty was all-important for clients. Although the agency was able to achieve TANF caseload decline in part through diversion and by freezing the income eligibility standard for cash assistance and the amount of the TANF cash grant, clients decried the meager grant amounts and the unrealistically low income-eligibility standards. Some recognized that these administrative decisions helped to produce the poverty they had to live with. Others criticized the "scare tactics" Oregon used to achieve the (administrators') goal of making "Oregon number one for welfare reform." They would have preferred that the state increase access to resources and services to help them manage the harsh effects of economic hardship and to support their goal of finding decent jobs, rather than "any job."

TANF in Oregon after 2000

We studied welfare restructuring in Oregon during three years when the economy was strong (1998–2000), when the TANF program was operating under a waiver from the most draconian features of PRWORA, and when the TANF block grant (its dollar amount pegged to federal expenditures on AFDC in 1994) provided more adequate funding for the JOBS program than has been the case since 2000. Whatever evidence adherents of welfare reform produced for success in the late 1990s faded in Oregon and nationally as the economy worsened, after welfare waivers expired (for Oregon in 2003), and in the wake of the more stringent TANF rules the Bush administration won in the 2005 federal Deficit Reduction Act (DRA).

Shortly after our research ended, Oregon, like the nation, suffered a significant recession, and the recovery was slow and limited, especially for low-income families. Most benefits of the recovery went to higher income workers, both nationally and in Oregon. It took until 2007 for the average Oregon household income to regain even the value of the income they had in 2000 (Leachman and

Margheim 2008, 5). Higher income households did post earnings gains in the post-2000 period, but earners in the bottom 60 percent of the wage and salary distribution saw their earnings lose ground to the rising cost of living (Leachman and Margheim 2008, 12). Fewer workers received employer-provided health insurance and, among those 45 percent of low-wage workers who did have some coverage, premium costs soared and coverage was more limited (Leachman and Margheim 2008, 33, 35).

Oregon continued to shed manufacturing jobs after 2000, even as the economy recovered, with job growth concentrated in the service sector, where wages and benefits are typically lower than many other sectors. Almost 21 percent of jobs in the computer and electronics industries, the shining-star sector of Oregon's economic growth in the 1990s, were lost following the collapse of the dot. com bubble (Leachman and Margheim 2008, 9). The grimmest job news began in 2008 with significant job losses posted each quarter, spiking in the last quarter as the national economy tanked. These are the labor market conditions that greeted families trying to become "self-sufficient" as they sought aid from or exited from Oregon's TANF program after 2000.

Not surprisingly Oregon made no appreciable progress in reducing poverty after 2000 (Boushey and Rosnick 2004). Poverty rates increased each year between 2000 and 2004, then fell slightly starting in 2005, before shooting up again in 2008. At the *peak* of Oregon's economic recovery, almost 13 percent—one in eight—Oregonians were poor (Leachman and Margheim 2008, 5). Even before the current crisis, one in three Oregon female-headed families with children lived below the poverty line (U.S. Bureau of the Census 2008b). Both in Oregon and the nation, low-income single mothers have suffered higher rates of job loss and longer spells of unemployment than other workers (Chapman and Bernstein 2003; Boushey and Rosnick 2004). Having a full time breadwinner doesn't insulate all families from poverty. One out of twenty such families lived below the poverty line in 2006–2007, a rate almost twice that for similar Oregon families in the late 1970s (Leachman and Margheim 2008, 5).

As mentioned above, TANF caseloads did climb modestly in Oregon after 2001. Nevertheless, actual caseload numbers remained historically low.[4] Rising caseloads indicate not just more, but deepening, poverty because the income-eligibility floor for TANF remained frozen at its 1991 level. This means families now have to be in "deep poverty," defined as income below 50 percent of the poverty threshold, to qualify for TANF. Thus, even though caseloads have risen in Oregon and other states, many needy families are not getting assistance. This may be because they have been scared away from TANF, or they know they cannot successfully comply with work requirements. It may be because they have been sanctioned off assistance or have reached the state or federally imposed time limits for help. (The federal lifetime limit is five years. The Oregon limit is two years, but the clock does not start ticking as long as the client is engaging in work-related activities). Whatever the cause, in 2005, less than half (48 percent) of the families who met states' income and other eligibility requirements received TANF (Coven 2005). Recent data show that number was only 21 percent in 2008 (DeParle and Erickson 2009, A-18).

As economic hardship intensified, welfare administrators in Oregon and many other states struggled to meet rising demand with significantly reduced resources. The value of states' TANF block grants plummeted because the block grant amount was pegged to the value of state grants in the mid-1990s. The value of Oregon's block grant fell 20 percent between 1997 and 2005 (Leachman, Merten, and Sheketoff 2005, 2). It was hard for most states to fill the gaps created by the decreasing value of the federal block grants because of the fiscal crises many states were facing. But there was also a demonstrable lack of political will to reconsider welfare policy and new, more limiting federal requirements for TANF programs, enacted by the Bush administration in 2006, restricted agency flexibility to respond to increased need.

The Oregon Center for Public Policy (OCPP) calculated that "total inflation adjusted spending from all federal and state sources on the four traditional self-sufficiency programs—childcare subsidies, employment services, cash assistance, and emergency assistance—fell from $744 million in 1993–1995 to $478 million in the 2003–2005 budget period" (Leachman, Merten, and Sheketoff 2005, 7).[5] These cuts resulted from both cuts in the Oregon Department of Human Services (ODHS) budget and policy decisions that funneled monies previously used for programs for poor families to "fill budget gaps in other state programs" (Leachman, Merten, and Sheketoff 2005, 1). For example, ODHS shifted millions of dollars that had been going into JOBS-related programs to children's protective services, where service demands had risen steeply. Some antipoverty advocates attributed the rising caseload in children's protective services to the stringency of welfare-to-work requirements and the inadequacy of child care services and resources for low-wage-earning families (Leachman, Merten, and Sheketoff 2005).

In 2001 the Oregon Department of Human Services was reorganized. Adult and Family Services (AFS) was merged with the Office for Services to Children and Families, and the new division was called Children, Adults and Families (CAF). CAF has since weathered a series of changes in leadership and in the division's mission, goals, programs, and services. Over time there was an unmistakable shift in the tone and content of agency leaders' public comments about welfare, poverty, and safety net programs. The optimism and claims of success of the 1990s were replaced by more frequent expressions of alarm about what was happening to families who were falling through the cracks in the state safety nets and publicly articulated worries by agency leaders about difficulties meeting the rising demand for services with proportionately fewer staff and reduced agency budgets.

In 2004 CAF division head Jean Thorne told her staff to brace for $207 million in program cuts that were going to result in service reductions (Thorne 2004). Several months later a new ODHS director thanked his staff for "absorbing" the increased need for services despite no corresponding increase in agency staff (Weeks 2004). Later messages announced major reductions in the Oregon Health Plan, the elimination of the Emergency Assistance program, and cuts in other safety-net programs. Later that year another new head of ODHS expressed concern that hard-working families were "falling through the cracks" in Oregon's woefully inadequate safety net:

> Never before have we seen so many at or near the poverty level....Our challenge is to continue to stay focused on addressing the conditions that are widely acknowledged to trigger poverty—economic insecurity and instability, lack of education, homelessness, hunger and food insecurity, divorce and separation, substance abuse and mental illness....Cutbacks and reductions the department has taken over the years [mean that] eligibility and access of the programs we do have are more limited now and many, many, many more Oregonians are and will continue to fall through the cracks of these programs. (Weeks 2004)

Weeks' message sounds very different from the declarations of success made regularly by AFS head Sandie Hoback in the late 1990s. Not only does he put poverty front and center, his list of poverty "triggers" goes beyond the "poor choices" of individuals to recognize the structural economic conditions of Oregon's economy and labor market.

This shift became more pronounced when the next agency head, Dr. Bruce Goldberg, used one weekly "Director's Message" to discuss the challenges facing the agency after congressional passage of the Deficit Reduction Act of 2005 that included reauthorization and revision of TANF. In a barely concealed critique of the federal government, he thanked his staff for once again having to "work smarter and more efficiently" and with a "cooperative spirit...regrettably ...absent from our federal partners" (Goldberg 2006a). And in another striking departure from earlier agency rhetoric, he explicitly defines as "myth" the belief that mothers on welfare are "poor because they have too many children, they like to be on welfare because it's an easy life, or, the most common of these— they're lazy and don't like to work." He laments the new federal rules that, he says, will "mean a huge cost and a huge workload, and all to solve a problem that doesn't exist, that is, in fact, a myth—that low-income people are too lazy to work" (Goldberg 2006b).

Oregon was subject to new federal welfare rules after passage of the Deficit Reduction Act of 2005. Among the most problematic of these new rules was the combination of higher work participation rate mandates (states now had to achieve participation rates of 50 percent for single-headed households and 90 percent for two-parent households) and a much narrowed list of "allowable [work] activities." Failure to meet these targets can mean a loss of up to 5 percent of the federal block grant.[6] A recent projection of "work participation rate gaps" by the National Conference of State Legislatures (NCSL)[7] showed Oregon having one of highest projected "gaps," at 41 percent, for 2007. Such a failure to meet the federal mandates could mean a penalty of up to $8 million (NCSL 2008). Oregon was not alone. Most states were projected to fall significantly short, with hundreds of millions of dollars of lost federal block grant funds at stake (NCSL 2008). The bottom line: The policy consequences of welfare restructuring have *worsened significantly* since we completed our research, with deleterious effects for clients and for the agency staff responsible for implementing these policies.

In this changing context, the new welfare agency leaders made some modest changes in Oregon's TANF program, although it remained fundamentally a "work first" program. The goal of "family stability" made a comeback as a central goal of the agency in the mid-2000s, reversing Hoback's 1998 decision to define it as a second-tier goal (see prologue). Another new model for case management was also introduced because, according to one of the trainers for the new model, the old one "wasn't working. The new leadership saw that" (Terran 2008, 101). With a caseload peopled by more families with multiple barriers to employment and family stability and the stiff new federal work participation rates, this new case management model aimed to foster more supportive, effective, and partnership-based relationships between case managers and clients. Case managers were encouraged to work from "clients' strengths" and to provide services in ways that are less punitive and discouraging" (Terran 2008, 101).[8] The agency also conducted an internal review of the sanction process ("disqualifications" and "conciliation") in the JOBS program. They concluded that the sanctions process was often "confusing and at times confrontational," so agency leaders replaced it with a "redesigned process entitled 're-engagement,'" allegedly designed to "create a more streamlined, strength-based, functional process to re-engage families in efforts to move them toward a more self-sufficient life" (ODHS 2007a, 1).

Given that our research ended before these changes were instituted, we cannot say if these changes in rhetoric were fully implemented. But there is no question that agency leaders did adopt a more critical stance on the earlier neoliberal welfare policy, including the coercive and, sometimes, highly punitive service-delivery tools that workers used during the period we observed. Administrators and workers labored under increasingly difficult circumstances caused by both budget cuts and reduced policy flexibility. In 2007 the agency announced an initiative called "LEAN," a management tool originating in the private sector, to "relentlessly pursue improvement and reduce waste" (ODHS 2007b). LEAN was occasioned by "a continuing growth in demand for services, along with a revenue stream that is not keeping pace [and the need for] more accountability" (ODHS 2007b). Thus, despite the recognition that their case management services were inadequate, the agency had even fewer staff with which to implement the new model. Caseloads of 90 clients per case manager, which even back in the 1990s were too large for staff to be effective with many clients, climbed to as high as 130–140 clients per case manager, according to a researcher who did interviews in the agency in 2008 (Terran 2008).

In the summer of 2007, state legislators ordered changes in Oregon's TANF to bring it into compliance with the new federal TANF rules. They mandated more intensive screening and assessment processes; established the sixty-month (five-year) lifetime time limits on benefits for adults with certain exemptions;[9] modified sanction practices; extended the period of exemption from work requirements for new parents; and changed other rules so that more clients who left TANF received Medicaid. The legislation established two new programs, both of which were supposed to help the state achieve the 50 percent work participation rate for clients on TANF. They created a state-only funded program for disabled adults, with DHS workers who helped eligible clients apply for SSI. These cases were subtracted from the total TANF caseload, removing some of the most difficult to employ from the mix of cases subject to federal mandates (and calculations!).

The legislature also created a "post-TANF" program that provides $150 per month (for a year) to employed ex-TANF clients (as long as their income remains below 250 percent of the poverty level). This added a whole group of employed clients to the TANF caseload, helping the state to reach the more stringent work participation rates. Before this legislation, a mere 2 percent of Oregon's TANF clients were employed because Oregon has had one of the lowest earnings limits for receipt of TANF among states (Leachman, Merten, and Sheketoff 2005). This new program has rapidly increased this proportion of working clients (Terran 2008). Similar programs to provide supplemental assistance to former TANF clients who are employed in low-wage jobs have been authorized or implemented in at least one-third of the other states (Schott 2008).

These changes clearly help "make work pay" for clients. But they also appear to be policy contortions designed to fit within the constraining combination of unrealistic federal rules and penalties, inadequate state and federal allocations for poor families, and other social and economic policies that affect the lives and fortunes of low- and moderate-income people in this country.

Reforming Welfare Reform

Welfare reform as enacted and implemented in the 1990s, and reinforced since 2005, drew on a particular set of economic assumptions and core American values—the dignity and value of paid work, personal responsibility, and an abiding faith in the institutions of a capitalist "free" market and marriage. Welfare reform (along with related neoliberal tax policies) constituted a U-turn away from the reigning liberal policies that assigned state and federal governments a role in protecting vulnerable people from the vicissitudes of the market and family dynamics, guaranteeing a modicum of economic security and providing public resources and services to challenge inequities and foster equal opportunity. Drawing on our and other research, we advocate policy changes to better align public policy with both the economic realities of our time and other core American values—fairness, equal opportunity, personal and shared (social) responsibility, and human dignity.

Our recommendations begin with the need to immediately reestablish a stronger safety net to cope with the devastating effects of the current economic crisis. We begin with a focus on recommended changes in TANF and then look beyond TANF to immediate and longer-term policy changes aimed at promoting greater economic security, more widely shared prosperity, and gender and racial equity.

In the immediate future, access to TANF should be reopened to all who are income eligible. We advocate a return to the principle of cash assistance as an entitlement for needy families. This would require a change in federal funding, abandoning the block grant and returning to a system of funding for the actual caseload. In the longer run, the main goal of TANF should be to help reduce poverty among families with children, recognizing that poverty reduction requires many other policies, including creating more living-wage jobs, encouraging and supporting postsecondary education, and providing better and less expensive child care. We discuss such proposals below. But, TANF has a contribution to make to poverty reduction by providing a safety net to prevent families from falling into deeper poverty and offering services that help individuals overcome the challenges that moor them in economic hardship.

This need not mean jettisoning the goals of promoting employment, self-sufficiency, and family stability. However, key strategies and practices *would* need to change, at both the federal and state levels. Performance measures, for example, should focus on alleviating poverty rather than rewarding caseload reduction, for example, by tracking decreases in the poverty rate among families leaving TANF. This would encourage welfare administrators and workers to use their resources and design their programs differently. Examples of successful innovation exist from the welfare-to-work era, including the mid-1990s JOBS program in Portland, Oregon, that compared favorably to other programs precisely because it paired investments in human capital and employment promotion, was decently funded, and focused on helping clients find "better" than minimum-wage, dead-end jobs (see chapter 2).

Given the many reasons that different families are poor, including those over which individual families have little to no control, successful poverty reduction programs will need a wide range of tools and strategies, well-trained staff free to develop varying plans with clients, adequate funding, and strong partnerships outside the agency. Welfare agency staff will need to be released from arbitrary and constraining caseload reduction targets and work participation rules (such as currently exist), allowing them to redirect their efforts away from constraining, coercive policies and toward services that will help families meet realistic family-friendly goals. Our research showed that carrots worked better than sticks with most clients, as discussed in chapter 5. Most clients who are not burdened with health problems or serious family problems prefer employment to welfare. With them, coercion is neither necessary nor a productive strategy of assistance. Diversion, time limits, sanctions, and rapid labor force attachment do not lead most clients to employment in decent jobs, and for those clients for whom employment is not a realistic goal, these policies foster desperation, severe poverty, and poor outcomes for their children.

A reformed TANF should offer income supports for single-parent and unemployed two-parent families at a level that helps to relieve grinding hardship and to stabilize the family so that employment, education or job training, safety, and recovery from illness or substance abuse is a viable next step. In Oregon, TANF cash eligibility and benefit levels should be raised to, at the very least, 1991 values when they were frozen at 66 percent of the poverty line. This increase would allow more poor families to qualify for assistance and allow those who enter paid jobs to keep some benefits as their incomes increase. A benefit increase would allow families time to develop realistic plans to improve their conditions, supported and advised through non–cookie cutter, humane practices of case management. This should also enable clients to take advantage of postsecondary education, job and vocational training, and subsidized work experience programs, with the support of cash and child care assistance, as well as other benefit and loan programs. Thus, low-income women would have the option to follow the paths to better jobs that have long been available to their more affluent peers.

Replacing caseload reduction with poverty reduction as the driving force of TANF policy means turning away from the exclusionary policies that played such a big role in falling TANF caseloads. Diversion practices that discourage clients from seeking help or delay benefits, policies that exclude legal immigrants from eligibility for TANF, and rules more onerous for two-parent than one-parent families all need to be changed. Our goal is not to encourage rising caseloads; it is to allow the fluctuating economic conditions of families, labor markets, and economies to determine caseload levels.

If TANF is to serve as one piece of a larger effective policy of poverty reduction, welfare administrators and workers need to understand and help clients overcome the effects of gender and race discrimination and injustice in the larger society. Research has documented that the current system has most disadvantaged women of color, including immigrants, who have borne the greatest burdens of welfare reform.[10] Policies that define legal immigrants as undeserving "outsiders" (Fujiwara 2006, 2008) need to be changed to allow them access to the full range of public resources and services available to other residents of this country. Real reform of welfare needs to put racial and gender equity on the radar screens of agency workers so they understand the different challenges clients confront and can develop services to better address the particular racialized and gendered obstacles affecting their clients' lives. Susan Gooden (2003) has suggested that welfare administrators develop and use performance measures that help assess equity in program implementation and outcomes. We support her suggestion and suggest collecting data by race on factors such as services offered; referrals to services, agencies, and jobs; resources allotted; percent employed; and type of job secured, including wages, benefits, and whether the job is permanent or contingent. This would give welfare administrators a greater understanding of how race shapes both employment opportunity and service delivery. Although CAF (formerly AFS) rhetorically values diversity, this does not mean that agency staff have either the understanding or the tools they need to take racism or gender subordination seriously as factors in the lives of their clients or as considerations in developing programs.

With the new goals we propose for TANF, more adequate funding, and the abolition of penalties for states not meeting restrictive work-participation targets, welfare administrators, managers, and workers will be able to take advantage of some of the lessons learned from more than a decade of welfare-to-work policy. When case managers can, on balance, be service providers and advocates for clients, rather than agents of surveillance and coercion, more effective and humane services can be developed. If agency administrators were held accountable to poverty reduction objectives, rather than caseload reduction, not only could they work collaboratively with agency staff, antipoverty advocates, and clients to redesign agency procedures and practices, but they could become more effective antipoverty advocates within the policy community and with partners in the business community. All of this implies policy changes that go well beyond those suggested for TANF.

Beyond Changes in TANF

Beyond changes in the TANF program are other critical changes in public policy that are needed to refocus public policy on reducing poverty, economic insecurity, and economic inequality. These include programs that make "work pay" for single mothers and others, programs to attend to the needs of children in low-income families, cash safety net programs other than TANF, and health and education programs that are essential if adults are to work and maximize their possibilities for better jobs and income. Even broad and generous supports, however, will not eliminate poverty. That would require a much greater supply of living-wage jobs and changes in many other tax, labor, and economic development policies.

Poverty is a class condition, but it is not race- and gender neutral. Program proposals may sound neutral but contain embedded race and gender assumptions that lead to differential effects for white women and women and men of color. Poverty is also linked to place: It is most prevalent in some parts of the country, such as some rural areas, deindustrialized towns, and central cities. Policies and programs need to be put together with these differences in mind.

In addition, policy implementation matters: It can range from punitive, coercive, disrespectful, and ineffective to fair, respectful, considerate, and effective. We saw just such differences in our observations in agency branches. We recommend that federal and state policy makers and administrators pay much more attention to how policies are implemented, with an eye to concerns about equity, human rights, and human dignity.

From "Work First" to "Children First"

An important guiding principle of a reformed welfare "reform" would be to replace the "work first" emphasis of TANF with policies that recognize and support both the paid and unpaid work needed to foster the well-being of children and others who cannot care for themselves. A strong family policy would better assist most parents in combining both forms of work and help families whose earnings are inadequate to better meet their children's needs for safety, decent housing, good nutrition, learning and education, and comprehensive health care.

AFDC was criticized because it gave poor mothers an option unavailable to many nonpoor women: support to stay home to raise their children. But TANF leans in the opposite direction, subjecting poor women to the mandate to put "work first" no matter what the effects on their children. When it comes to ensuring their children's well-being, poor women should have no fewer options than other mothers. Strong family-supporting policies (not a biased rhetoric about "family values") need to be implemented *across* the class spectrum.

In the immediate future, we recommend raising the Employment Related Day Care (ERDC) subsidy so that low-income women can better access high-quality child care for their children. This includes expanding eligibility for ERDC and developing more affordable copayments so that parents are not forced to "choose" second-class care. Program rules should allow ERDC to be used not just to subsidize employment-related child care but also to subsidize care needed when a parent is engaged in education or vocational/job training programs. Raising the subsidy also allows child care providers, who are usually women and often also parents of young children, to better support *their* families and will help attract more qualified workers into the field of child care. In addition, policy makers should strengthen regulation of both center- and family based child care and offer incentives for and training for child care workers to increase the overall quality of care available to all families. Finally, we need to significantly expand the available slots for high-quality child care and ensure that ability to pay does not determine which children have high-quality care. Otherwise we reinforce the current pattern in which many poor children reach K-12 public education already behind their more affluent peers, a gap that is difficult to close and fosters educational inequities from early on.

Given that many TANF recipients use welfare as an effective parental leave and that income-strapped low- and moderate-income families often cannot afford to take advantage of the unpaid leaves mandated by the Family Medical Leave Act (FMLA),[11] we advocate paid family leave. One year of paid parental leaves for all births and adoptions would ensure that children begin life with a secure bond to a parent who is not struggling to make ends meet on a low-wage job. Paid leaves should include fathers as well as mothers, to be divided between the parents as they wish, with the caveat that the father needs to take a minimum amount of leave (perhaps three months) to make the family eligible for an additional portion of the leave. The objective here is to encourage paternal participation and gender equity, as other countries such as Norway, Sweden, and Iceland have done (Ellingsaeter and Leira 2006). Employment should not be a criterion of eligibility.

Changes are also needed in the Child Tax Credit (CTC). The CTC currently provides a $1,000 per child tax credit to families to help defray the costs of child rearing. Because it is currently only a partially refundable tax credit, millions of low-income families are left out of the benefits of this credit. They either receive no credit or cannot get its full value because of the way the tax credit is structured (Aron-Dine 2008). By leaving out the very families who most need help with child-rearing expenses while subsidizing family expenses for higher income families, the CTC reproduces inequality, rather than serving as a modest form of redistribution. Making the CTC fully refundable would help enormously.

Because gender and race so profoundly shape income distribution in this country, as long as access to high-quality child care is largely dependent on market forces, children in female-headed families and/or in families of color will continue to be disadvantaged. The changes we propose will help relieve low-income parents of some of the costs of child care and child rearing and reduce the inordinate stress experienced by many, especially financially strapped female heads of household. Moreover, children are not the only dependents who require unpaid care work. Families, and again mostly women, must also find ways to provide unpaid care for or help pay the costs of care for elderly family members who can no longer live safely on their own and for disabled or acutely or chronically ill relatives. Until our public policies address the "care crisis" (Rosen 2007) in society today, not only will children and others lose out, but the women who struggle to meet the inadequately supported care needs of families will continue to make sacrifices others do not, often resulting in labor market disadvantages.

Making Work Pay

The cruelest irony of "work first" welfare reform is the gap between the rhetoric and the realities of employment as a route to self-sufficiency and escaping poverty. For low-wage workers, hard work doesn't necessarily pay, and good jobs—with decent wages, predictable hours, and benefits—are hard to find and get. Although AFS, and welfare departments across the country, understood the need to help "make work pay," these agencies can only (and partially) make up for the facts that too few living-wage, benefit-providing jobs are available, and the supply of such good jobs is contracting, sharply since late 2008. Thus, to "make work pay," policy changes are needed that directly affect the wage and compensation packages of workers. First and foremost the minimum wage should be raised so it comes much closer to a living wage, including automatic cost of living increases so it will maintain its value. Although many clients had jobs that paid more than the minimum wage, minimum wage policies tend to "trickle up," exerting an upward pressure on all wages. We discuss such a proposal in more detail below.[12]

Another immediate policy proposal is reform of the federal and state Earned Income Tax Credit (EITC). The federal EITC is currently the single most effective antipoverty program the government offers, at least as measured by its role in providing additional income to low-income families. We recommend ensuring that the value of the federal EITC continues to keep pace with rising costs and inflation and that it remains refundable (so that families with no tax liability still receive the value of the credit). We also recommend that efforts be made to increase the number and value of state EITCs. Currently only twenty-four states offer state EITCs, and only twenty-one of them are refundable. The value of state EITCs vary greatly, ranging from 3.5 percent (Louisiana) of the value of the federal credit to 40 percent (Washington, D.C.); Oregon's EITC is on the low end of the continuum, at 6 percent of the federal credit, but it is refundable (Levitis and Koulish 2008). All states need to develop robust, refundable EITCs.

Beyond making work "pay," public policies should make work "work" better for families, particularly for the women who bear the brunt of the work-family balance problems that are endemic in this society. While there has been extensive research and advocacy about the need for "family friendly" work policies, those that have been implemented are mostly enjoyed by higher wage and salaried employees. Most low-wage working women are left to fend for themselves, with much less flexibility and fewer employer-provided benefits (from health insurance and retirement benefits to sick leave, paid family and medical leave, and paid vacations) to help them manage their multiple responsibilities. This exacerbates the other gender- and race-based inequalities that impact them. As long as employers are free to decide if they will provide these benefits to their employees and discriminate by offering them only to some (usually higher level) workers, the most "disposable" workers and families—precisely those who end up at the welfare office—will continue to seek help from the government to make up for what their employers fail to provide.

A Stronger Safety Net

We propose a more robust safety net that goes beyond TANF to protect against family and individual economic crises caused by loss of income or income inadequate to cover ongoing needs. Need for a safety net may arise from illness, poverty-level wages, gendered care obligations, race-limited labor force opportunities, disability, unemployment, and businesses' need for flexibility in the low-wage labor market. An overhauled safety net would offer income supports for short-term crisis needs, such as paying for a car repair to ensure transportation to work, but it would also realistically address longer-term needs.

To this end, Emergency Assistance should be funded by the federal government in cooperation with the states to assist with such crisis needs and forestall longer term economic disaster for families. More immediately, Oregon should restore its Emergency Assistance program that was ended in 2004 (Leachman, Merten, and Sheketoff 2005, 13). An assistance program for adults without young children should be established to provide for unemployed people who do not qualify for unemployment insurance, such as women who have been out of the labor force while caring for their children or those who have had unsteady work in the low-wage economy.

At the same time, Unemployment Insurance (UI) eligibility rules need to be amended to include part-time workers, those with short-term jobs or contract work, and those without sufficient earnings to qualify. In 2007 in Oregon, only about one in three unemployed workers collected UI; low-wage workers are half as likely as higher paid workers to receive this benefit (Leachman and Margheim 2008, 37, 38). Women are particularly disadvantaged by the current rules of the UI program. Because they are more likely to be in low-wage jobs, work part-time, or have temporary jobs, often because of their care responsibilities, women in Oregon were much less likely than men to collect UI (37% of unemployed women received UI compared to 46% of men) (Leachman and Margheim 2008, 38).

The Workers' Compensation program also needs to be strengthened and expanded, as does access to Supplemental Security Income (SSI) and Social Security Disability Insurance (SSDI). Most of these programs are, in effect, entitlements for those who meet the eligibility criteria. Food Stamps, arguably the most successful and most widely used safety-net program, is an entitlement program. Eligibility for Food Stamps should be expanded to again include full-time students, and the levels of benefits should be raised so that the country can do a better job of staving off food insecurity and hunger.

Access to Health Care and Quality Education

We assume that health care is a basic human right. Employed or not, individuals and families in a wealthy industrialized nation should not have to take on crushing debt to obtain decent medical care or to forgo medical care because they cannot afford treatment when they or their children are sick. Dealing with this issue requires federal as well as state action. As this book goes to press the Obama administration is actively seeking health care reform, sure to be a highly contested issue. In the immediate future, we support state action; in Oregon this would include a return to previous Oregon Health Plan funding levels and rules of inclusion. Registration for OHP for those not receiving TANF, which was closed in 2004, should be reopened to all, and income limits for eligibility should be raised so a wider swath of the low-income population qualifies. In 2006 over 42 percent of Oregon's working-age adults below the poverty line were without health insurance (Leachman and Margheim 2008, 35).

Moreover, the OHP eligibility guidelines should be restructured to provide for a slower phasing out of coverage as incomes rise, so families do not abruptly lose medical care with a slight rise in income. Oregon, like many other states, is developing a plan to revamp its health care system to address some of these issues.[13] The State Children's Health Insurance Program (SCHIP) was reauthorized and expanded by Congress in early 2009, beginning the process of providing medical care to all children (Pear 2009).

We also assume that access to education is critical for individuals across the income spectrum. Postsecondary and/or technical education is a more reliable long-term strategy than rapid labor force attachment for helping individuals position themselves for better paying jobs. As an immediate policy change in Oregon and other states that refused to count education as an allowable work activity, we advocate allowing education to count as work-related activity for TANF eligibility, at least as long as work requirements are in place. As the cost of higher education rises, working-class, and even many middle-class, students are being priced out of participation. Expansion of educational grant programs, such as the federal Pell grants, would ease access for a wider group of low-income people. Increased numbers of tuition reduction and scholarship programs would increase access also. Student loan programs should be closely monitored to prevent the exploitation of low-income people by high interest rates and by bogus offers of vocational training, which happened to some of the women we interviewed.

Universal Programs—Better Solutions

Most of the policies discussed above are intended to meet the needs of people with limited incomes. Such policies and programs are needs based, means tested, and often targeted at particular groups of people, including single mothers and their minor children. Eligibility criteria are often complex, stringent, and stigmatizing, with the result that people in need are frequently excluded, as our discussions above illustrate. A different approach to meeting common human needs, based on the belief in social and economic rights, is the provision of universal benefits for which all are eligible. In addition, no invidious distinctions are made between more or less deserving beneficiaries (Neubeck 2006). Free public education is the prime example of a universal benefit in the United States. Social Security is an almost universal program that provides for all who have worked for pay and for whom Social Security taxes have been paid. Those who have never worked or for whom the tax has not been paid, such as some domestic workers, are not covered. Thus Social Security has a criterion of eligibility that excludes as well as includes.

Middle- and upper-class families, including the most wealthy, already enjoy universal income supports. Many of these are hidden, buried within the tax code, such as tax deductions that subsidize home ownership, college and retirement savings, and health care (Abramovitz and Morgen 2006; Howard 2008). Universal programs have certain advantages over needs-based programs: They help more families and create more powerful, broader constituencies for public programs. When everyone has a right to a benefit, more people have a stake in the program. Free public education and Social Security are universal programs with widespread support. Universal programs have a high legitimacy level and cannot be challenged as giving away scarce money to the undeserving. Universal programs also have a better record of eradicating poverty than needs based programs. For example, in the United States, poverty among older Americans has decreased dramatically as a result of Social Security (Mishel, Bernstein, and Boushey 2003). Most other wealthy industrialized nations have many more universal programs than the United States, including health care, child allowances, and day care programs, as we have already noted. These other countries also have lower poverty rates than the United States (Mishel, Bernstein, and Boushey 2003). The following reform suggestions are for universal programs and policies that can benefit low-income and middle-class people and reduce poverty rates.

Medical Care

We support the establishment of a universal, single-payer health care plan for the United States. Such a plan would open access to everyone in the country. It would lower costs by lowering time and personnel spent on approvals and billing, replacing multiple and complex bureaucracies with one set of forms and rules. It would also lower costs by eliminating the health care dollars going to profits for insurance and pharmaceutical companies. It would reduce poverty by eliminating bankruptcies due to extremely high medical costs not covered by insurance. It would, in all probability, increase the quality of medical care for those who now rely on emergency rooms or who go without, contributing to the reduction of poverty related to poor health.

A Living Wage

We advocate raising the federal minimum wage to the level of a living wage, at least a wage high enough so that a full-time, year-round worker can earn enough to have income above the poverty line for a family of two. There are many proposals for such a wage. Debates about what that wage would be (in different communities) entail both political and economic questions. Greatly expanding the availability of living-wage jobs and ensuring that access to these jobs is not negatively affected by gender, race, or class inequities are probably the most important antipoverty policies this country could develop. The question of how to build support for a higher minimum wage and a greater supply of living-wage jobs is complex given the current economic crisis. One way to encourage such jobs is to restore labor protections for unions that would allow them to regain some of the leverage they had in the middle decades of the twentieth century. Another is to use labor and tax law to create positive incentives for employers to treat workers better. If policy makers are to really impact wage and benefit levels in this country, they will have to address a wide swath of issues, including trade, tax, immigration, and economic development policies.

A Universal Child Allowance

We believe the United States should establish a universal monthly child allowance payable to a mother upon the birth of her child and continuing until the child is eighteen years old. A child allowance would replace the Child Tax Credit, making the same benefits available to families in all income categories. The amount of this allowance should equal the basic cost added to the family budget with the addition of a child. Eighty-eight other countries offer child allowances in some form and in varying amounts (Seccombe 1999). As many other nations recognize, investment in children contributes to the future economic, civic, and social well-being of a nation. These costs should be shared by those who benefit (i.e., all citizens of the nation) rather than shouldered nearly exclusively by the child's parents.

Free or Affordable Public Education

We advocate improvements in K-12 public education funding and the extension of free or very low cost public education to preschooling and to postsecondary schooling as a long-term goal. Three decades of neoliberal policies have eroded the quality of public education in many cash-starved communities. Free public education through the twelfth grade was established in the United States when the high school diploma was the terminal degree for most people, qualifying them for most jobs. This is no longer true: A bachelor's degree or a two-year associate's degree is now basic education for most jobs that pay fairly well. There are precedents in U.S. history for free or very low cost public higher education. For example, the New York City Colleges were free at one time, and some state universities had very low tuition. Contemporary precedents also exist: Many other wealthy industrialized countries have free or very low cost higher education. We realize that this proposal runs counter to patterns of funding and access to higher education in the last couple of decades. But it is time to reconsider the issue as more and more young people leave college with tremendous debt, beginning adult life on the edge of poverty.

Are We Just Dreaming?

As this book is going to press, state leaders across the country, facing massive state budget deficits, are proposing draconian cuts in public programs. These include slashing critical safety net programs needed to help the most vulnerable families weather this economic crisis. The media has focused its attention on California Governor Arnold Schwarzenegger's proposal to *eliminate* the California Work Opportunity and Responsibility to Kids (CalWORKs) program, California's version of TANF and welfare-to-work. While the cuts proposed for Oregon's public assistance programs are not this severe, they are deep and will be extraordinarily painful unless the federal government steps in at a much higher level than it has already. And California and Oregon are not alone.

Are we just dreaming, proposing fundamental changes in the context of this economic crisis? We think not. Moments such as this one expose the glaring fault lines in current public policy. Still, formidable barriers exist to realizing even the most minimal of the above proposals for reforming TANF and other support programs, reducing poverty, and working toward greater economic equality. The disproportionate power of corporate interests in shaping public policy is perhaps the most formidable of these obstacles. Through their extraordinary political influence, teams of lobbyists, and think tanks, corporations have supported the shredding of the social safety net, demanded large cuts in corporate taxes and reduced government regulation, and vigorously opposed comprehensive social programs and a more equal distribution of the national wealth (Johnston 2003; Phillips 2008). Their message of the superiority of market fundamentalism has been aimed at a public who are told that in an era of intensified globalization, maintaining U.S. competitiveness requires widespread sacrifice, including a reversal of the even modest redistributive policies that this country had over much of the twentieth century. It may well be that without campaign finance and lobbying reform it will be difficult to gain much traction for the proposals we have made here.

On the other hand, the extent and severity of the current economic crisis have eroded confidence that the country is on the right track. Challenges to neoliberal assumptions and policies have gained legitimacy as the consequences of market fundamentalism, deregulation, tax policies that favor wealthy investors, decimation of the public infrastructure and public programs, a slashed social safety net, and trade policies that reward outsourcing and job migration outside the United States have become highly visible. However, with hundreds of billions of dollars going to government bailouts to financial institutions and the auto industry, and more than $800 billion allocated to stimulate economic recovery, competition will be fierce for the kinds of dollars needed to enact the policies we propose. In this environment it would be foolish to imagine that all, or many, of our proposals are likely to be enacted. So why even make them?

Reform of our social safety net and broader redistribution policies are needed now to *simultaneously* spur economic recovery, avoid further economic catastrophe for millions of ordinary families, and begin to reverse the extreme economic polarization that was integral to, and fueled, the fiscal excesses and policy mistakes of the recent era. The reforms would also strengthen the public sector and add public-sector jobs, a strategy that has worked in the past both to counter and to cope with economic crisis. Although the revenue necessary to implement these programs is substantial, it *can* be generated if redistributive tax and other policies are enacted so that prosperity is more broadly shared once the recovery begins. This is exactly what happened in the aftermath of the Great Depression when, over several decades, this country combined strong economic growth and a more equitable sharing of the resulting prosperity than has been the case since redistributive policies were reversed, beginning around 1980.

At the heart of this book is the insight that perspective matters, and we have shown how even among those immersed in the social welfare system, administrators, workers, and clients experience and interpret policies differently based, in part, on their positions in gendered, racialized class relations. One of many of the troubling consequences of the intensifying economic inequality of the past thirty years has been the polarization of perspective, along with income and wealth. Reforming our welfare system so that it more effectively serves as both an integral component of the social safety net and as a springboard for individuals to work themselves out of poverty will require that the needs, experiences, and perspectives of those near the bottom of the income and wealth distribution can be heard by and taken seriously by those in positions to make, implement, and assess policy.

Reforming welfare, rebuilding a strong social safety net, and developing universal social programs are not radical proposals, but they will be fiercely contested and they are unlikely to all happen at once. However, as we see our way out of the depths of this crisis, we need to envision an economic future that promotes race, class, and gender equality, departs from the dramatic income polarization of recent decades, and builds a stake for everyone in a revitalized economy. Perhaps the only silver lining in this economic crisis is that it has created an opening for a serious reconsideration of the failings of market fundamentalism. A large and diverse constituency of individuals, families, businesses, nonprofit organizations, and public institutions has demonstrated that they want change. Many advocate fundamental change. The Obama administration faces enormous challenges to be sure. But they have a mandate for change that should not be ignored.

The main barriers to achieving the policies we advocate are neither a deficit of smart policy proposals, nor their price tags. The main obstacle is politics, especially the enormous political power of the well-endowed opposition. But even among advocates for change within progressive movements, there is too frequently a failure to address the deep divisions of race, gender, and class that have constituted both blinders and barriers to the strong coalitions needed to move the country in a new direction. These reform proposals will not go far unless many organizations, communities, and individuals come together to question the wisdom and fairness of the path we are on and to demand and work for change. These include groups that represent the collective interests of working people such as unions and the larger labor movement, organizations of the poor and advocates for the poor, civil rights and racial justice groups, immigrants and welfare rights coalitions, women's organizations, sexual minorities, veterans, and advocates for children, the elderly, and the sick and disabled.

Public policy is too important to be left to the policy makers. Studying and watching welfare reform unfold and be differently assessed and experienced by groups with different stakes in and perspectives on the policy process is a stark reminder of why we need a far more inclusive process for envisioning, crafting, and evaluating public policy. Welfare reform as we have known it may not have been a success, but it can offer a new generation who care about social justice and shared prosperity important lessons, particularly if they have to respond to the demands of a re-energized progressive movement for economic security and equality.

Appendix

SITUATING OURSELVES

The team that carried out the ethnographic research was comprised of seven women.[1] The project leaders, both affiliated with the Center for the Study of Women in Society at the University of Oregon, were Joan Acker and Sandra Morgen, a sociologist and anthropologist, respectively.[2] Jill Weigt and Lisa Gonzales were graduate students in the department of sociology at the University of Oregon and since we began writing, Jill has become an assistant professor in sociology at California State University—San Marcos.[3] Kate Barry, then head of the Women's Center at Lane Community College, and Suzanne Williams, an independent scholar who later became an instructor in the sociology department at Lane Community College, are both sociologists.[4] Sonja Vegdahl was an assistant professor of Social Work at Concordia College. Six of the team members are white women, one a Latina. Our class backgrounds are not uniform, representing a spectrum from (some) raised poor to (most of us) comfortably middle class. Of the team members, Acker, Morgen, and Weigt, the coauthors of this book, were the only ones involved in the study from beginning to end. Although Weigt began the study as a graduate student, her long-term involvement in all aspects of the study, as well as her professional development, positions her as a fully equal collaborator in the writing of this book.

We understand that a recitation of our gender, race, and class identities does not make transparent—either to the reader or to ourselves—the complex ways that our individual and collective social locations have influenced the analysis in this book. As authors we share social locations as white women, mothers, and social scientists, for example, but we differ in terms of class, generation, past experience with welfare agencies, ethnicity, and our relative power as research team members. Although we are all white and all mothers, for example, what those identities mean or our daily practices of mothering are very different. During the research and writing of the book Joan's adult children lived in other states and Sandi's children were in high school (and lived at home) and then in college and/or the labor force (and no longer lived at home). Jill's children were preschoolers and then elementary school-aged so she was providing a different kind of care on a daily basis.

Joan and Sandi are both from middle-class backgrounds, but class experiences were mediated by history and family specifics. By standard sociological indicators of socioeconomic status, Jill hails from upwardly mobile working-class origins. We are each feminists, and our feminism has helped to shape our views of the world and the research we do. But what feminism means and the ways we (have) practice(d) feminism in our daily lives and activities are different. We are all academics, but Joan is a professor emerita, Sandi is a full professor, and Jill was both a graduate student and then a tenure-track (now tenured) faculty member at a teaching university at different points during this work.

Our theoretical and political investments are compatible, but they are not identical. Those differences were sometimes challenging as we saw or analyzed things differently, or as they affected the intellectual and emotional nature of our relationships, but they also greatly enriched the research and writing processes.

How our individual and collective identities, histories, politics, disciplinary training, and other everyday responsibilities shaped the research is a more complex matter. Each of these surely affected how we were perceived by welfare administrators, workers, and clients. They affected how comfortable we were and what we saw as we observed different interactions between workers and clients or administrators and workers, and our rapport and interpretations of our interviews with workers and clients. For example, Joan had worked in public welfare and has a master's degree in social work. This experience gave her a different view of the stresses involved in doing the work of welfare. The differences that emerged from all of this variously shaped our discussions, our analyses, and how and what we wrote individually and collectively.

Perhaps what is most important is that we chose to do this research and write this book because we were deeply troubled by how we imagined, and then saw, these new welfare policies affecting low-income families. We were also concerned about what these new policies would mean for the public-sector workers whose jobs, while very different from our own, were also affected by the economic and political dynamics of neoliberalization.

So we began this research with skepticism about the voluble claim that "work is always better than welfare" and the less explicit assumption that recipients of public assistance were not (or had not in the past been) working, either as paid employees or unpaid providers of care for their families. While our stances and practices as researchers were not "objective" (in the positivist sense of values neutrality), we have tried to convey accurately what we learned from the people who so generously gave of their time to talk to us and let us watch them at work.

Notes

PROLOGUE

1. States vary dramatically in the proportions of welfare-eligible families (by income) who receive TANF. Oregon, for example, mirrored the national average exactly with 21 percent of poor adults and children receiving cash assistance. This variance is significantly influenced by *how* states chose to organize welfare programs in the wake of federal welfare reform, that is, what rules and regulations they adopted and how they implemented those rules. According to the *New York Times,* the share of poor children and parents that received welfare was 10 percent or less in fifteen states in 2008: Alabama, Arkansas, Colorado, Florida, Georgia, Idaho, Illinois, Louisiana, Mississippi, North Carolina, Oklahoma, South Carolina, Texas, Utah, and Wyoming. Some states were much more generous. In three states the share of poor families' children and parents receiving cash assistance was twice the national average (42 percent) or more: California, Maine, and Vermont (DeParle and Erickson 2009).

INTRODUCTION

1. Pub. L. 104-193, 110 Stat. 2105.

2. This name, like all those of the women and men we interviewed for this book, is a pseudonym.

3. Handler and Hasenfeld 2006; Kilty and Segal 2006; Urban Institute 2006.

4. Albelda and Withorn 2002; Nelson 2002; Schram and Soss 2002.

5. Adult and Family Services (AFS) was renamed Children, Adults, and Families (CAF) Division of the Oregon Department of Human Services (ODHS) after we completed our study. We will use its former name in this book to be consistent with what it was called while we were doing our research.

6. Book-length accounts based on ethnography include, e.g., Davis 2006; DeParle 2004; Dodson 1999; Hays 2002; Kingfisher 2002; Marchevsky and Theoharis 2006; Reese 2005; Seccombe 1999.

7. Cf., Clarke 2004; Goode and Maskovsky 2001; Kingfisher 2002; Piven 2002; Schram 2006.

8. The Deficit Reduction Act or Pub. L. 109-171, 120 Stat. 4 was enacted February 8, 2006. Reauthorization of TANF was one of its provisions. However the main intent and impact of the legislation was to cut forty billion dollars from entitlement programs such as Medicare and Medicaid, change student loan formulas, and mandate other cost-savings measures.

9. Brodkin 1986; Lurie 2006; Ridzi 2009.

10. Cf., Cherry 2007; Handler and Hasenfeld 2006; Kilty and Segal 2006.

11. Cf., Blank and Haskins 2001; Hamilton 2002; Loprest and Zedlewski 2006.

12. Davis 2006; Fujiwara 2008; Henrici 2006; Kingfisher 2002; Lein et al. 2007; Marchevsky and Theoharis 2006; Scott et al. 2004; Seccombe 1999.

13. See, e.g., Brodkin 1997; Lurie 2006; Ridzi 2009.

14. See chapter 3 for more discussion of this aspect of the research, including a lengthier discussion of methodology.

15. The observations in Bridgetown were over eleven months, between April 1998 and March 1999. Observations at Woodside and Coastal spanned six months each, between March 1998 and December 1998. Field notes were pooled, team meetings were opportunities for comparing notes, and data analysis was done, in the main, by the authors of this book.

16. JOBS is the name given to state's employment and training programs for public assistance recipients or applicants. JOBS staff are often employees of organizations other than AFS who receive subcontracts to provide job readiness services. However, some JOBS employees have work stations inside AFS branch offices and others work out of other locations.

17. Access to these branches necessitated the approval of the executive staff of AFS *and* of the branch managers. We explained the study to workers at staff meetings, emphasizing that we were there not mainly/only to study their interactions with clients but also to explore how welfare restructuring was affecting them as workers. We also asked permission from individual workers to observe their work and, of course, secured their consent for individual interviews.

18. We discuss *diversion* in various parts of the book. Essentially, diverted clients were those who filed an application for TANF but who did not ultimately get on TANF, although they frequently did receive some financial and other services as part of the assessment process.

19. The Oregon Survey Research Lab (OSRL) at the University of Oregon conducted the telephone survey, which was designed by the Center for the Study of Women in Society (CSWS) Welfare Research Team, representatives from AFS, and the director of OSRL. Each of the telephone interviews took about an hour to administer.

20. Jill Weigt conducted, as part of the research for her doctoral dissertation, these additional interviews. See Weigt 2002.

21. Feminist epistemologists have argued that theories about the nature of knowledge have been constructed from positions within male-defined and dominated arenas of power. Women's experience and voice were absent or invisible from such positions. Understanding of the nature of knowledge was faulty because of this absence. Feminists of color made similar criticisms of feminist theorizing from the perspectives of white, middle-class women; cf., Collins 2000; Harding 2004; Naples 2003.

22. Avery and Peffley 2003; Clawson and Trice 2000; deMause and Rendell 2007; Gilens 1999; Hancock 2004; Lens 2002.

23. Increased reporting about poverty in New Orleans, revealed to the world by the storm Katrina, often followed the racist interpretations of poverty in the media at large.

24. This includes Bhavnani 2001; Brewer 1993; Collins 2000; Crenshaw 1991; Dill and Zambrana 2009; Fujiwara 2008; Glenn 1999; McCall 2005; Mullings 1997; Zinn and Dill 1996

25. We are not alone in our disappointment with much of the research that has been done to assess the outcomes and processes of welfare reform. Marchevsky and Theoharis, for example, critique one of the largest studies of welfare reform, the Urban Change Project, funded by over $26 million from public and private sources, for uncritically adopting the assumptions of work-first welfare reform, neglecting the "structural context of recipient's lives and choices," and parading as objective science on the basis of the positivist research methodologies that give the appearance of being "politically neutral and value-free" (2006, 208).

26. An earnings disregard is that portion of the wages earned monthly by a welfare recipient that is disregarded, i.e., not counted, when welfare workers determine a family's eligibility for welfare. A higher earnings disregard allows a breadwinner to earn more in wages without losing benefits or having their benefits decreased. This effectively encourages low-wage employment.

27. Federal TANF rules require that families who receive child support while on TANF must sign over that support to the state. A "pass through" program is one in which a state redistributes some or all of its share of that money (a portion goes to the federal government) back to the family. From 1984 to 1996 states had to "pass through" the first fifty dollars of collected child support. States were not allowed to count that fifty dollars when determining income-eligibility for AFDC. Both these rules were changed by PRWORA.

28. The welfare *leaver* was defined in these studies as someone who left or was diverted from TANF at a particular moment in time and who stayed off TANF for a defined period of time. For a critique of these studies, see, e.g., Morgen 2002.

CHAPTER 1

1. But see more comprehensive feminist histories of the U.S. welfare state; e.g., Abramovitz 1996; Gordon 1994; Mittelstadt 2005; Quadagno 1994. An excellent source on comparative welfare state scholarship is O'Connor, Orloff, and Shaver 1999.

2. Much research exists on the history of assistance to the poor. Many authors identify the 1834 Poor Law Reform in Great Britain and similar efforts in the United States as critical turning points in how governments dealt with the economic insecurity, poverty, and dislocation resulting from the development of capitalist economies. See, in addition to Polanyi (1957), e.g., Piven and Cloward (1993).

3. Abramovitz 1996; Gordon 1994; Katz 1996.

4. Abramovitz 1996; Kornbluh 2007; Mink 1998; Quadagno 1994; Roberts 1997.

5. Keynesian economics is more complex, encompassing, and far-reaching than this reductive statement. See the collected works of John M. Keynes.

6. Abramovitz 1996; Gordon 1994; Mink 1998; Williams 2003.

7. P.L. 74-271, 49 Stat. 620; or Title IV of the Social Security Act of 1935.

8. There have been many changes to this program over time. We do not attempt to catalogue all the changes. However, the name change does signal the program's gradual (though minimal) recognition of the need to provide some support to the caretakers of poor children. In 1950 the federal government began to provide some support to the caretaker relative, almost always the mother. In 1961 the program was changed to allow for minimal support of an unemployed parent and in 1962 for a second parent in a family with an incapacitated or unemployed parent.

9. Kornbluh 2007; Piven and Cloward 1993; Roberts 1997. Thanks to welfare rights activism in the 1960s many of these practices were changed. Thus, the racial composition of the welfare rolls more closely reflected the racial demographics of poverty.

10. Limitations on women's service in the U.S. Armed Forces due to military policy meant that few were direct beneficiaries of the housing and education benefits. Exclusionary military recruitment and discharge procedures disenfranchised African Americans and other people of color from benefits, compounding the effects of segregation on access to higher education and housing (Lutz 2001; Williams 2003). This meant that even the relatively limited number of men of color who were eligible to receive G.I. Bill benefits could not use them or benefit as much from the mobility and asset accumulation consequences of education and home ownership.

11. Availability of these benefits to white, male veterans, but not to most veterans of color or women, is one cause of the huge disparities in the accumulation of family assets (wealth) between white families and families of color that continue to this day.

12. Kornbluh 2007; Piven and Cloward 1971; West 1981.

13. Many conservatives have opposed social welfare for decades. That the attack on welfare became so concerted and successful after the 1980s speaks more to the growing

power of conservatives in national and state politics than to a shift in conservative thought about social welfare in that period.

14. Morgen and Weigt 2001; O'Connor 2001; Phillips 1990.

15. Avery and Peffley 2003; Mink 1998; Roberts 1997.

16. Piven and Cloward (1993) also discuss the symbolic importance of AFDC.

17. Clucas, Henkels, and Steel 2005; Ellis 2002; Morgen 2006.

18. For more information see the AIFE website http://www.fullemployment.org/.

19. Oregon's JOBS Plus program placed people on TANF (and some who were on Unemployment Insurance) in limited-duration training positions with private employers. The employer received a state subsidy to help reimburse the cost of hiring the "trainee" for the short-term job with state dollars equivalent to the welfare, Food Stamps, and/or Unemployment Insurance benefits that, otherwise, the individual would have received as public assistance. The premise of the program was that these training jobs would provide the experience necessary for trainees to move into unsubsidized positions at the end of the program.

CHAPTER 2

1. We understand "the State" to be an assemblage of sectors of government; public institutions and agencies; practices, processes, and relations of ruling; and public-sector workplaces characterized by organizational hierarchies, managerial strategies, wage and salary scales, job descriptions, and working conditions. States are, and are embroiled in, complex political, economic, and social processes that include relations within the public sector and relations between the public and private sectors. However, given processes of privatization, the distinction between State and non-State or public and private institutions and relations is permeable and in flux as neoliberalization transforms the very meanings, contours, missions, and capabilities of State institutions and practices—a point we mention, but do not have the space to fully develop, here.

2. This is no coincidence. The agency is proud of and works intentionally toward having a diverse workforce.

3. This compares favorably to figures for all state agencies that indicate that 41.5% of employees in mid- or upper-level management were women and 8.7% were persons of color (Adult and Family Services 2000, p. 33).

4. MDRC is a "nonprofit, nonpartisan social policy research" organization that has conducted large-scale evaluation research of policies and programs, including welfare-to-work programs, since the early 1970s. More than half of its annual budget of over $35 million in 2004 was from grants and contracts with local, state, and federal agencies. MDRC conducts evaluation research based on a method it pioneered of randomly assigning study participants into control and experimental groups to evaluate program design. They tout this method as similar to the gold-standard experimental studies done in medicine, "the same highly reliable methodology that is used to test new medicines." http://www.mdrc.org/about_what_is_mdrc.htm (accessed September 14, 2008).

5. Of the seven study sites, four, including Portland, had labor force attachment programs, and seven had various education-focused programs. Portland's program, however, was unlike the other three, emphasizing "labor force attachment" in two ways distinguished by study authors: (1) it offered GED preparation classes to clients whom case managers believed would benefit from them, and (2) case managers ostensibly encouraged clients to find "good" jobs that paid above minimum wage.

6. They observed that in the "program group" in Portland, "staff encouraged people to seek and accept 'good' full-time jobs paying more than the minimum wage with benefits

and potential for advancement" (Scrivener et al. 1998, ES-7). They favorably compared the Portland "program group" to other sites in terms of relatively stronger job development and placement services, greater success in helping clients without high school diplomas to complete GEDs, and more focused limited training programs available to some clients (Hamilton et al. 2002, ES-3). Eschewing a claim of causality, the report argues that Portland's combination of a "strong employment message," a "willingness to impose sanctions," and "strong job development and placement services" were "influential factors" in the program's successful outcomes (Scrivener et al. 1998, ES-21).

7. This prompt, which essentially recycles the AFS motto "work is better than welfare, always," was inserted into the survey by an AFS representative. The exact wording of this question was "From your point of view, do you think you are better off working or on cash assistance?" We had already developed (and did ask) several other questions that we believed would give respondents an opportunity to give an overall assessment of how their families were doing. But AFS insisted we include this question.

8. Our team developed an independent media strategy for disseminating the research in the final study. The result was that the press tended to present a more complex picture of welfare reform than at the point of the interim report. The lead editorial in *The Oregonian* on January 28, 2001, bore the headline "Welfare reform's successes: A study by the UO points to problems, but some of the system's accomplishments are undeniable." Other newspapers bore headlines such as "Poverty struggle remains" (*Statesman Journal,* Salem, January 25, 2001); "Welfare reform no cure-all" (*The Register Guard,* Eugene, January 25, 2001); and "Welfare-to-work study uncovers income problems" (*The Oregonian,* Portland, January 25, 2001).

9. Because the poverty rate differs depending on both the number of related persons in a household and whether the household head is older or younger than 65, 200 percent of the poverty rate differs for different household configurations. For example, using data from 2000, 200 percent of the poverty line was $17,918 for a single adult under 65; $23,738 for a two-person household including one child under age 18; and $27,748 for a three-person household, including two children under 18. For a chart with the poverty rates for all household types in 2000 see Dalaker 2001.

10. For 2000, additional goals were set to reduce the first-time demand for public assistance among young adults by decreasing rates of teen pregnancy, teen drug use, and juvenile crime and increasing school graduation and placement rates for young adults.

11. The exact wording of AFS goals, measurable outcomes, and performance measures changed somewhat over the years of our observation of the agency. This list appeared in the September 1999 Quarterly Performance Update, published by the Department of Human Services, Adult and Family Services Division. We chose to use this version because it was published roughly halfway through the period of our research.

12. Some of the trainings we observed included workshops on relating to clients more effectively, domestic violence, and how to use the new AFS policy manual.

13. Unfortunately, over the years a combination of budget woes and changes in the ideological framework of Oregon's legislative leadership resulted in periods of contraction, often severe, of subsidized health coverage for low-income working families in Oregon.

CHAPTER 3

1. Elena Lopez, Latina case manager, twenty-four years experience with AFS.

2. Donald Henderson, case manager, fourteen years experience with AFS.

3. Our work in this chapter builds on that of Brodkin 1997; Handler and Hasenfeld 1997; Kingfisher 1996; Lipsky 1980; Lurie 2006; Meyers, Glaser, and MacDonald 1998.

4. We are sometimes deliberately vague about occupational and demographic information in order to protect the identities of these workers.

5. The Emergency Assistance (EA) program provides "temporary financial assistance and supportive services to eligible families during crisis or emergent situations when other resources are not immediately available. The most common emergent situation among EA applicants is homelessness" (AFS 1998b, Emergency Assistance A-1). When PRWORA was enacted, instead of the EA program being funded by a 50% federal match, the funding came from the TANF block grant dollars. Along with the change in funding, states were granted much greater flexibility in program eligibility. In October 1998 the maximum benefit was $350 for clients applying for benefits at AFS, except in cases of domestic violence or disaster relief, in which case $1,200 was available.

6. The Child Support Program (CPS) is described in the policy manual as fostering self-sufficiency by "fostering the value that primary responsibility for the support of dependent children rests with their parents, including their non-custodial parents. CPS establishes legal paternity for dependent children when needed, and establishes, modifies, and enforces child support orders on behalf of dependent children" (AFS 1998b: Child Support Program A-1).

7. Demographic breakdowns were not available for all AFS workers statewide.

8. In September 1998, persons of color were 20.3% of AFS staff, compared with 9.6% of State of Oregon employees and 8.7% of the state labor force (Adult and Family Services 1998).

9. We do not have details on the types of public assistance received by workers. We do know that some received Food Stamps only during a brief financial crisis or while they were students. Receiving Food Stamps was common among college students prior to restrictions on the program introduced in the 1980s.

10. Even the top annual wage for case managers ($33,768) was significantly below the 1999 mean annual income of white men in the western United States ($39,981) (U.S. Bureau of the Census 2008a).

11. These were unpaid jobs given to TANF recipients with little work experience to help prepare them to enter the labor force.

12. These percentages are our calculations based on agency data for size of staff in two periods, 1993–1995 and 1999–2001. Thus, the percentages do not represent staff reductions in particular years.

13. Although "case manager" was a new job category, many case managers with long experience at the agency told us that they had always worked intensively with clients, and while their jobs had not changed substantially, the rhetorical support for case management and, in some cases, the resources to back it up were new additions to the package.

14. Data for Bridgetown branch area and larger community calculated from the American Community Survey, 1996. Data cited in this paragraph are for 1996.

15. U.S. Census Bureau, Small Area Income and Poverty Estimates for Oregon Counties 1998. www.census.gov/cgi-bin/saipe/saipe.cgi.

16. Ibid.

17. Calculated as total branch TANF caseload divided by number of case managers in each branch.

18. Statewide, TANF cases declined by 56% during this period. Percentages calculated by authors from Oregon Department of Human Services data. http://www.dhsresources.hr.state.or.us.

19. Supplemental Security Income is the federal program administered through the Social Security Administration to assist people who have permanent disabilities.

20. In 2000 Oregon had a higher hunger rate and a higher food insecurity rate than almost all other states, according to a U.S. Department of Agriculture study (Leachman 2001). What impact the reduction of welfare caseloads might have on the amount of hunger in the population is unclear. Advocate groups make a strong case for connection.

21. The neoliberal ideological valorization of privatization explains the nationwide practice of subcontracting, often to private firms, the responsibility for jobs and employment services.

CHAPTER 4

1. These signs were present in most Oregon welfare offices in the late 1990s until antipoverty advocates convinced AFS to remove the signs in 1999.

2. Davis 2006; Gooden and Douglas 2006; Neubeck and Cazenave 2001.

3. Fording 2003; Gooden and Douglas 2006; Schram 2003; Soss et al. 2001.

4. See, e.g., Frankenberg 1993; Lipsitz 1998; Page and Thomas 1994.

5. See, e.g., Hancock 2004; Mink 1999; Roberts 2002.

6. Compare this number of cases with the experience of one of the authors (Joan Acker) in doing intensive social casework: In her experience, thirty cases at any one time was considered to be the absolute maximum that any social worker could handle effectively.

7. Many of the Food Stamp errors were not about the amount of the Food Stamp award but concerned small details such as these, which counted as errors for the purposes of the federal audit.

CHAPTER 5

1. One group of AFS clients is not well represented in this chapter—"the hard to serve," who have not successfully moved off the TANF roles. They were not the target of the study sample, which included only those who had left or been diverted from TANF or Food Stamps.

2. These numbers are for the in-depth sample; although they are similar to the telephone survey sample in which 58% of respondents were employed at both survey contacts (13% at the first but not the second contact, 8% at the second but not the first contact), and 19% were not employed at either contact. In this sample, 61% of those not employed at the first interview had worked for wages within the previous year (Acker et al. 2001).

3. In much of the text we will revert to glossing the sample as women, although there are a small number of men (3) included in the sample. We do this to constantly remind the reader that we are, for the most part, talking about women. When we quote a man, we will note his gender.

4. Burnham 2001; Gooden 1998; Neubeck and Cazenave 2001; Schram, Soss, and Fording 2003.

5. The costs of higher education are beyond the budgets of many low-income families. A 2006 national study estimates the current net cost of public universities and colleges as the equivalent of about 57% of the net income of a family in the bottom quintile of the United States; this compares to 17% and 7% for middle- and high-income families, respectively (Callan 2006). However, in Oregon, advocates for changes in this policy did finally succeed, armed with the results of this study, in opening the door to higher education for more TANF recipients. In 2003 Oregon's governor signed the "Parents as Scholars" program that allowed 1% of the TANF caseload to count postsecondary education toward the work requirement.

6. Brandwein 1999; Raphael 2000; Rennison and Wechans 2000; Richie 1996.

7. For similar sentiments documented in other studies, see Dodson 1999, Kingfisher 1996, and Seccombe 2007.

CHAPTER 6

1. Chase-Lansdale and Pittman 2002; Monroe and Tiller 2001; Scott et al. 2004.

2. Cherry 2007; Loprest 2001; Peterson, Song, and Jones-DeWeever 2003.

3. The quality of jobs has been assessed by a number of researchers. Kalleberg, Reskin, and Hudson (2000), for example, found that in the 1990s one in seven U.S. jobs lacked all of the criterion used to code a "good" job: wages over $6.00 an hour, health benefits, and a pension.

4. This finding may be influenced by the timing of our study in relation to the restructuring process. Case managers informed us that they were only beginning to work with long-term recipients, those who were presumed to have the most serious "barriers" to employment. Thus, those we interviewed were probably disproportionately short-term clients of TANF.

5. Spalter-Roth et al. 1995; Susser 1996.

6. Loprest 2001, 2003; Richer, Savner, and Greenberg 2001.

7. Oregon ranked ninth highest among fifty states in 1998 (with a rate of 5.58%), fifth highest in 1999 (with a rate of 5.45%), and ninth again in 2000 (with a rate of 6.5%) (U.S. Bureau of Labor Statistics 1999).

8. Chaudry 2004; Henly and Lyons 2000; Kalil et al. 2000; Presser and Cox 1997; Scott, London, and Hurst 2005.

9. E.g., Brush 2006; Cherlin 2003; Coontz and Folbre 2002.

10. The term partnering here refers to involvement in intimate relationships, both cohabiting and non-cohabiting, that entail some degree of day-to-day logistical and/or financial interdependence. None of the interviewees revealed to us that they were in same-sex partnerships; thus, all of the partnerships discussed involve heterosexual relationships.

11. The high rate of partnership at the last interview may be, in part, an artifact of being able to locate individuals who were slightly more financially stable than others.

CONCLUSION

1. E.g., Albelda and Withorn 2002; Handler and Hasenfeld 2006; Horton and Shaw 2002; Kilty and Segal 2006; Marchevsky and Theoharis 2006; Morgen and Maskovsky 2003.

2. E.g., Abramovitz 2000; Kilty and Segal 2006; Mink 1999; Piven 2001; Roberts 2002; Schram 2006.

3. E.g., Cherry 2007; Haskins and Sawhill 2007; Mead 2007; Sawhill et al. 2002.

4. The TANF caseload was at its lowest level in 2001 when statewide there were 16,517 TANF cases (Oregon Department of Human Services [ODHS] 2008). As we pointed out in chapter 1, this was a 61% drop from the top caseload level of 42,000 cases in 1994, before PRWORA. By 2003, when the postboom recession was most severe, TANF served 18,462 families. The caseload remained about the same until 2008 when in July of that year it climbed to 21,256, an increase of 14.9% from the year before (ODHS 2008).

5. These data are complicated. Some of the decrease results from declining caseloads. However OCPP is accurate in attributing a significant portion of this decline to fiscal realities and policy decisions to reduce spending on these particular programs for poor families.

6. Whether and how much actual loss states will face is still unclear. There have been changes in the rules since 2005 and considerable wrangling and negotiation between states and the federal government.

7. These were based on the baseline TANF participation rate in fiscal year 2004 (before passage of the Deficit Reduction Act), the rate gap for 2007, and the potential loss of income to states if states lost the full 5%.

8. Terran's study is interesting, but she was able to interview only a small number of case managers. Many declined to be interviewed because their outsized caseloads were so large that they did not even have time for a one-hour interview. Needless to say, the combination of higher caseloads and more intense pressures to be supportive, engaged, and humane could be experienced as dichotomous pressures.

9. The months in which the adult on the grant had certain barriers to work would not be counted toward the limit, and children can continue to receive benefits after the parent has reached the limit.

10. Davis 2006; Fujiwara 2006, 2008; Gooden and Douglas 2006.

11. The United States was one of the four countries out of a total of 173 countries studied that did not offer some form of guaranteed paid leave for mothers after childbirth (Heymann 2001). The United States' Family Medical Leave Act (FMLA) currently offers 12 weeks of job-guaranteed unpaid leave to employees who have worked 1,250 hours in the past 12 months for an employer with over 50 employees in a 75-mile radius. Experts estimate that only about 50 percent of the *employed* population are covered by FMLA (i.e., they work for employers with 50 or more employees) and are also eligible for FMLA (i.e., they have been with their employer for the previous year and worked at least 1,250 hours). Some also estimate that only about 20 percent of new mothers are covered and eligible for the FMLA (Fass 2009). This low percentage probably results from high rates of employment of young women in small, service sector firms as well as in businesses such as convenience stores and restaurants that often offer part-time work. The proportion of new mothers actually using the FMLA is probably much lower because many are in low wage jobs and cannot afford to take an unpaid leave.

12. Review of the many proposals about how to calibrate the minimum wage to be a family-sustaining wage is beyond the scope of this work. However, our point is that without such strategies to ensure that employment is a meaningful route to self-sufficiency, "work first" welfare policies will be empty promises.

13. See, e.g., Oregon Health Fund Board, http://healthfundboard.oregon.gov.

APPENDIX

1. Others who worked on the project at different points, but who were not involved with either the observations in welfare offices or the in-depth interviews, include the following: Terri Heath, project manager for the survey portion of the study; Patty Gwartney, then head of the Oregon Survey Research Lab at the University of Oregon, oversaw a staff that did the telephone interviews for both waves of the telephone survey, and contributed to the design of the surveys; and Holly Langan, an undergraduate work-study student and then a graduate student in public policy at the University of Oregon, worked on the project in a variety of ways, including data analysis and clerical tasks.

2. Acker and Morgen were the principal investigators. In collaboration with other members of the research team, they were responsible for the design of the overall study, including the ethnographic study of three welfare offices and interviews with welfare workers and the telephone survey and in-depth interviews with TANF and Food Stamp clients. Acker and Morgen did observations and conducted interviews in two of the welfare offices—the ones we call Coastal and Woodside. They also conducted interviews with TANF and Food Stamp clients.

3. Jill Weigt did observations at the Bridgetown office and conducted in-depth interviews. Of the team members, Jill was in the field the longest, not only because the observations at Bridgetown were conducted over a longer period of time but also because she did a third round of interviews with a subsample of the in-depth sample for her dissertation. Lisa Gonzales joined the team during the in-depth interview portion of the study and conducted in-depth interviews.

4. Both Kate and Suzanne did observations in Bridgetown and Woodside and conducted some of the interviews with welfare workers. The Women's Center at Lane Community College was a unit that worked with many low-income women transitioning to community college. Kate's work there brought her into contact with hundreds of current and former welfare recipients, and she was also involved in statewide activities related to services for "women in transition" to community college.

Bibliography

Abramovitz, Mimi. 1996. *Regulating the Lives of Women*. Boston: South End Press.

———. 2000. *Under Attack, Fighting Back: Women and Welfare in the United States*. New York: Monthly Review Press.

Abramovitz, Mimi, and Sandra Morgen. 2006. *Taxes Are a Woman's Issue: Reframing the Debate*. New York: The Feminist Press.

Acker, Joan. 1988. "Gender, Class and Relations of Distribution." *Signs* 13 (3): 473–497.

———. 1990. "Hierarchies, Jobs, Bodies: A Theory of Gendered Organizations." *Gender & Society* 4 (2): 139–158.

———. 2006. *Class Questions, Feminist Answers*. Lanham, MD: Rowman and Littlefield.

Acker, Joan, Sandra Morgen, and Lisa Gonzales. 2002. *Policy Matters: Welfare Restructuring, Work, and Poverty: Policy Implications from Oregon*. Eugene: Center for the Study of Women in Society, University of Oregon. http://csws.uoregon.edu/?page_id=91

Acker, Joan, Sandra Morgen, Terri Heath, Kate Barry, Lisa Gonzales, and Jill Weigt. 2001. "Oregon Families Who Left Temporary Assistance for Needy Families (TANF) or Food Stamps: A Study of Economic and Family Well-Being, 1998–2000," vols. I & II. A report to Adult and Family Services, State of Oregon. Eugene: Center for the Study of Women in Society, University of Oregon. http://csws.uoregon.edu/?page_id=93

Acs, Gregory (2008). "Low Wage Workers in the United States: Status and Prospects." Testimony before the Committee on Ways and Means Subcommittee on Income Security and Family Support, United States House of Representatives. Urban Institute. http://www.urban.org/UploadedPDF/901190_Acs_low-wage_workers.pdf.

Adult and Family Services (AFS). 1996. Quarterly Performance Update, December. Salem, OR: Department of Human Services.

———. 1997. "A Short History of Welfare Reform in Oregon." Salem, OR: Department of Human Services.

———. 1998a. Quarterly Performance Update. September. Salem, OR: Department of Human Services.

———. 1998b. Family Services Manual. Emergency Assistance A-1. Child Support Program A-1. Salem, OR: Department of Human Services.

———. 2000. Quarterly Performance Update, December. Salem, OR: Department of Human Services.

Albelda, Randy. 2002. "What's Wrong with Welfare-to-Work?" In *Work, Welfare, and Politics: Confronting Poverty in the Wake of Welfare Reform*, edited by Frances Fox Piven, Joan Acker, Margaret Hallock, and Sandra Morgen, 73–80. Eugene: University of Oregon Press.

Albelda, Randy, and Chris Tilly. 1997. *Glass Ceilings and Bottomless Pits: Women's Work, Women's Poverty*. Cambridge, MA: South End Press.

Albelda, Randy, and Ann Withorn, eds. 2002. *Lost Ground: Welfare Reform, Poverty and Beyond*. Boston: South End Press.

American Institute for Full Employment. 1996. *Full Employment Newsletter* 1 (July).

Aron-Dine, Aviva. 2008. Improving the Refundable Child Tax Credit: An Important Step Toward Reducing Child Poverty. Washington, DC: Center on Budget and Policy Priorities, May 19. http://www.cbpp.org/10-24-07tax.pdf.

Aron-Dine, Aviva, and Isaac Shapiro. 2007. Share of National Income Going to Wages and Salaries at Record Low in 2006. Washington, DC: Center on Budget and Policy Priorities, March 29. http://www.cbpp.org/8-31-06inc.

Avery, James, and Mark Peffley. 2003. "Racial Context, Public Attitudes, and Welfare Effort in the American States." In *Race and the Politics of Welfare Reform*, edited by Sanford F. Schram, Joe Soss, and Richard C. Fording, 131–150 Ann Arbor: University of Michigan Press.

Bernstein, Jared, Chauna Brocht, and Maggie Spade-Aguilar. 2000. *How Much Is Enough? Basic Family Budgets for Working Families.* Washington, DC: Economic Policy Institute.

Bhavnani, Kum-Kum. 2001. *Feminism and "Race."* Oxford: Oxford University Press.

Blank, Rebecca, and Ron Haskins, eds. 2001. *The New World of Welfare.* Washington, DC: Brookings Institution Press.

Block, Fred, Richard Cloward, Barbara Ehrenreich, and Frances Fox Piven. 1987. *The Mean Season: The Attack on the Welfare State.* New York: Pantheon Books.

Boushey, Heather, Chauna Brocht, Bethney Gundersen, and Jared Bernstein. 2001. *Hardships in America: The Real Story of Working Families.* Washington, DC: Economic Policy Institute.

Boushey, Heather, and David Rosnick. 2004. *For Welfare Reform to Work, Jobs Must Be Available.* Washington, DC: Center for Economic and Policy Research. April 1. http://www.cepr.net/documents/publications/welfare_reform_2004_04.pdf.

Brady-Smith, Christy, Jeanne Brooks-Gunn, Jane Waldfogel, and Rebecca Fauth. 2001. "Work or Welfare? Assessing the Impacts of Recent Employment and Policy Changes on Very Young Children." *Evaluation and Program Planning* 24: 409–425.

Brandwein, Ruth. 1999. *Battered Women, Children, and Welfare Reform: The Ties That Bind.* Thousand Oaks, CA: Sage.

Brewer, Rose. 1993. "Theorizing Race, Class and Gender: The New Scholarship of Black Feminist Intellectuals and Black Women's Liberation." In *Theorizing Black Feminisms: The Visionary Pragmatism of Black Women,* edited by Stanlie James and Abenia Busia, 13–30. New York: Routledge.

Brodkin, Evelyn. 1986. *The False Promise of Administrative Reform: Implementing Quality Control in Welfare.* Philadelphia: Temple University Press.

———. 1997. "Inside the Welfare Contract: Discretion and Accountability in State Welfare Administration." *Social Science Review* 71:1–33.

Brown, Michael K., Martin Carnoy, Elliott Currie, Troy Duster, David B. Oppenheimer, Marjorie M. Shultz, and David Wellman. 2003. *White-Washing Race: The Myth of a Color-Blind Society.* Berkeley: University of California Press.

Brush, Lisa. 2001. "Poverty, Battering, Race and Welfare Reform." *Journal of Poverty* 5:67–89.

———. 2006. "Safety and Self-Sufficiency: Rhetoric and Reality in the Lives of Welfare Recipients." In *The Promise of Welfare Reform: Political Rhetoric and the Reality of Poverty in the Twenty-First Century,* edited by Keith Kilty and Elizabeth Segal, 183–192. New York: Haworth Press.

Burd-Sharps, Sarah, Kristen Lewis, and Eduardo Borges Martins. 2008. *The Measure of America: American Human Development Report.* New York: Columbia University Press.

Burnham, Linda. 2001. "Welfare Reform, Family Hardship, and Women of Color." *Annals of the American Academy of Political and Social Science* 577 (1): 38–48

Butler, Sandra, and Mary Katherine Nevin. 1997. "Welfare Mothers Speak: One State's Effort to Bring Recipient Voices to the Welfare Debate." *Journal of Poverty* 1:25–61.

Callan, Patrick. 2006. "College Affordability: Colleges, States Increase Financial Burdens on Students and Families." Measuring Up: The National Report Card on Higher Education, http://measuringup.highereducation.org/commentary/collegeaffordability.cfm.

Cancian, Francesca, and Stacey Oliker. 2000. *Caring and Gender.* Thousand Oaks, CA: Pine Forge Press.

Cancian, Maria, Robert Haveman, Daniel Meyer, and Barbara Wolfe. 2002. *Before and After TANF: The Economic Well-Being of Women Leaving Welfare.* Madison, WI: Institute for Research on Poverty.

Center for American Women and Politics. 2008. Women in Elective Office in 2008. New Brunswick, NJ: Rutgers University. http://www.cawp.rutgers.edu/fast_facts/levels_of_office/documents/elective.pdf.

Center for the Study of Women in Society Research Team. 2000. Memo to Adult and Family Services, January 18.

Chapman, Jeff, and Jared Bernstein. 2003. "Falling through the Safety Net: Low-Income Single Mothers in the Jobless Recovery." Economic Policy Institute, Issue Brief 191, April 11. http://www.epi.org/publications/entry/issuebriefs_ib191/.

Chase-Lansdale, P. Lindsay, and Laura Pittman. 2002. "Welfare Reform and Parenting: Reasonable Expectations." *Future of Children* 12:167–185.

Chaudry, Ajay. 2004. *Putting Children First: How Low-Wage Working Mothers Manage Child Care.* Newbury Park, CA: Russell Sage.

Cherlin, Andrew. 2003. "Should the Government Promote Marriage?" *Contexts* 2 (4): 22–29.

Cherry, Robert. 2004. "Assessing Welfare Reform Data: A Comment on Christopher." *Feminist Economics* 13 (2): 185–195.

———. 2007. *Welfare Transformed: Universalizing Family Policies That Work.* New York: Oxford University Press.

Christopher, Karen. 2004. "Welfare As We [Don't] Know It: A Review and Feminist Critique of Welfare Reform Research in the United States." *Feminist Economics* 10 (2): 143–171.

Clarke, John. 2004. *Changing Welfare, Changing States: New Directions in Social Policy.* Thousand Oaks, CA: Sage.

Clawson, Rosalee, and Rakuya Trice. 2000. Poverty As We Know It: Media Portrayals of the Poor. *Public Opinion Quarterly* 64:53–64.

Clucas, Richard, Mark Henkels, and Brent S. Steel. 2005. *Oregon Politics and Government: Progressives versus Conservative Populists.* Lincoln: University of Nebraska.

Collins, Patricia Hill. 2000. *Black Feminist Thought.* New York: Routledge.

Coontz, Stephanie, and Folbre, Nancy. 2002. *Marriage, Poverty, and Public Policy: A Discussion Paper from the Council on Contemporary Families.* Prepared for the Fifth Annual Council on Contemporary Families Conference, April 26–28. http://www.contemporaryfamilies.org/subtemplate.php?t=briefingPapers&ext=marriagepovertypublicpoli.

Coven, Martha. 2005. *An Introduction to TANF.* Washington, DC: Center on Budget and Policy Priorities. http://www.cbpp.org/1-22-02tanf2.htm.

Crenshaw, Kimberle Williams. 1991. "Mapping the Margins: Intersectionality, Identity Politics and Violence Against Women of Color." *Stanford Law Review* 43 (6): 1241–1279.

Crouse, Gil. 1999. "State Implementation of Major Changes to Welfare Policies, 1992–1998." Washington, DC: Office of Human Services Policy, Assistant Secretary for Planning and Evaluation, US Department of Health and Human Services.

Dalaker, Joseph. 2001. "Poverty in the United States 2000." U.S. Census Bureau, Current Population Reports, Series P.60-214. U.S. Government Printing Office: Washington, DC. http://www.census.gov/prod/2001pubs/p60-214.pdf

Davis, Dana-Ain. 2006. *Battered Black Women and Welfare Reform: Between a Rock and a Hard Place.* Albany: State University of New York Press.

DeParle, Jason. 2004. *American Dream: Three Women, Ten Kids, and a Nation's Drive to End Welfare.* New York: Penguin.

———. 2009. "Welfare Aid Isn't Growing as Economy Drops Off." *New York Times,* February 2, A1.

DeParle, Jason, and Matthew Erickson. 2009. Variations in Government Aid Across the Nation. *New York Times,* May 10, A18.

Deloitte Touche. 1990. *Oregon New JOBS: Oregon Adult and Family Services Division,* vol. 1. October 15. Salem, OR: Department of Human Services.

deMause, Neil, and Steve Rendell. 2007. "The Poor Will Always Be with Us—Just Not on the TV News: A FAIR (Fairness and Accuracy in Reporting) Study." http://www.fair.org/index.php?page=3172.

Dill, Bonnie Thornton, and Ruth Zambrana, eds. 2009. *Emerging Intersections: Race, Class, and Gender in Theory, Policy, and Practice.* Piscataway, NJ: Rutgers University Press.

Dodson, Lisa. 1999. *Don't Call Us Out of Name: The Untold Lives of Women and Girls in Poor America.* Boston, MA: Beacon Press.

Dodson, Lisa, and Leah Schmalzbauer. 2005. "Poor Mothers and Habits of Hiding: Participatory Methods in Poverty Research." *Journal of Marriage and Family* 67 (4): 949–959.

Dressel, Paula. 1992. "Patriarchy and Social Welfare Work." In *Human Services as Complex Organizations,* edited by Yeheskel Hasenfeld, 205–223. Newbury Park, CA: Sage.

Edin, Kathryn, and Laura Lein. 1997. *Making Ends Meet: How Single Mothers Survive Welfare and Low Wage Work.* New York: Russell Sage Foundation.

Ellingsaeter, Anne Lise, and Arnlaug Leira, eds. 2006. *Politicising Parenthood in Scandinavia: Gender Relations in Welfare States.* Bristol, UK: Policy Press.

Ellis, Richard. 2002. *Democratic Delusions: The Initiative Process in America.* Lawrence: University Press of Kansas.

Esping-Andersen, Gosta. 1990. *The Three Worlds of Welfare Capitalism.* Princeton, NJ: Princeton University Press.

Estes, Sarah Beth, and Jennifer Glass. 1996. "Job Changes Following Childbirth: Are Women Trading Compensation for Family Responsive Work Conditions?" *Work and Occupations* 23 (4): 405–436.

Fass, Sarah. 2009. "Paid Leave in the States: A Critical Support for Low-Wage Workers and Their Families." New York: National Center for Children in Poverty, Columbia University. http://www.nccp.org/publications/pdf/text_864.pdf

Folbre, Nancy. 1991. *The Invisible Heart: Economics and Family Values.* New York: The New Press.

Fording, Richard. 2003. "'Laboratories of Democracy' or Symbolic Politics?: The Racial Origins of Welfare Reform." In *Race and the Politics of Welfare Reform,* edited by

Sanford F. Schram, Joe Soss, and Richard C. Fording, 72–94. Ann Arbor: University of Michigan Press.

Frankenberg, Ruth. 1993. *White Women, Race Matters: The Social Construction of Whiteness*. Minneapolis: University of Minnesota Press.

Fraser, Nancy, and Linda Gordon. 1994. "A Geneology of Dependency: Tracing Key Word in the U.S. Welfare State." *Signs* 19 (2): 309–336.

Fujiwara, Lynn. 2006. Immigrants, Welfare, and the Persistence of Poverty. In *The Promise of Welfare Reform: Political Rhetoric and the Reality of Poverty in the Twenty-First Century*, edited by Keith Kilty and Elizabeth Segal, 237–248. New York: Haworth Press.

———. 2008. *Mothers without Citizenship: Asian Immigrant Families and the Consequences of Welfare Reform*. Minneapolis: University of Minnesota Press.

Garey, Anita Ilta. 1999. *Weaving Work and Motherhood*. Philadelphia: Temple University Press.

Gilens, Martin. 1999. *Why Americans Hate Welfare: Race, Media, and the Politics of Anti-poverty Policy*. Chicago: University of Chicago Press.

Glenn, Evelyn Nakano. 1999. "The Social Construction and Institutionalization of Gender and Race: An Integrative Framework." In *Revisioning Gender*, edited by Myra Feree, Judith Lorber, and Beth Hess, 3–43. Thousand Oaks, CA: Sage.

Goldberg, Bruce 2006a. Director's Message. Oregon Department of Human Services. March 3. http://www.oregon.gov/DHS/news/messages/2006messages/2006-0303.shtml.

———. 2006b. Director's Message. Oregon Department of Human Services. July 14. http://www.oregon.gov/DHS/news/messages/2006messages/2006-0714.shtml.

Goldschmidt, Neil. 1989. *Oregon Shines*. Salem: Oregon Progress Board. http://egov.oregon.gov/DAS/OPB/os_intro.shtml.

Gonzales, Lisa, Ken Hudson, and Joan Acker. 2007. "Diverting Dependency: The Effects of Diversion on the Short Term Outcomes of TANF Applicants." *Journal of Poverty* 11 (1): 83–106.

Goode, Judith, and Jeff Maskovsky. 2002. *The New Poverty Studies: The Ethnography of Power, Politics and Impoverished People in the United States*. New York: New York University Press.

Gooden, Susan. 1998. "All Things Not Being Equal: Differences in Caseworker Support toward Black and White Welfare Clients." *Harvard Journal of African American Public Policy* 4:79–110.

———. 2003. "Contemporary Approaches to Enduring Challenges: Using Performance Measures to Promote Racial Equality under TANF." In *Race and the Politics of Welfare Reform*, edited by Sanford F. Schram, Joe Soss, and Richard C. Fording, 254–275. Ann Arbor: University of Michigan Press.

Gooden, Susan, and Nakeina Douglas. 2006. "Ever Present, Sometimes Acknowledged, But Never Addressed: Racial Disparities in U.S. Welfare Policy." In *The Promise of Welfare Reform: Political Rhetoric and the Reality of Poverty in the Twenty-First Century*, edited by Keith Kilty and Elizabeth Segal, 207–222. New York: Haworth Press.

Gordon, Linda. 1994. *Pitied, But Not Entitled: Single Mothers and the History of Welfare, 1890–1935*. New York: Free Press.

Hamilton, Gayle. 2002. *Moving People from Welfare to Work: Lessons from the National Evaluation of Welfare-to-Work Strategies*. New York: Manpower Demonstration Research Corporation. http://aspe.hhs.gov/hsp/NEWWS/synthesis02/.

Hancock, Ange-Marie. 2004. *The Politics of Disgust: The Public Identity of the Welfare Queen*. New York: New York University Press.

Handler, Joel F., and Yeheskel Hasenfeld. 1997. *We the Poor People: Work, Poverty, and Welfare*. New Haven: Yale University Press.

———. 2006. *Blame Welfare, Ignore Poverty and Inequality*. New York: Cambridge University Press.

Haney, Lynne. 2004. "Introduction: Gender, Welfare, and States of Punishment." *Social Politics* 11 (3): 333–362.

Harding, Sandra. 2004. *The Feminist Standpoint Theory Reader: Intellectual and Political Controversies*. New York: Routledge.

Harrington, Michael. 1968. *The Other America: Poverty in the United States*. New York: Simon and Schuster.

Harris, Leslie. 1999. *Valuing Families: The State of Oregon's Families*. Eugene: Center for the Study of Women in Society, University of Oregon.

Harvey, David. 2005. *A Brief History of Neoliberalism*. Oxford: Oxford University Press.

Haskins, Ron. 2007. *Work over Welfare: The Inside Story of the 1996 Welfare Reform Law*. Washington, DC: Brookings Institution Press.

Haskins, Ron, and Isabel Sawhill. 2007. Introduction to *The Next Generation of Anti-Poverty Policies*. Special issue of *The Future of Children* 17 (2): 3–16. Washington, DC: Brookings Institution Press.

Henly, Julia R., and Sandra Lyons. 2000. "The Negotiation of Child Care and Employment Demands among Low-Income Parents." *Journal of Social Issues* 56:683–706.

Henrici, Jane. 2006. *Doing Without: Women and Work after Welfare Reform*. Tucson: University of Arizona Press.

Heymann, Jody. 2001. *The Widening Gap: Why America's Working Families Are in Jeopardy and What Can Be Done about It*. New York: Basic Books.

Hoback, Sandie. 1999. "Oregon Uses Kinder Approach to Welfare." *The Register Guard*, May 7.

———. 1999. *Presentation to the Joint Committee on Ways and Means, Human Resources Subcommittee*. Salem, OR: Department of Human Resources, Adult & Family Services Division.

———. 2000. "News Around AFS." *AFS Update*. Salem, OR, January 21.

Horton, John, and Linda Shaw. 2002. "Opportunity and Control: Living Welfare Reform in Los Angeles County." In *Work, Welfare and Politics: Confronting Poverty in the Wake of Welfare Reform*, edited by Frances Fox Piven, Joan Acker, Margaret Hallock, and Sandra Morgen, 197–212. Eugene: University of Oregon Press.

Howard, Christopher. 1997. *The Hidden Welfare State: Tax Expenditures and Social Policy in the United States*. Princeton, NJ: Princeton University Press.

———. 2008. *The Welfare State Nobody Knows: Debunking Myths about U.S. Social Policy*. Princeton, NJ: Princeton University Press.

Jacobs, Jerry A., and Kathleen Gerson. 2004. *The Time Divide: Work, Family, and Gender Inequality*. Cambridge: Harvard University Press.

Johnston, David Cay. 2003. *Perfectly Legal: The Covert Campaign to Rig Our Tax System to Benefit the Super Rich—and Cheat Everybody Else*. New York: Portfolio.

Jones-DeWeever, Avis. 2006. *Tenth Anniversary of Welfare Reform*. Washington, DC: Institute for Public Accuracy. August 10. http://accuracy.org/newsrelease.php?articleId=1335.

Jones-DeWeever, Avis, and Barbara Gault. 2006. *Resilient and Reaching for More: Challenges and Benefits of Higher Education for Welfare Participants and Their Children*. Washington, DC: Institute for Women's Policy Research no. D466. http://www.iwpr.org/pdf/D466.pdf.

Kalil, Ariel, Heidi Schweingruber, Marijata Daniel-Echols, and Ashli Breen. 2000. "Mother, Worker, Welfare Recipient: Welfare Reform and the Multiple Roles of

Low-Income Women." In *Coping with Poverty: The Social Contexts of Neighborhood, Work, and Family in the African American Community,* edited by Sheldon Danziger and Ann Chih Lin, 201–222. Ann Arbor: University of Michigan Press.

Kalil, Ariel, Kristen Seefeldt, and Hui-Chen Wang. 2002. "Sanctions and Material Hardship under TANF." *Social Service Review* 76 (4): 642–662.

Kalleberg, Arne, Barbara Reskin, and Ken Hudson. 2000. Bad Jobs in America: Standard and Nonstandard Employment Relations and Job Quality in the United States. *American Sociological Review* 65 (2): 256–278.

Katz, Michael B. 1996. *In the Shadow of the Poorhouse: A Social History of Welfare in America.* New York: Basic Books.

Keynes, John Maynard. 1971–1989. *The Collected Writings of John Maynard Keynes.* London: Macmillan.

Kilty, Keith M., and Elizabeth A. Segal, eds. 2006. *The Promise of Welfare Reform: Political Rhetoric and the Reality of Poverty in the Twenty-First Century.* New York: Haworth Press.

Kim, Marlene. 2000. "Women Paid Low Wages: Who They Are and Where They Work." *Monthly Labor Review,* Bureau of Labor Statistics (September), 26. http://www.bls.gov/opub/mlr/2000/09/art3full.pdf.

Kingfisher, Catherine. 1996. *Women in the American Welfare Trap.* Philadelphia: University of Pennsylvania Press.

———. 2002. *Western Welfare in Decline: Globalization and Women's Poverty.* Philadelphia: University of Pennsylvania.

Kornbluh, Felicia. 2007. *The Battle for Welfare Rights: Politics and Poverty in Modern America.* Philadelphia: University of Pennsylvania Press.

Kurz, Demie. 2002. "Poor Mothers and the Care of Teenage Children." In *Child Care and Inequality: Rethinking Carework for Children and Youth,* edited by Francesca Cancian, Demie Kurz, Andrew London, Rebecca Reviere, and Mary Tuominen, 23–26. New York: Routledge.

Leachman, Michael. 2001. *Hunger in Oregon.* Silverton: Oregon Center for Public Policy. http://www.ocpp.org/2001/01hunger.htm.

Leachman, Michael, and Joy Margheim. 2008. *Rolling Up Our Sleeves: Building an Oregon that Works for Working Families.* Silverton: Oregon Center for Public Policy.

Leachman, Michael, and Sara Merten. 2007. *Opportunities for Improving Oregon's TANF Program: A Checklist Comparing HB 2469 and HB 2180 on Nine Key Policy Options.* March 13. Silverton: Oregon Center for Public Policy.

Leachman, Michael, Sara Merten, and Chuck Sheketoff. 2005. *The TANF Shell Game: Oregon Uses Funds for Helping Poor Families Be Self-sufficient to Cover Other Budget Holes.* Silverton: Oregon Center for Public Policy.

Legal Momentum. n.d. *Why NOW Legal Defense Opposes Federal Marriage Promotion in TANF Reauthorization.* http://www.legalmomentum.org/assets/pdfs/marriagebackgrounder.pdf.

Lein, Laura, Deanna Scheznayder, Karen Douglas, and Daniel Schroeder. 2007. *Life After Welfare: Reform and the Persistence of Poverty.* Austin: University of Texas Press.

Leira, Arnlaug. 1992. *Welfare States and Working Mothers.* Cambridge: Cambridge University Press.

Lens, Vicki. 2002. "Public Voices and Public Policy: Changing the Societal Discourse on Welfare." *Journal of Sociology and Social Work* 24 (1): 137–154.

Levitis, Jason, and Jeremy Koulish. 2008. "State Earned Income Tax Credits: 2008 Legislative Update." Washington, DC: Center on Budget and Policy Priorities. http://www.cbpp.org/6-6-08sfp.htm.

Lipsitz, George. 1998. *The Possessive Investment in Whiteness: How White People Profit from Identity Politics.* Philadelphia: Temple University Press.

Lipsky, Michael. 1980. *Street Level Bureaucracy: Dilemmas of the Individual in Public Services.* New York: Russell Sage Foundation.

London, Andrew, Ellen Scott, Kathryn Edin, and Vicki Hunter. 2004. "Welfare Reform, Work-Family Tradeoffs, and Child Well-Being." *Family Relations* 53:148–158.

Loprest, Pamela. 2001. *How Are Families That Left Welfare Doing? A Comparison of Early and Recent Welfare Leavers. Assessing the New Federalism, Series B, 36.* Washington, DC: Urban Institute.

———. 2003. *Fewer Welfare Leavers Employed in Weak Economy.* Washington, DC: Urban Institute. http://www.urban.org/url.cfm?ID=310837.

Loprest, Pamela, and Sherila Zedlewski. 2006. *The Changing Role of Welfare in the Lives of Low-Income Families with Children.* Washington, DC: Urban Institute. http://www.urban.org/url.cfm?ID=311357.

Lurie, Irene. 2006. *At the Front Lines of the Welfare System: A Perspective on the Decline in Welfare Caseloads.* Albany, NY: Rockefeller Institute Press.

Lutz, Catherine. 2001. *Homefront: A Military City and the American Twentieth Century.* Boston: Beacon Press.

Marchevsky, Alejandra, and Jeanne Theoharis. 2006. *Not Working: Latina Immigrants, Low-Wage Jobs, and the Failure of Welfare Reform.* New York: New York University Press.

Maskovsky, Jeff, and Judith Goode. 2001. Introduction to *The New Poverty Studies: The Ethnography of Power, Politics, and Impoverished People in the United States,* edited by Judith Goode and Jeff Maskovsky, 1–36. New York: New York University Press.

Maskovsky, Jeff, and Catherine Kingfisher, eds. 2001. "Introduction to Globalization, Neoliberalism and Poverty in Mexico and the United States." *Urban Anthropology and Studies of Cultural System and World Economic Development* 30 (2–3): 105–123.

McCall, Leslie. 2005. "The Complexity of Intersectionality." *Signs* 30 (3): 1771–1800.

McDonald, Katrina Bell, and Elizabeth M. Armstrong. 2001. "De-romanticizing Black Intergenerational Support: The Questionable Expectations of Welfare Reform." *Journal of Marriage and Family* 63 (1): 213–223.

Mead, Lawrence. 2007. "Why Welfare Reform Succeeded." *Journal of Policy Analysis and Management* 26 (2): 370–374.

Menjivar, Cecilia. 2000. *Fragmented Ties: Salvadoran Immigrant Networks in America.* Los Angeles: University of California Press.

Mezey, Jennifer, Rachel Schumacher, Mark H. Greenberg, Joan Lombardi, and John Hutchins. 2002. "Unfinished Agenda: Child Care for Low-Income Families Since 1996. Implications for Federal and State Policy." Washington, DC: Center for Law and Social Policy. http://clasp.org/publications/unfinished_agenda_full_report.pdf.1.

Meyers, Marcia, Bonnie Glaser, and Karin MacDonald. 1998. "On the Front Lines of Welfare Delivery: Are Workers Implementing Policy Reforms?" *Journal of Policy Analysis and Management* 17 (1): 1–22.

Michaux, Michelle. 2008. When Welfare Worked: A Community Approach to Welfare Reform. *Polity* 40: 1–23.

Mink, Gwendolyn. 1998. *Welfare's End.* Ithaca: Cornell University Press.

———. 1999. *Whose Welfare?* Ithaca: Cornell University Press.

Mishel, Lawrence, Jared Bernstein, and Sylvia Allegretto. 2007. *The State of Working America: 2006–2007.* Washington, DC: Economic Policy Institute.

Mishel, Lawrence, Jared Bernstein, and Heather Boushey. 2003. *The State of Working America 2002/2003*. Ithaca: Cornell University Press.

Mittelstadt, Jennifer. 2005. *From Welfare to Workfare: The Unintended Consequences of Liberal Reform, 1945–1965*. Chapel Hill: University of North Carolina Press.

Moffitt, Robert A. 2002. *From Welfare to Work: What the Evidence Shows*. Washington, DC: Brookings Institution. http://www.brookings.edu/papers/2002/01welfare_moffitt.aspx.

Monroe, Pamela, and Vicky Tiller. 2001. "Commitment to Work Among Welfare-Reliant Women." *Journal of Marriage and Family* 63 (3): 816–828.

Morgen, Sandra. 2002. "The Politics of Welfare and Poverty Research." *Anthropological Quarterly* 75 (4): 745–757.

———. 2006. "Anti-Tax Politics and Processes of DeKeynesianization: The Neo-liberal Homo Economicus as Asocial and Amoral?" Presented at the annual meeting of the American Anthropological Association, San Jose, CA, November 16.

Morgen, Sandra, Joan Acker, Jill Weigt, and Lisa Gonzales. 2006. "Living Economic Restructuring at the Bottom: Welfare Restructuring and Low-Wage Work." In *The Promise of Welfare Reform: Rhetoric or Reality?*, edited by Keith Kilty and Elizabeth Segal, 81–94. New York: Haworth Press.

Morgen, Sandra, and Jeff Maskovsky. 2003. "The Anthropology of Welfare 'Reform': New Perspectives on U.S. Urban Poverty in The Post-welfare Era." *Annual Review of Anthropology* 32: 315–337.

Morgen, Sandra, and Jill Weigt. 2001. "Poor Women, Fair Work, and Welfare-to-Work That Works." In *The New Poverty Studies: The Ethnography of Politics, Policy and Impoverished People in the U.S.*, edited by Judith Goode and Jeff Maskovsky. New York: New York University Press.

Mullings, Leith. 1997. *On Our Own Terms: Race, Class and Gender in the Lives of African American Women*. New York: Routledge.

Naples, Nancy. 1997. "The New Consensus on the Gendered Social Contract: The 1987–1988 U.S. Congressional Hearings on Welfare Reform." *Signs* 22 (4): 907–945.

———. 2003. *Feminism and Method: Ethnography, Discourse Analysis, and Activist Research*. New York: Routledge.

National Conference of State Legislatures (NCSL). 2008. State TANF Work Participation Rates Gaps to Avoid Federal Penalties in FFY 2007. http://www.ncsl.org/statefed/welfare/workpart.htm.

Nelson, Julie. 2006. *Economics for Humans*. Chicago: University of Chicago Press.

Nelson, Margaret K. 2002. "Declaring Welfare 'Reform' a Success: The Role of Applied Social Science." *Journal of Poverty* 6 (3): 1–27.

Neubeck, Kenneth. 2006. *When Welfare Disappears: The Case for Economic Human Rights*. New York: Routledge.

Neubeck, Kenneth, and Noel Cazenave. 2001. *Welfare Racism: Playing the Race Card Against America's Poor*. New York: Routledge.

Northwest Policy Center. 2001. *Northwest Job Gap Study: Searching for Work that Pays*. Seattle: University of Washington, Evans School of Public Affairs. http://www.dept.washington.edu/npc/.

O'Connor, Alice. 2001. *Poverty Knowledge: Social Science, Social Policy, and the Poor in Twentieth Century U.S. History*. Princeton, NJ: Princeton University Press.

O'Connor, Julia, Ann Orloff, and Sheila Shaver. 1999. *State, Markets, Families: Gender, Liberalism and Social Policy in Australia, Canada, Great Britain and the United States*. Cambridge: Cambridge University Press.

Oliker, Stacey. 1990. "Discourses on Motherhood in Welfare Reform." Presented at the annual meeting of the American Sociological Association, Washington, DC, August 22.

———. 2000. "Examining Care at Welfare's End." In *Care Work: Gender, Labor, and the Welfare State,* edited by Madonna Harrington Meyer, 167–185. New York: Routledge.

———. 2002. "Challenges for Studying Care after AFDC." In *Families at Work: Expanding the Bounds,* edited by Naomi Gertsel, Dan Clawson, and Robert Zussman, 289–301. Nashville, TN: Vanderbilt University Press.

Oregon Center for Public Policy. 1999. "Many Of Oregon's Low Income Parents Lack Health Insurance." http://www.ocpp.org/1999/pr990209.htm.

———. 2002. "Recession Takes Its Toll: Oregon's Poverty Rate Flat; Number of Poor Grows; Median Income Unchanged." September 24. www.occp.org/2002/nr020924.htm.

Oregon Commission for Child Care. 1998. "Vital Links, Next Steps: 1999–2001." Report to the Governor and the Legislature. Salem: Oregon Employment Department.

Oregon Department of Human Services (ODHS). 2007a. *Annual Performance Progress Report. FY 2004–2005.* http.//www.oregon.gov/DHS/.

———. 2007b. "DHS Transformation Initiative: The LEAN Connection." http://www.dhs.state.or.us/tools/transformation/lean.html.

———. 2008. "Food, Cash, and Housing. Historical Statewide Caseloads—Past 10 Years." http://dhsresources.hr.state.or.us:591/histcases/fmpro?-db=histcase.fp3&-format=histcase.htm&-view.

Oregon Progress Board. 1989. *Oregon Shines.* http://egov.oregon.gov/DAS/OPB/os.shtml#Oregon_Shines__1989.

———. 2000. "Oregon Update: Oregon Minorities A Summary of Changes in Oregon Benchmarks by Race and Ethnicity 1990-1998." http://www.oregon.gov/DAS/OPB/docs/Parity/RE2000pdf.

———. 2002. A Brief History of the Oregon Progress Board. http://www.oregon.gov/DAS/OPB/docs/history.PDFc.

Oregon Welfare Reform Work Group. 1995. *An Investment Opportunity: Redesigning Oregon's Public Assistance System to Reduce Poverty by Placing More Oregonians in Jobs.* Salem, OR, March 28. http://aspe.hhs.gov/progsys/oregon/history/chap4.htm.

(The) *Oregonian.* 1993. "A Fairer Shot at Workfare." July 16, D08.

Padin, Jose A. 2005. "The Normative Mulattoes: The Press, Latinos, and the Racial Climate on the Moving Immigration Frontier." *Sociological Perspectives* 48 (1): 49–75.

Page, Helan, and R. Brooke Thomas. 1994. "White Public Space and the Construction of White Privilege in U. S. Health Care: Fresh Concepts and a New Model of Analysis." *Medical Anthropology Quarterly* 8 (1): 109–116.

Parrott, Sharon, and Arloc Sherman. 2007. "TANF Results Are More Mixed Than Is Often Understood." *Journal of Policy Analysis and Management* 26 (2): 374–381.

Pateman, Carole. 1988. *The Sexual Contract.* Stanford, CA: Stanford University Press.

———. 2005. "Another Way Forward: Welfare, Social Reproduction, and a Basic Income." In *Welfare Reform and Political Theory,* edited by Lawrence M. Mead and Christopher Beem, 34–64. New York: Russell Sage Foundation.

Pear, Robert. 2009. "Obama Signs Children's Health Insurance Bill." *New York Times,* February 5. http://www.nytimes.com/2009/02/05/us/politics/05health.html?_r=1&pagewanted=print.

Peterson, Janice, Xue Song, and Avis Jones-DeWeever. 2003. *Life After Welfare Reform: Low-Income Single Parent Families, Pre- and Post-TANF.* Washington, DC: Institute of Women's Policy Research. http://www.iwpr.org/pdf/d446.pdf.

Phillips, Kevin. 1990. *The Politics of Rich and Poor: Wealth and the American Electorate in the Reagan Aftermath.* New York: Random House.

———. 2002. *Wealth and Democracy: A Political History of the American Rich.* New York: Broadway Books.

———. 2008. *Bad Money: Reckless Finance, Failed Politics, and the Global Crisis of American Capitalism.* New York: Viking.

Pierson, Christopher. 2007. *Beyond the Welfare State: The New Political Economy of Welfare.* University Park: Penn State University Press.

Piña, Darlene, and Laura Canty-Swapp. 1999. "Melting Multiculturalism: Legacies of Assimilation Pressures in Human Service Organizations." *Journal of Sociology and Social Welfare* 26 (4): 87–113.

Piven, Frances Fox. 2001. "Welfare Reform and the Cultural Reconstruction of Low-wage Labor Markets." In *The New Poverty Studies: The Ethnography of Power Politics, and Impoverished People in the United States,* edited by Judith Goode and Jeff Maskovsky, 135–151. New York: New York University Press.

———. 2002. "Welfare Policy and American Politics." In *Work, Welfare and Politics: Confronting Poverty in the Wake of Welfare Reform,* edited by Frances Fox Piven, Joan Acker, Margaret Hallock, and Sandra Morgen, 19–33. Eugene: University of Oregon Press.

Piven, Frances Fox, Joan Acker, Margaret Hallock, and Sandra Morgen, eds. 2002. *Work, Welfare and Politics: Confronting Poverty in the Wake of Welfare Reform.* Eugene: University of Oregon Press.

Piven, Frances Fox, and Richard A. Cloward. [1971] 1993. *Regulating the Poor.* Second Vintage ed., New York: Vintage Books.

Polanyi, Karl. 1957. *The Great Transformation.* Boston: Beacon Press.

Presser, Harriet. 2003. *Working in a 24/7 Economy: Challenges for American Families.* New York: Russell Sage Foundation.

Presser, Harriet, and Amy G. Cox. 1997. "The Work Schedules of Low-Educated American Women and Welfare Reform." *Monthly Labor Review* 120 (4): 25–43.

Quadagno, Jill. 1994. *The Color of Welfare: How Racism Undermined the War on Poverty.* New York: Oxford University Press.

Raphael, Jodi. 2000. *Saving Bernice: Battered Women, Welfare and Poverty.* Boston: Northeastern University Press.

Reese, Ellen. 2005. *Backlash Against Welfare Mothers: Past + Present.* Berkeley: University of California Press.

Reitman, Meredith. 2006. "Uncovering the White Place: Whitewashing at Work." *Social and Cultural Geography* 7 (2): 267–282.

Rennison, Callie L., and Sara Wechans. 2000. *Special Report: Intimate Partner Violence.* Washington, DC: Bureau of Justice Statistics, May. http://www.ojp.usdoj.gov/bjs/pub/pdf/ipv.pdf.

Richer, Elise, Steve Savner, and Mark Greenberg. 2001. Frequently Asked Questions About Working Welfare Leavers. Washington, DC: CLASP. http://s242739747.onlinehome.us/publications.php?id=2&year=2001#0.

Richie, Beth. 1996. *Compelled to Crime: The Gender Entrapment of Battered Black Women.* New York: Routledge.

Ridzi, Frank. 2009. *Selling Welfare Reform: Work-First and the New Common Sense.* New York: New York University Press.

Riger, Stephanie and Susan L. Staggs. 2004. "Welfare Reform, Domestic Violence, and Employment." *Violence Against Women* 10 (9): 961–990.

Roberts, Dorothy. 1997. *Killing the Black Body: Race, Reproduction, and the Meaning of Liberty.* New York: Pantheon Books.

———. 2002. *Shattered Bonds: The Color of Child Welfare.* New York: Basic Books.

Roschelle, Anne R. 1997. *No More Kin: Exploring Race, Class, and Gender in Family Networks.* Thousand Oaks, CA: Sage.

Rosen, Ruth. 2007. "The Care Crisis." *The Nation* 284 (10): 11–16.

Rubin, Lillian. 1994. *Families on the Fault Line.* New York: HarperCollins.

Sawhill, Isabel, R. Kent Weaver, Ron Haskins, and Andrea Kane. 2002. *Welfare Reform and Beyond: The Future of the Safety Net.* Washington, DC: Brookings Institute.

Schott, Liz. 2008. Using TANF or MOE Funds to Provide Supplemental Assistance to Low-Income Working Families. Washington, DC: Center on Budget and Policy.

Schram, Sanford. 1995. *Words of Welfare: The Poverty of Social Science and the Social Science of Poverty.* Ann Arbor: University of Minnesota Press.

———. 2003. "Putting a Black Face on Welfare: The Good and the Bad." In *Race and the Politics of Welfare Reform,* edited by Sanford Schram, Joe Soss, and Richard Fording, 196–221. Ann Arbor: University of Michigan Press.

———. 2006. *Welfare Discipline: Discourse, Governance, and Globalization.* Philadelphia: Temple University Press.

Schram, Sanford, and Joe Soss. 2002. "Success Stories: Welfare Reform, Policy Discourse and the Politics of Research." In *Lost Ground: Welfare Reform, Poverty and Beyond,* edited by Randy Albelda and Ann Withorn, 57–78. Boston: South End Press.

Schram, Sanford, Joe Soss, and Richard Fording. 2003. *Race and the Politics of Welfare Reform.* Ann Arbor: University of Michigan Press.

Scott, Ellen, Kathryn Edin, Andrew London, and Rebecca Kissane. 2004. "Unstable Work, Unstable Income: Implications for Family Well-Being in the Era of Time-Limited Welfare." *Journal of Poverty* 8:61–88.

Scott, Ellen, Kathryn Edin, Andrew London, and Joan Maya Mazelis. 2001. "My Children Come First: Welfare-Reliant Women's Post-TANF Views of Work-Family Trade-Offs and Marriage." In *For Better and For Worse: Welfare Reform and the Well-Being of Children and Families,* edited by Greg Duncan and P. Lindsay Chase-Lansdale, 132–152. New York: Russell Sage Foundation.

Scott, Ellen, Andrew London, and Allison Hurst. 2005. "Instability in Patchworks of Child Care When Moving from Welfare to Work." *Journal of Marriage and Family* 67:370–387.

Scott, Ellen, Andrew London, and Nancy A. Myers. 2002a. "Dangerous Dependencies: The Intersection of Welfare Reform and Domestic Violence." *Gender and Society* 16:878–897.

———. 2002b. "Living with Violence: Women's Reliance on Abusive Men in Their Transitions from Welfare to Work." In *Families at Work: Expanding the Bounds,* edited by Naomi Gertsel, Dan Clawson, and Robert Zussman, 302–316. Nashville, TN: Vanderbilt University Press.

Scrivener, Susan, Gayle Hamilton, Mary Farrell, Stephen Freedman, Daniel Friedlander, Marisa Mitchell, Jodi Nudelman, and Christine Schwartz. 1998. *National Evaluation of Welfare-to-Work Strategies: Implementation, Participation Patterns, Costs, and Two-Year Impacts of the Portland (Oregon) Welfare-to-Work Program.* Washington, DC: U.S. Department of Health and Human Services.

Seccombe, Karen. 1999. *"So You Think I Drive a Cadillac?": Welfare Recipients' Perspectives on the System and Its Reform.* Boston: Allyn and Bacon.

———. 2007. *"So You Think I Drive a Cadillac?" Welfare Recipients' Perspectives on the System and Its Reform.* 2nd ed. Boston: Allyn and Bacon.

Sherman, Arloc, Shawn Fremstad, and Sharon Parrott. 2004. *Employment Rates for Mothers Fell Substantially During Recent Period of Labor Market Weakness.*

Washington, DC: Center on Budget and Policy Priorities, June 22. http://www.cbpp.org/archiveSite/6-22-04ui.pdf.

Shulman, Beth. 2003. *The Betrayal of Work: How Low-Wage Jobs Fail 30 Million Americans and Their Families.* New York: The New Press.

Smith, Dorothy. 1987. *The Everyday World as Problematic.* Boston: Northeastern University Press.

———. 2005. *Institutional Ethnography: A Sociology for People.* Lanham, MD: AltaMira Press.

Soss, Joe, Richard C. Fording, and Sanford F. Schram. 2008. "The Color of Devolution: Race, Federalism, and the Politics of Social Control." *American Journal of Political Science* 52 (3): 536–553.

Soss, Joe, Sanford Schram, Thomas Vartanian, and Erin O'Brien. 2001. "Setting the Terms of Relief: Explaining State Policy Choice in the Devolution Revolution." *American Journal of Political Science* 45 (2): 378–395.

Spalter-Roth, Roberta, Beverly Burr, Heidi Hartmann, and Lois Shaw. 1995. *Welfare That Works: The Working Lives of AFDC Recipients.* Washington, DC: Institute for Women's Policy Research.

Spriggs, William E. 2007. "The Changing Face of Poverty in America." *The American Prospect* 18 (5): A5–A7.

Stack, Carol. 1974. *All Our Kin: Strategies for Survival in a Black Community.* New York: Harper and Row.

Steuerle, C. Eugene, and Gordon Mermin. 1997. "The Big-Spending Presidents." *Urban Institute Brief No. 11. The Future of the Public Sector Series,* April 1. Washington, DC: Urban Institute. http://www.urban.org/publications/307052.html.

Stuart, Elaine. 1997. "Oregon Option: Welfare Reform." In *State Innovations Briefs: New and Best Practices in State Government.* Lexington, KY: The Council of State Governments, December.

Sunstein, Cass. 2006. *The Second Bill of Rights: FDR's Unfinished Revolution and Why We Need It More Than Ever.* New York: Perseus Books.

Susser, Ida. 1996. The Social Construction of Poverty and Homelessness in U.S. Cities. *Annual Review of Anthropology* 25:411–435.

Tapogna. John. 1998. "Making the Transition to Self-Sufficiency in Oregon." Portland, OR: ECONorthwest. http://www.rvi.net/~ccn/old%20pages/econwrpt.htm.

Tapogna, John, and Tara Witt. 2002. "Making the Transition to Self-Sufficiency in Oregon." In *Work, Welfare and Politics, edited by* Frances Fox Piven, Joan Acker, Margaret Hallock, and Sandra Morgen. Eugene: University of Oregon Press.

Terran, Eve. 2008. "Oregon Welfare Programs and the Adoption of Dr. Ford's Collaborative Model of Case Management." Master's thesis, Conflict and Dispute Resolution Program, School of Law, University of Oregon.

Thomas, Susan L. 1995. "Exchanging Welfare Checks for Wedding Rings: Welfare Reform in New Jersey and Wisconsin." *Affilia* 10 (2): 120–137.

Thompson, Jeff, and Michael Leachman. 2000. *Prosperity (or Poverty) in Perspective: The State of Working Oregon 2000.* Silverton: Oregon Center for Public Policy, September.

———. 2002. *Boom, Bust, and Beyond: The State of Working Oregon.* Silverton, OR: Oregon Center for Public Policy.

Thorne, Jean. 2004. *Director's Message.* Salem: Oregon Department of Human Services, January 6. http://www.oregon.gov/DHS/news/messages/2004messages/2004-0106.shtml.

U.S. Bureau of the Census. 2008a. Historical Income Tables, table P6, "Regions of White People by Mean Income and Sex: 1967–2007." www.census.gov/hhes/incomes/histinc/p06W.html.

———. 2008b. *Income, Poverty and Health Insurance Coverage in the U.S.* Current Population Reports. Washington, DC. www.census.gov/prod/2008pubs/p60-235pdf.

U.S. Bureau of Labor Statistics. 1999. "Unemployment Rate Fifty State Rankings, 1998 and 1999." http://www.state.ok.us/osfdocs/budget/table9.pdf.

———. 2008. *Women in the Labor Force: A Data Book.* Report 1011, table 6, p. 19. http://www.bis.gov/cps/wlf.databook-2008.pdf.

U.S. Department of Health and Human Services (DHHS). 2006. "Successes Marked on 10th Anniversary of Welfare Reform." August 21. www.hhs.gov/news/press/2006pres/20060821.html.

———. 2008. *Caseload Data 2008.* http://www.acf.hhs.gov/programs/ofa/data-reports/caseload/caseload_current.htm.

Urban Institute. 2006. *A Decade of Welfare Reform: Facts and Figures. Assessing the New Federalism.* Washington, DC: Urban Institute. June. http://www.urban.org/UploadedPDF/900980_welfarereform.pdf.

Weaver, Kent. 1999. "The Role of Policy Research in Welfare Debates, 1993–1996." Inequality Summer Institute '99. http://www.hks.harvard.edu/inequality/Summer/Summer99/privatepapers/Weaver.PDF.

Weeks, Gary. 2004. Message from DHS Director Gary K. Weeks. Salem, OR: Department of Human Services. January 28.

Weigt, Jill M. 2002. "The Work of Mothering: Welfare Reform and the Care Work of Poor and Working Class Women." PhD diss., Department of Sociology, University of Oregon, Eugene.

———. 2006. "Compromises to Carework: The Social Organization of Mothers' Experiences in the Low-Wage Labor Market after Welfare Reform." *Social Problems* 53 (3): 332–351.

West, Guida. 1981. *The National Welfare Rights Movement: The Social Protest of Poor Women.* New York: Praeger

Williams, Linda Faye. 2003. *The Constraint of Race: Legacies of White Skin Privilege in America.* University Park: Penn State University Press.

Winston, Pamela. 2002. *Welfare Policymaking in the States: The Devil in Devolution.* Washington, DC: Georgetown University Press.

Zaslow, Martha, S.M. McGroder, and Kristin Moore. 2000. *National Evaluation of Welfare-to-Work Strategies: Impacts on Young Children and Their Families Two Years after Enrollment (Summary Report).* Washington, DC: U.S. Department of Health and Human Services, Administration for Children and Families and Office of the Assistant Secretary for Planning and Evaluation, and the U.S. Department of Education.

Zinn, Maxine Baca, and Bonnie Thornton Dill. 1996. "Theorizing Difference From Multiracial Feminism." *Feminist Studies* 22 (2): 321–332.

Index